ROUTLEDGE LIBRARY EDITIONS: AFGHANISTAN

Volume 3

THE TRAGEDY OF AFGHANISTAN

THE TRAGEDY OF AFGHANISTAN
The Social, Cultural and Political Impact of the Soviet Invasion

Edited by
BO HULDT AND ERLAND JANSSON

LONDON AND NEW YORK

First published in 1988 by Croom Helm Ltd

This edition first published in 2020
by Routledge
2 Park Square, Milton Park, Abingdon, Oxon OX14 4RN

and by Routledge
52 Vanderbilt Avenue, New York, NY 10017

Routledge is an imprint of the Taylor & Francis Group, an informa business

© 1988 Swedish Institute of International Affairs

All rights reserved. No part of this book may be reprinted or reproduced or utilised in any form or by any electronic, mechanical, or other means, now known or hereafter invented, including photocopying and recording, or in any information storage or retrieval system, without permission in writing from the publishers.

Trademark notice: Product or corporate names may be trademarks or registered trademarks, and are used only for identification and explanation without intent to infringe.

British Library Cataloguing in Publication Data
A catalogue record for this book is available from the British Library

ISBN: 978-0-367-14305-3 (Set)
ISBN: 978-0-429-29389-4 (Set) (ebk)
ISBN: 978-0-367-26518-2 (Volume 3) (hbk)
ISBN: 978-0-429-29378-8 (Volume 3) (ebk)

Publisher's Note
The publisher has gone to great lengths to ensure the quality of this reprint but points out that some imperfections in the original copies may be apparent.

Disclaimer
The publisher has made every effort to trace copyright holders and would welcome correspondence from those they have been unable to trace.

THE TRAGEDY OF AFGHANISTAN

The Social, Cultural and Political Impact of the Soviet Invasion

Edited by
BO HULDT
ERLAND JANSSON

CROOM HELM
London • New York • Sydney

© 1988 Swedish Institute of International Affairs
Croom Helm Ltd, Provident House,
Burrell Row, Beckenham, Kent BR3 1AT

Croom Helm Australia, 44-50 Waterloo Road,
North Ryde, 2113, New South Wales

Published in the USA by
Croom Helm
in association with Methuen, Inc.
29 West 35th Street,
New York, NY 10001

British Library Cataloguing in Publication Data

The Tragedy of Afghanistan: the social, cultural
   and political impact of the Soviet invasion.
   1. Afghanistan — Social conditions
   I. Huldt, Bo   II. Jansson, Erland
   958'.1044   HN670.6.A8
   ISBN 0-7099-5708-4

Library of Congress Cataloging-in-Publication Data

Huldt, Bo. 1941–
   The tragedy of Afghanistan: the social, cultural, and political
impact of the Soviet invasion/Bo Huldt and Erland Jansson.
      p. cm.
   Bibliography: p.
   Includes index.
   ISBN 0-7099-5708-4
   1. Afghanistan — History — Soviet occupation, 1979– 2. Afghanistan
— Social conditions. I. Jansson, Erland, 1947– . II. Title.
DS371.2.H84   1988
958'.04 — dc 19
                                                                87-33287
                                                                    CIP

Printed and bound in Great Britain by Mackays of Chatham Ltd, Kent

CONTENTS

Introduction   **Bo Huldt** and
Erland Jansson

PART I: Ethnicity and the New Nationalism

1. When Muslim Identity Has Different Meanings: 3
   Religion and Politics in Contemporary
   Afghanistan
   Asger Christensen

2. Cultural Changes among the Mujahidin and   20
   Muhajerin
   Louis Dupree

3. Concepts of Personal, Moral and Social   38
   Disorder among Durrani Pashtuns in
   Northern Afghanistan
   Nancy and Richard Tapper

4. The Kushans – An Afghan Search for Roots   55
   Richard N. Frye

5. Ethnic Factors in Afghanistan's Future   62
   Eden Naby

PART II: Afghan Learning and Education

6. Past and Present Education in Afghanistan –   75
   A Problem for the Future
   Sayd B. Majrooh

7. Scholars, Saints and Sufis in Modern   93
   Afghanistan
   Bo Utas

8. Modern Political Culture and Traditional   106
   Resistance
   Olivier Roy

Contents

9. Afghan Education during the War   113
   Batinshah Safi

PART III: The War

10. Modernisation from Below: The Afghan   121
    Resistance between the Fight for Liberation
    and Social Emancipation
    Jan-Heeren Grevemeyer

11. A Local Perspective on the Incipient   148
    Resistance in Afghanistan
    Jan Ovesen

12. The Afghan Resistance: Achievements and   155
    Problems
    Mohammad Es'haq

13. An Assessment of the New Mujaheddin Alliance   164
    Sabahuddin Kushkaki

PART IV: Ecology

14. Ecology and the War in Afghanistan   175
    Terje Skogland

15. Effects of the War on Agriculture   197
    Mohammad Qasim Yusufi

PART V: The Exile

16. What Happens to Honour in Exile? Continuity   219
    and Change among Afghan Refugees
    Inger W. Boesen

17. Afghan Nomads Trapped in Pakistan   240
    Bernt Glatzer

18. The Role of the VOLAGs   248
    Nancy Hatch Dupree

Index   263

INTRODUCTION

Bo Huldt and Erland Jansson

The Soviet invasion of Afghanistan in December 1979 stunned the world. It put a definite end to detente and ushered in a new period of superpower confrontation. Although we may now be witnessing a change of climate again, from confrontation to co-operation between the superpowers, the kind of detente that was thought to emerge in the 1970s will not return and the Afghanistan conflict remains a key obstacle to a relaxation of international tension.

When considering this fact of high politics one may wonder at the relative lack of public attention to Afghanistan and to the plight of the Afghan people. In the democratic West none of the popular mobilisation of opinion of the Vietnam years has materialised. Despairing commentators have also accused the political leaders in the West of accepting the inclusion of Afghanistan into the Soviet bloc as final - or at least as no concern of theirs. The fate of Ethiopia or Mandchuria-China during the interwar and League of Nations years may come to mind.

Scholars who previously devoted themselves to the study of Afghanistan now find themselves cut off from their old field of research and therefore turn to new ones. Afghan scholars remaining in their country find themselves reduced to silence. Many of those who have fled their country have been absorbed by Western society. Others, who remain in close proximity to the conflict, dedicate themselves to the Afghan cause by applying their special skills to educational work or information activities. However, they work under very

Introduction

difficult conditions and with little support from their colleagues in the Western world.

The result is that while the need for information about Afghanistan is now greater than ever it is getting more and more difficult to get reliable information. In December 1985 a seminar was arranged at the Swedish Institute of International Affairs on the theme 'Afghanistan - A Threatened Culture'. Rather than focusing on the superpowers and the international aspects of the conflict the aim of the seminar was to get a broad picture of what the war has meant for Afghanistan, its people and its culture. A second aim was to explore the possibilities of co-operation between Western scholars and their Afghan colleagues now residing in Pakistan.

This volume is based on the proceedings of that seminar, and the chapters presented here are more or less revised versions of papers presented at the seminar. One thing all the participants had in common - their concern for Afghanistan and sympathy with the Afghan people. Otherwise their background varied greatly. This variety the organisers felt was an asset for a seminar of this kind and, indeed, necessary. No attempt has been made to publish the proceedings in a strictly uniform mould.

As regards the contents, there is a great variety of perspectives and approaches. While some of the articles are primarily concerned with presenting research results, others largely deal with the problems of research that still needs to be done. Others yet discuss practical measures to support the Afghans, inside the country or in exile.

Another thing that will be quite striking to the reader is that while developments prior to December 1979 are comparatively well covered, this group of distinguished experts had rather less to tell about what has happened after the Soviet invasion. In this way, too, the present volume is an invitation to further research.

Yet another thing which should be mentioned in this context is that the papers were completed or revised at different points in time, some as early as autumn 1985, others a year later. This explains some discrepancies between the papers.

The Swedish Institute of International Affairs

Introduction

thus publishes this volume in the hope that it will contribute to a better knowledge of Afghanistan among those looking for information and that it will inspire more research within the academic community.

For the Swedish Institute of International Affairs the subject has a specific significance. The Institute is presently engaged in a major research project on 'The Soviet Union and Its Neighbours - Aspects of Security' with the ambition to review the postwar development of Soviet-Rimland relations. While Soviet-neighbour relations in Europe and in Asia are certainly different we should not disregard the possibility of a more general Soviet strategy and posture towards the neighbours and, above all, towards the neighbouring small states. The Soviet superstate - whether as existing empire or as possible commonwealth - is presently thought to be in a state of transition with not only 'glasnost' but also 'perestrojka', restructuring, as key-words. While analyses of Soviet security and foreign policy tend to focus on 'expansionism' or 'entrenchment' of positions once taken, and few experts predict a speedy Soviet retreat from Afghanistan, one may still be entitled to speculate about policies for 'contraction' and 'disengagement' as guidelines for an overextended superpower.

Still, while thus not forgetting the wider and global ramifications of the conflict under study here we should once again recall that in focus remains the fate of Afghanistan - its people and its culture.

The editors of this book would like to make due acknowledgements of the support received from the Swedish Council for Research in the Humanities and Social Sciences and the Nordic Cooperation Committee for International Politics, including Conflict and Peace Research.

Bo Huldt and Erland Jansson
Stockholm

PART I

ETHNICITY AND THE NEW NATIONALISM

WHEN MUSLIM IDENTITY HAS DIFFERENT MEANINGS: RELIGION AND POLITICS IN CONTEMPORARY AFGHANISTAN

Asger Christensen

'For Islam, honour, and homeland' (Islam de para, namus de para, votan de para) are the concepts usually employed when refugees or guerrillas belonging to Afghanistan's largest ethnic group, the Pakhtun,(1) explain their opposition to the present regime in Kabul and its Soviet allies. Together these three categories define the conceptual realm which provides meaning and raison d'etre for the Afghan resistance struggle: the defence of territory and cultural tradition against interference from an opponent considered to be an infidel (kafir). Yet, although the majority among both the Pakhtun and the other ethnic groups in Afghanistan appear to agree to defend their beliefs and way of life against the Kabul regime and the Soviet forces of occupation, this does not mean that a consensus exists even within the separate ethnic groups, concerning the conceptualisation of the cultural tradition which is defended. The Afghan resistance, and in particular that of the Pakhtun, is split into a large number of political parties and groups, who differ more or less profoundly from each other both with regard to what they view as proper Islam, and with regard to the kind of society they envisage in a liberated Afghanistan. In what follows I shall attempt to outline how the very same categories - Islam, honour, and homeland - which provide the impetus for resistance are also the ones which must be considered, if the political and organisational fragmentation of the resistance is to be explained.

Religion and Politics

Diversity within Islam

Islam does not contain any distinction between a religious and a secular sphere of life, but strives instead to create a total way of life based on the guidelines, directives and prohibitions which are given by God in the Koran or are contained in legends of the life of Muhammed, the hadith. However, the fact that the overwhelming majority of Afghans consider themselves Muslim and regard the Koran and hadith as the supreme authority concerning all contexts of existence, does not mean that Islam in Afghanistan constitutes an unequivocal or static phenomenon.

The presence of both of the major Muslim sects, the Sunni and the Shi'a, provides the basic diversity within Islam in Afghanistan. Neither Sunni nor Shi'a constitute monolithic systems of belief. Instead both contain internal sectarian differences like that between Imamis and Ismailis among the Shi'a, or those which separate the different Sufi tariqa and also separate the followers of these from the other believers among the Sunni. Moreover, the adherents of both Sunni and Shi'a Islam come from culturally diverse ethnic groups, who consequently in praxis realise mutually distinct versions of a Muslim way of life. All of these versions contain elements which deviate from or even contradict the message of the Koran and hadith, but people experience this condition very differently, and the practical consequences which they draw also vary considerably.

The Pakhtun provide an example of this kind of diversity. They regard themselves as descendants from a common ancestor by the name of Qaiz, who lived at the time of Muhammed, and who was converted to Islam by the Prophet himself. The Pakhtun thus associate and equate their very origin and identity as a people with their Muslim identity, and they contrast this with all the other ethnic groups in Afghanistan, whose Muslimity is not original, but who are later converts. At the same time, however, this notion of common descent also constitutes the basis of a tribal social order, which contains norms and modes of conduct that depart from Islam in several important respects.(2) This schism is part of Pakhtun cultural consciousness and is explicitly formulated as when the tribal notions of honourable behaviour, pakhtunwali, are contrasted with the sayings of the Koran in the proverb 'Pakhtun half use the Koran, half pakhtunwali' (Pukhtane nim Quran mani, nim pukhtunwali mani).(3) Most Pakhtun do not consider this conflict specially problematic, and many just appear to accept it as a fact of life, while others experience it as a fundamental existential dilemma and strive to solve it in different ways. Some attempt to do this by practising a personal life-style that places greater emphasis on the precepts of Islam, or attach themselves to a religious figure respected for his piousness and learning from whom they receive spiritual guidance, as for example one of the leaders (Pirs) of a Sufi tariqa. Yet others who wish to eliminate the discrepancy they experience, seek a political solution through a transformation of society which brings it in correspondence with what they view as proper Islam.

Such differences of opinion concerning the relationship between what is understood as proper Islam and the existing social order can be found within all sections of the Afghan population, and it was also present in the attitudes which people held with regard to the increasing 'modernisation' and 'westernisation' of Afghan society.

So, instead of providing unity of belief and a shared unequivocal conception of how society should be, the role of Islam as the basic conceptual frame of reference and the ultimate source of legitimation means that social and political matters are commonly understood and discussed in religious terms. The concepts of Islam have always been sufficiently ambiguous to allow different interpretations of their meaning and thus to allow mutually divergent political views to be seen as religiously legitimate by their exponents and followers. The result is that attempts to mobilise people for political action through religiously legitimate appeals, or to convince them of the correctness of certain kinds of conduct, invariably take place in a context which contains divergent or even alternative appeals, that are likewise held to be derived from Islam.

Afghan history contains many examples of political confrontations based on different interpreta-

Religion and Politics

tions of Islam.(4) One of the most illustrative of these conflicts took place in the context of the expansion and consolidation of Afghan state authority during the reign of Amir Abdur Rahman (c.1880-1901). In addition to harsh military and administrative measures his attempts to strengthen the authority of the state also involved a religious policy which entailed the propagation of a new interpretation of Islam (cf. Ghani, 1978). The main feature of this interpretation was the attempt to provide state authority with religious legitimacy by defining the good Muslim as identical with the good subject who accepted this authority. Through a combination of repression and rewards the state managed to gain the support of a number of prominent religious personalities who promoted its version of Islam. But at the same time this version was rejected by others who proclaimed the ruler heretic, and who thereby lent religious legitimacy to the extensive popular resistance against the attempts made by the state to expand and strengthen its control.

The situation today exhibits certain parallels to that of the reign of Amir Abdur Rahman. Ever since seizing power through the coup d'etat in April 1978 the new 'revolutionary' regime has striven to present itself as Muslim. Its decrees and other official proclamations have all been introduced by an invocation of God, and like its nineteenth-century predecessor, it has repressed and eliminated part of the religious establishment while at the same time attempting to ally itself with other religious figures who were willing to provide the regime and its policies with religious legitimation. However, the extensive popular opposition against the new regime demonstrates that this policy has been far from successful and that most people instead identify themselves with the resistance and consider it the legitimate representative of Islam.

Honour - Autonomy and Rivalry

One of the most important reasons for this state of affairs is the one which prompted the resistance against the centralising policies of Amir Abdur Rahman, and it is expressed in the second of the categories that the Pakhtun use to explain the current resistance struggle - their honour. For them, honour is associated with the maintenance of autonomy and integrity, be that in relation to other members of the local community or to outside powers such as the state. While the notions of honour (nang) appear most elaborated among the Pakhtun, where they constitute the core of the tribal value system pakhtunwali (cf. Janata and Hassas, 1975), the association of honour and autonomy is also shared by the other rural ethnic groups in Afghanistan.

The attempt to strengthen state authority at the expense of local autonomy at the end of the last century, and to introduce such measures as taxation and military conscription, met with open resistance from practically all the ethnic groups in the country (cf. Kakar, 1971). But although the central government succeeded in expanding its influence considerably compared to its predecessors, there nevertheless remained considerable sections of the rural population who managed to retain much of their former autonomy, and who, moreover, have been able to do so right up to the present.

The current resistance struggle began as a number of mutually isolated and unrelated attempts to defend this local autonomy against increasing interference from the new 'revolutionary' regime. Clashes between the local population and inexperienced, newly-appointed officials, who often acted in a dogmatic and high-handed fashion, were seen by the government as 'counter-revolutionary' resistance and met with military reprisals. The result was that as early as the summer of 1978, a few months after the coup d'etat and before the reforms affecting the rural population had been made public, the actions of the new regime had already fostered a growing popular resistance. At the beginning of October this resistance reached such a level in the province of Kunar in Eastern Afghanistan, that the Afghan army had difficulties handling the situation and had to be supported by Soviet military advisers (Christensen, 1983: 11). The dependency of the new regime on Soviet civil and military aid - a dependency which deepened and became more manifest as the resistance increased - thus made it appear as foreign-dominated and un-Islamic to many

Religion and Politics

Afghans long before the Soviet invasion in December 1979.

However, as mentioned above, the Pakhtun notion of honour has yet another dimension. Just as the maintenance of honour leads to resistance against the imposition of outside control, it is also a source of rivalry on the local level concerning influence, leadership and control over resources. The notion of honour is closely linked to the idea that all (male) Pakhtun are equal (sial) because of their common descent. Honour is preserved by asserting equality vis-a-vis other Pakhtun, be they close or distant kinsmen. The realisation of this involves above all the maintenance of the autonomy and integrity of the household (korunei) through the ability to protect (and control) the women, the house and the land belonging to it, three categories that are united in the same concept of honour - namus. In the eyes of Pakhtun society, then, it is not enough that the individual is a Pakhtun merely through descent, but he also has to do Pakhto (pakhto kavol) by upholding namus in order to preserve his equality and status as a real Pakhtun tribesman.

Equality thus has a dual nature for the Pakhtun: on the one hand it is something which is ascribed and given, yet on the other hand it also has to be confirmed through achievement. This duality is the source of the ambiguity, tension and frequent hostility which pervades the relations between even close collateral agnates, because the effort to secure the premised equality by upholding honour and autonomy may either be pursued through relations to others involving co-operation and conjunction, or competition and attempted dominance (Christensen, 1984: 72).

The ambiguity inherent in the relationship between patrilineal kinsmen is clearly expressed in the concepts used by Pakhtuns. Despite the often stated ideal of solidarity between agnates, the verb siali kavol, which literally means 'to make equality', has the meaning of 'competition', and the term for patrilateral cousin, tarbur, has the connotation of 'enemy', while tarburwali denotes the rivalry often existing between collateral agnates.

So political relations are shaped and conditioned by an organisational context provided by a patrilineal descent system with a strong normative emphasis on solidarity, but where at the same time the actual relations between agnates are crucially influenced by variable interests, which may either bring them together as allies, or separate them as competitors and opponents. The result is that landholding descent groups sharing the same village or local community are usually split in rival factions headed by big-man type leaders who compete with each other in building and consolidating a following among both kin and non-kin. Political allegiance cuts across patrilineal descent relations, and the political groupings confronting each other consist of more or less unstable factions and coalitions of factions based on situationally coincidental interests. While patrilineal descent groups are not mobilized in any consistent pattern of balanced opposition (cf. Barth 1959) descent segments of varying size nevertheless do emerge within the overall context of this factional rivalry (cf. Christensen 1982: 37 ff).

Variations on such a factional mode of politics are also found outside the areas inhabited by Pakhtuns (cf. Azoy 1982: Canfield, 1973), and this pattern of political organisation has implications which reach beyond that of local politics. One such implication is that despite the resentment of state interference, the rivalry caused by the attempt to uphold autonomy and honour also lends ambiguity to the relationship between the local population and the state.

Thus, throughout this century successive Afghan regimes who have tried to gain control over what they regarded as the Pakhtun yaghistan, or 'land of rebels' (Caroe, 1958: 347), have all managed to exercise some kind of influence by means other than those of direct military intervention. By various measures including direct financial subsidies, the granting of administrative functions to favoured individuals, or a generally privileged treatment compared to what is given to others, the regimes have been able to establish alliances with persons and groups at the local level. As a result of the pervasive rivalry and attendant competition for the prestigious position of local political leadership, there will always be some among those who aspire to local leadership, who will find it advantageous to ally themselves with whatever

Religion and Politics

regime is in power. For the local leader in question, however, such alliances do not necessarily entail any acceptance of the wider implications of state authority. His ties to government and administrators are more likely to be founded on tactical considerations concerning the benefits and support which can be derived from the state, and the followers who can be attracted by acting as middlemen between them and the state authorities.

Although still uneven and often marginal, the influence of the state apparatus in Afghanistan has nevertheless been felt in practically every corner of the rural hinterland since the period of state consolidation at the end of the nineteenth century. Since the state is something to be reckoned with, the participants in the competition for local leadership generally attempt to establish ties with the state authorities in their province, and, if possible, with those in the political centre in Kabul as well, which can be used to strengthen the leader and provide benefits for his allies and followers. The means used to establish such friendly relations and to obtain easy access to provincial authorities include hospitality and bribes to different officials, as well as cooperation in various matters. In addition, an increasing number of the families of local political importance have family members employed in government service as office workers, teachers and army officers whose connections with the regime in power or with rival cliques and groupings in the capital may yield immediate or future results.

The frequent political upheavals and changes which have taken place in Kabul during this century have been accompanied by corresponding alternations in the alignments between the state and local leaders in the provinces. Following these changes, the leaders most closely attached to the former regime have usually been discarded as allies by its successors, who, instead, have promoted and favoured new constellations of rising local leaders, often comprising the rivals of the previously dominant ones (cf. Christensen, 1982: 42 ff).

This form of political organisation and process also provided the framework of both the support for and the opposition against the new 'revolutionary' regime after the coup d'etat in April 1978. Allegiance and opposition to the new regime thus cuts across class divisions, and in the rural areas both supporters and opponents are made up of factions comprising feudal landowners, small landholders, tenants, and the landless (Christensen, 1983: 6 ff).

Support for the new regime appears in particular to have come from those factions who before the coup d'etat were the underdogs in the competition for local political influence, and who did not have close relations with the previous regime. Some of the families heading these factions had members who had joined the People's Democratic Party of Afghanistan, and who now received promotion within the administration and the army. As the new regime did not have any organisational foothold among the rural population, its influence in the countryside following the coup was critically dependent on such alliances with local factional leaders. In the years following seizure of power the new regime has consistently striven to maintain and if possible expand these alliances, and to this end it has used a number of means, including frequent meetings in the capital with local leaders, bribes and gifts, or promises to refrain from interference in local affairs.

But the pattern of local factional rivalry has another important implication besides that of creating conditions for alliances between local leaders and the state. Factional rivalry also prevents the resistance against outside interference from uniting within a more encompassing framework, because few factional leaders are prepared to relinquish their autonomy and submit to the authority of someone whom they consider their equal. To the extent that the resistance against outside threats is united in the current resistance struggle, and has been so in the past, this has been achieved through religious and not secular leadership. Both religious figures such as Sayyeds, Akhunzadas, Mians, Pirs, Maulawis, and occasionally even village mullahs have frequently managed to transcend their customary role as spiritual teachers, mediators, and magico-religious healers and have been able to use their spiritual reputation and following as a basis for exercising political influence. But their ability to function as political leaders and to

Religion and Politics

rally people behind them through appeals to Islam is always subjected to the inherent diversity of attitudes, interpretations and interests which exist in Afghan society, and therefore even their leadership remains partial and incomplete as well as relatively unstable. It is partial and incomplete because their message and version of Islam is not accepted by everybody. At the same time it is relatively unstable, because only part of their following may be motivated by a shared religious attitude. Others may have joined mainly because of more mundane political considerations, which make their continued support dependent on the success of the religious-cum-political leader, and on his ability to safeguard their interests. So even though religious leaders may be able to build more encompassing followings this does not mean that factional rivalry is neutralised or superseded; instead it is transferred to another level of organisation, where it is expressed in the support for different religious leaders.

The Divided Resistance

Within the current resistance such political divisions based on different interpretations of Islam exist among both Sunni and Shi'a. Within each of these major sects the many political groupings appear to be divided into two main categories, of which only those among the Sunni will be discussed here.(5)

The political groups and parties constituting the first of these main categories have evolved from traditional religious forms of organisation and leadership like the Sufi tariqas. Thus, members of the leading Mujaddedi family within the Naqshbandia tariqa now head the National Liberation Front (Jabha-e najat-e melli-e Afghanistan), while members of the Gailani family from the Qaderia tariqa constitute the leadership of the National Islamic Front (Mahaz-e melli-e islami-e Afghanistan). Formerly, these families played an important role in the religious and political life of Afghanistan, and both are related by marriage to the exiled royal family. The members of each party are largely drawn from the religious followers of the Sufi tariqa from which the party has evolved, and since both tariqa have a considerable

Religion and Politics

number of adherents among Pakhtun in Eastern Afghanistan, this is also the region where they are most influential. The two parties thus represent different segments of the traditional religious and political establishment. Both seek the co-ordination of the resistance in a broad national front, and they favour the restoration of the monarchy and the establishment of a pluralistic political system, while at the same time stressing the need for strengthening Islam.

The second main category is composed of so-called 'fundamentalist' organisations like the Islamic Party (Hizb-e Islami) headed by the former engineering student, Gulbuddin Hekmatyar, and the Islamic Union (Jamiat-e Islami) which is led by Burhannudin Rabbani, who formerly held a teaching position in theology and Islamic law at the University of Kabul. These parties both want a radical transformation of Afghan society to make it conform to their conception of Islam, and each party regards itself as the leading force in this process. They look upon the Sufi background of the National Liberation Front and the National Islamic Front as something which is ideologically suspect. At the same time they consider the leaders of these parties to be partly responsible for the present situation in Afghanistan because of their former association with the monarchy whose policies the 'fundamentalists' view as excessively liberal.

These 'fundamentalist' parties represent a new phenomenon in Afghan politics. Like their opponents on the Afghan left, the 'fundamentalists' as a political movement are mainly the creation of the radicalisation which took place among sections of the intelligentsia and urban middle class from the end of the sixties and onwards as a reaction to their frustrated aspirations after employment, political influence and economic development. But Marxism and 'fundamentalist' Islam share more than being alternative and opposed ideological solutions to the same social problems. Besides a common historical background it would appear that their urban origins and their radical, uncompromising dogmatism make both basically unacceptable as political solutions to the rural population.

Thus, as early as the middle of the seventies 'fundamentalist' Islamic revolutionaries tried to

Religion and Politics

mobilise the rural population against the Daud regime, but without success, despite the financial and military support they allegedly received from the then president of Pakistan, Ali Bhutto. Nor did this change before the coup d'etat in April 1978. 'Fundamentalist' agitators, who were named Panj Pirei by the local population after the madressa of Panj Pir outside Peshawar where they had been educated, were actively preaching against the government in the province of Kunar in 1977 and early '78. But although the authorities were unable to catch them, the Panj Pirei, on the other hand, did not attract sufficient followers to pose any serious problem. The local mullahs looked upon them as a threat to their own position, while people in general either ignored them or considered them somewhat heretic.(6)

It was only after the coup d'etat, when the interference in local affairs and the increasing repression by the new regime had created a growing opposition in the countryside, that the 'fundamentalist' groups managed to gain popular support.

All the resistance organisations mentioned above and others as well are to be found among the Pakhtun, but far from all Pakhtun resistance leaders are members or followers of such organisations. Many local leaders among the Pakhtun do not appear to be ready to relinquish their autonomy and submit to the authority and interference of the religious leadership of these organisations. The Pakhtun conception of their own original Muslimity introduces a certain ambiguity to their relative ranking vis-a-vis religious figures, and they tend to consider themselves as being on a par with people of religious status. So, although individual religious figures may acquire considerable prestige because of their piety, learning, or holy descent, they are not automatically considered superior or entitled to wield authority over the lives of others. This situation and the fact that the following of the religious leaders in the current resistance struggle may be based either on shared ideology or on more mundane political considerations, would seem to indicate that in addition to the two ideological tendencies within the resistance which have been described above, there exists a third: that of those Pakhtun tribesmen who do not

Religion and Politics

view the discrepancies between Islam and pakhtunwali as particularly problematical, and who consequently do not feel the need for spiritual guidance and political leadership by religious figures.

Homeland - Emerging National Consciousness

As we have seen, the following of the major resistance organisations, like the four mentioned above, is either based on common ideology or derives from more immediate and mundane political interests. From their headquarters in Peshawar in Pakistan these resistance organisations, and a couple of others beside them, maintain international contacts with governments or with kindred Islamic organisations both in Pakistan and in the Arab world. These contacts provide them with access to some of the resources, money, and to a certain extent also weapons, which are badly needed by the active resistance groups inside Afghanistan. In exchange for material support the resistance organisations expect political allegiance from the groups receiving it. Thus, although the overall context is different, the position of the major resistance organisations and of their leadership nevertheless, to a large extent, derives from their ability to assume what is essentially the traditional role of successful local leaders: that of the middleman or broker who creates a following through patronage. This kind of dependency and the resulting organisational fragmentation of the active resistance struggle is deeply resented by many Afghans, who regard the resistance organisations in Peshawar as being too self-seeking and therefore refer to the six largest of them as spag dukanan - the six shops.

Yet, at the same time there is a tendency towards increased co-operation between some of the active resistance groups inside Afghanistan. A new generation of leaders has emerged from the resistance struggle and has in many cases replaced or overshadowed the traditional local leadership. Some of the most able of these leaders have managed to maintain relations with a resistance organisation in Peshawar, which gives them access to resources and arms, without allowing this to compromise their freedom of action, and have succeeded in uniting all

Religion and Politics

or most of the resistance groups in a particular province or region. This tendency is most developed in areas dominated by non-Pakhtun ethnic groups, whereas the Pakhtun resistance apparently remains fragmented. The most prominent examples of such unification, cutting across both political and ethnic divisions, are the resistance fronts headed by Massoud in the Panjshir valley, Sabiullah in the region around Mazar-i Sharif, and Ismail Khan and Allahuddin in the provinces of Herat, Ghor, Farah and Nimruz in Western Afghanistan.

So, whereas resistance groups formerly used to restrict their actions to the particular locality or region they consider their homeland, the existence of a certain amount of co-operation between the three large fronts of Northern and Western Afghanistan, as well as the sentiments expressed by Afghan refugees in Pakistan, indicate that the struggle is increasingly seen as one of national liberation.

Conclusion

In the preceding discussion I have tried to substantiate the argument that the categories of Islam, honour and homeland, which constitute the raison d'etre of the current Afghan resistance struggle, are also the source of its ideological and organisational heterogeneity. This paradox derives from the fact that although the three categories are simultaneously present in the political discourse and apparently serve to define the shared cultural tradition and way of life of the Pakhtun, these categories do not constitute a consistent ideology or system of meanings.

This lack of consistency is inherent in the categories, and exists on different levels. First of all, the precepts of Islam and the notions of pakhtunwali differ in ways which cannot be resolved without compromising one of the systems. Second, the concepts of Islam leave room for interpretation and accommodation of different views of how the believers should arrange their existence. Third, pakhtunwali is also ambiguous, because the maintenance of honour may pose the dilemma of choice between autonomy and agnatic solidarity, both of which are considered important values by the Pakhtun. Finally, the dilemma of choice

Religion and Politics

posed by the notion of honour generates factional rivalry, which provides a social setting that allows different solutions of the ideological inconsistencies to function as alternatives.

Viewed from this perspective Pakhtun culture in the sense of a unified, consistent, and shared ideology does not exist. Culture and ideology instead have to be understood as heterogeneous systems of meanings which contain inherent contradictions, ambiguities, and dilemmas that are resolved in different ways by the members of the society in question. Moreover, such alternative ideological versions are always associated with, and defined by, specific interests, which they in turn serve to legitimate.

Notes

This chapter was presented at the Symposium on Islam: State and Society held at the University of Aarhus from 31 August to 1 September 1984. Fieldwork was conducted during 1977 to 1978 in the Kunar Province and a supplementary shorter visit was undertaken in February-March 1981 to Afghan refugees in Pakistan and to Kunar. The research was funded by the Danish Research Council for the Humanities.

1. Pakhtun, who are also called Pashtun or Pathan, number about 6 million of the approximately 15 million inhabitants of Afghanistan. Their main settlement areas are in the eastern and southern parts of the country overlapping the border with Pakistan's North-West Frontier Province and Baluchistan, where an additional 6 million Pakhtun live.
2. The relationship between formal Islamic injunctions and Pakhtunwali is described by Boesen (1979/80) and Anderson (1980).
3. Other proverbs expressing the same conflict can be found in Enevoldsen (1967) and Anderson (1980).
4. Concerning such confrontations among the Pakhtun see Caroe (1958: 299 ff and 198 ff) and Spain (1963: 86 ff).
5. The political and ideological division among the Shi'a Hazara has been described by Roy (1983).

Religion and Politics

6. Besides referring to their proponents' ideological connections to 'fundamentalist' Islam in Pakistan, the name Panj Piri also carried the connotation of heresy, because it was used with the implication that the Islamic revolutionaries followed the fifth (:panj) Pir instead of one of the four established legal schools within Sunni Islam, i.e. the Hanafite, Malikite, Shafiite or Hanbalite.

References

Anderson, J.W. (1984) 'How Afghans define themselves in relation to Islam', in Revolutions and Rebellions in Afghanistan, M.N. Shahrani and R.L. Canfield (eds), Berkely: University of California.

Azoy, G.W. (1982) Buzkashi - Game and Power in Afghanistan, Philadelphia

Barth, F. (1959) 'Segmentary opposition and the theory of games: A study of Pathan organization', Journal of the Royal Anthropological Institute, vol. 89.

Boesen, I.W. (1979/80) 'Women, honour and love - Some aspects of Pashtun women's life in Eastern Afghanistan', Folk, vol. 21/22.

Canfield, R.L. (1973) 'Faction and conversion in a plural society: Religious alignments in the Hindu Kush', Ann Arbor.

Caroe, O. (1958) The Pathans 550 BC - AD 1957, London.

Christensen, A. (1982) 'Agnates, affines and allies: Patterns of marriage among Pakhtun in Kunar, North-East Afghanistan, Folk, vol. 24.

––– (1983a) 'Afghanistan - ikke kontrarevolution, men befrielseskamp, Jordens Folk, vol. 18, no. 1.

––– (1983b) 'Politik og religion i Afghanistan', IF Internationalt Forum, no. 3.

––– (1984) '"Udvikling" ovenfra - modstand nedefra: Socialisme og stammefolk i Afghanistan, Stofskifte - tidskrift for Antropologi, no. 10.

Enevoldsen, J. (1967) Oh mane - skynd dig - stig op og skin, Herning.

Ghani, A. (1978) 'Islam and state-building in a tribal society: Afghanistan 1880-1901'. Modern

Asian Studies, vol. 12, no. 2.
Janata, A. and R. Hassas (1975) 'Ghairatman – der gute Pashtune: Exkurs uber die Grundlagen des Pashtunwali', Afghanistan Journal, vol. 2, no. 3.
Kakar, H. (1971) Afghanistan: A study in international political developments 1880-1896, Kabul.
Roy, O. (1983) 'L'essor du khomeynisme parmi la minorite chiite, Le Monde Diplomatique, April 18.
Spain, J.W. (1963) The Pathan borderland, The Hague.

2

CULTURAL CHANGES AMONG THE MUJAHIDIN AND MUHAJERIN

Louis Dupree

For thousands of years the land we now call Afghanistan was in the centre of the action and the meeting-place of four ecological and cultural zones: the Middle East, Central Asia, South Asia and the Far East. Palaeolithic man lived in the caves of northern Afghanistan as early as 100,000 years ago and probably earlier. North Afghanistan possibly also sits in the zone of development of the domestication of the wheat/barley/sheep/goat/cattle complex, the Neolithic Revolution which gave mankind control of its food supply about 11,000 years ago. Post-World War II excavations indicate intimate commercial relations between the Bronze Age civilisations of Afghanistan, Central Asia, West Asia and the Indus Valley during the fourth to second millennia BC (Allchin and Hammond, 1978; L. Dupree, 1980; N.H. Dupree, 1983).

Another important event in world history was Alexander the Great's passage through the region in the fourth century BC. Out of a mixture of the sensuous Indian, humanistic Classical, and vigorous Central Asian-Sino-Siberian ideologies rose the Buddhism practised in most of the modern Far-Eastern and Southeast-Asian worlds. As a result of extensive contacts, particularly from the first to the fifth centuries AD, the Mahayana school and its attendant art styles travelled across Afghanistan into Central Asia and through the Dzungarian Gates to Mongolia, China, Korea and eventually to Japan. The caravan trails moved along the luxury-trade Silk Route, which connected ancient Cathay with the Mediterranean classical world of the Roman Empire (Rowland, 1970).

Islam had exploded into the region by the mid-seventh century AD and remains an important element in modern cultural and political patterns. Traditionally an area through which armies passed on their way to somewhere else, Afghanistan nevertheless witnessed the rise of several indigenous empires. The Ghaznavid (tenth-twelfth centuries AD), probably the most important, was a true renaissance of juxtaposed military conquests and cultural achievements (Bosworth, 1963).

Political instability, brought on by the destructive Mongol and Turco-Mongol invasions of the thirteenth to fourteenth centuries AD, and recurring localised, fratricidal wars broke up the land-based Silk Route trade, and by the fifteenth century European navigators were seeking new sea routes to the East, which led to the rediscovery, exploration, exploitation and development of a new world.

Asian imperialists (the Europeans did not invent imperialism!), mainly Persian Safavids and Indian Moghuls, fought over the Afghan area in the sixteenth to seventeenth centuries. In 1747 the last great Afghan empire rose under the leadership of Ahmad Shad Durrani, crowned king in Kandahar.

Continued fratricidal wars and the intrusion of European imperialism characterised nineteenth-century Afghanistan. British armies invaded Afghan territories in response to real or imagined threats to India as Czarist armies moved into the khanates of Central Asia, including lands claimed by Afghan amirs.

The creation of modern Afghanistan began during the reign of Abdur Rahman Khan (c.1880-1901). While external powers (Britain and Russia) drew the boundaries of Afghanistan, the Amir attempted to spread his influence (if not actual control) over the myriad ethnolinguistic groups and tribal kingdoms included inside his boundaries, a process of 'internal imperialism' (Kakar, 1979).

So, until the late nineteenth century, the Afghans, and most other areas in Afro-Asia, were largely dominated by patterns of political fusion and fission, which refers to the following sequence of events: a charismatic leader would arise in a tribal society and by using military power, diplomatic intrigue and judiciously arranged marriages, he would unite several tribes into a confederation, which would spread as far as its accumulated power permitted.

With (and sometimes before) the death of the emperor, fission would occur, and the great empire once again would segment into a multiplicity of tribal kingdoms. Later, another charismatic leader would arrive, and the process would begin again.

British and Russian imperialism, however, blocked Abdur Rahman, spoiling any plans he may have had to spill over into India, Persia or Central Asia, and thus create another Afghan empire. European imperialism had replaced Asian imperialism in the region.

The British, with at least the tacit consent of the Russians, controlled Afghanistan's foreign relations until 1919, when the Afghans gained the right to conduct their own foreign affairs after the Third Anglo-Afghan War in May 1919. (For a discussion of Afghan historical patterns, v. L. Dupree 1980.)

Four twentieth-century patterns wove contrapuntally in and out of the Afghanistan scene: economic development, alternating political repression and reform, neutrality in two world wars and non-alignment in between, until the Soviet invasion of December 1979. Some may argue that Soviet influence became paramount after the so-called ingelab-i-Saur, but until the 1979 intervention the leaders of the Democratic Republic of Afghanistan (DRA) perceived themselves as being non-aligned - with a tilt toward the USSR. So what else is new? Most so-called non-aligned nations tilt one way or the other, sometimes changing to suit their own interests.

But what is important for us is what has happened to overall cultural patterns since the Soviet invasion.

Much has been written about external intervention in the First Russo-Afghan War (1979-?). But little attention has been paid to internal Afghan cultural reactions to events since the 1978 leftist coup, which ushered in the era of the DRA. (See Select Bibliography).

To begin to explore how and why the culture reacted as it did without external interference, we should look briefly at what constitutes a peasant-tribal society, with emphasis on the Afghan scene.

Statistics in the non-Western world are notoriously inaccurate, so any used in this chapter will be what statisticians refer to as 'intelligent estimates', which really means 'wild guesses based on inadequate data'.

I shall only occasionally allude to the Afghan urban scene. The rural, peasant-tribal segments accounted for between 90-95 per cent of the pre-1978 population, and currently make up at least similar percentages among the Afghan refugees.

Although many common cultural elements exist between the urban and rural sectors (more than many literate, citified Afghans wish to admit), there are major differences among those with Western (including Soviet) educations. These urban types often react in predictable Western ways, but just as often revert to traditional rural Afghan values under stress situations.

I propose to outline the attributes of the Afghan peasant-tribal society under six major categories: multilingual; non-literacy; basic food production; lack of mobility; no adolescence; kinship replaces government. Each of these attributes is 180 degrees away from the patterns entrenched in Western, industrialised, developed (however defined) nations.

(1) Multilingual

Several language families and numerous dialects are represented in Afghanistan. Language lends itself to a perpetuation of ethnicity and when ethnic pride is reinforced by physical and religious differences, discriminations and dislikes are intensified.

In the Western world, usually a single language dominates the scene in any given country. Language has always been one of the major unifying factors in the creation of a nation-state in the Western sense.

(2) Non-literacy

The literate section of the Afghan nation has never reached 10 per cent. Literacy is not the only factor leading toward national unity, but it is certainly important. Multilingualism combines with non-literacy to form powerful forces against unification in non-Western societies.

(3) Basic food production

In Afghanistan, as well as in most other Third World countries, the majority of the people live in an agricultural or herding cycle (or combinations of the two). In spite of this, most pre-industrial nations are food-deficient countries. By contrast, the USA can feed itself to obscene obesity and have enough left over to feed most of the pre-industrial world. Technology, climate and soil partly account for this agricultural miracle.

(4) Lack of mobility

In most pre-industrial nations, the pattern is a lack of economic, social and political mobility. If an Afghan man is born into a farming family, the odds are he will be a farmer. He will either marry a father's brother's daughter, or someone as close to that relationship as possible. Alternately, he will marry a distant kinswoman, usually through an agreement by the two families involved and without consultation with the two main actors. Politically, a man is born into a leader or follower kin-group.

None of the above are hard and fast rules, and in Afghan history farmers have risen to become commercial entrepreneurs, men have married women outside their own ethnic groups, and peasants have become kings, and kings, peasants.

But the major patterns have been the lack of mobility discussed above.

(5) No adolescence

Child socialisation in developed nations occur mainly outside the family, and children are being subjected to extra-family education at younger and younger ages, with the family becoming less and less important.

In rural Afghanistan, and to a lesser extent urban Afghanistan, child socialisation takes place inside the nuclear and extended families and usually includes certain collateral relatives.

(6) Kinship replaces government

The above five attributes lead to the conclusion that the reciprocal, functioning rights and obligations between governed and government in Western societies are retained in kin-orientated, territorial groups in rural Afghanistan and other pre-industrial societies (Dupree and Albert, 1974).

Cultural Responses to the War

Having briefly discussed the Afghan peasant-tribal society, I now submit that there are several ways of discussing Afghan cultural patterns as witnessed by other chapters in this book. In addition, there are regional variations under each theme. Therefore, with these caveats I shall give several examples of how Afghan culture has reacted to the war.

(1) Rhetoric

The initial rhetoric of the DRA disturbed many in the countryside. The phraseology in Dari, Pashto, Turkic dialects, etc., was reminiscent of the noises coming out of the USSR into Afghanistan for decades. Many Afghans, rural and urban alike, immediately tagged the label 'Communist' on to those who had seized power, overthrown the Republic of Afghanistan (RA), and killed the Prime Minister Daoud and most of his family. The irony is that the DRA announced virtually the same reforms proposed by the Daoud regime, but Daoud had used acceptable Dari and Pashto terminology, whereas the DRA translated much of the Marxist-Leninist dialectic directly into local languages.

Also ironic, the DRA insisted it was not 'Communist', and announced a unique brand of socialism, suitable to Afghanistan. I believed them, although the leadership, especially Hafizullah Amin, went out of his way in international conferences to heap excessive praise on the USSR. I called Amin the 'unguided missile of the Soviet Union'.

In any event, both Amin and Nur Mohammed Taraki, the Khalq leaders, are now dead, partly because they were not subservient to the USSR, and partly because the reforms proposed with the unacceptable rhetoric

The Mujahidin and Muhajerin

sounded (in many cases) anti-Islamic and anti-Afghan culture. Amin and Taraki seemed to go out of their way to alienate every segment of Afghan society.

(2) Revolts: the seasonal aspects of Afghan tribal warfare and government over-reaction

The DRA coup d'etat occurred on 24-25 April 1978, and the government immediately began a series of arrests, mainly of Western (including some Soviet) educated Afghans. However, repressions and tortures are nothing new in Afghan history.

Little resistance to the regime occurred between late April and late August 1978. The leaders of the DRA felt confident that, even if the rural population did not actively support them, at least the countryside would remain passive. This proved to be a major miscalculation.

In late August 1978, revolts occurred in Nuristan (a mountainous region in eastern Afghanistan on the Pakistani border) and rapidly spread. The timing of the insurgencies was culturally and ecologically sound.

From early spring to early fall, the economic cycle dominates the Afghan countryside, and the intensity of the agricultural and herding activities forces people to work co-operatively. Also, it is difficult to farm and fight at the same time. A period of relative leisure drifts in during the fall season and lasts until early spring when the economic cycle begins again. During the slack season, blood feuds sometimes recommence.

But if the central government has instituted culturally (or economically) objectionable policies, the country people often put aside their own squabbles and march on the nearest government outposts. Initially, the object is not to overthrow the government, but to express an opinion.

The response of the government should always be culturally-orientated. It should send just enough troops into the field to check the revolt, and then call for a Loya Jirgah, a great national assembly which includes tribal and regional notables, religious leaders, top government civil servants, military officers, and others in power. The Loya Jirgah representatives should discuss the problems which set off the revolt. A consensus should be reached before spring, and all concerned return to their respective occupations.

However, in the fall of 1978, the DRA cadre over-reacted with their Russian advisers, aircraft, napalm and bombs. The government bombed villages in Nuristan and elsewhere and shed much blood. A badal (blood feud) quickly developed between the people and the DRA, precluding a short-term, peaceful solution.

Some specialists predicted the insurgents would cease fighting and go back to farming and/or herding as spring approached in 1979. But too much blood had been spilled, and no one 'placed the stone on the mountain', a traditional sign that local feuds should end and farming begin. The annual ecological cycle often governs warfare in pre-industrial societies. Native Americans (formerly referred to as 'American Indians') had a similar custom to end seasonal fights: they 'buried the hatchet'.

Most insurgents returned to the annual economic cycle in the spring of 1979, but many remained in the field to fight. This was another cultural signal to the regime in Kabul: 'Now we insurgents are fighting to overthrow the government'. By early fall 1979, it became obvious that unless the Soviets directly intervened militarily the government in Kabul would eventually collapse.

(3) The cultural responses

The Soviet invasion surprised many - including me. I did not believe the Soviets would invade because among other things it would establish a new ballgame: this would be the first, direct, post-World War II Soviet military aggression on an independent, non-aligned nation. We cannot consider Czechoslovakia and Hungary in the same category. They had been previously occupied, and in spite of how the Czechs and Hungarians may have felt, most of the world accepted the Soviet action with only overt protests.

Before the Soviet invasion only a small percentage of the Afghan population was actively engaged in revolt. After 24 December 1979 virtually the entire Afghan nation resisted the foreign invader.

The Mujahidin and Muhajerin

The Afghan kin-political system had responded in a traditional manner. The formalised segmentary <u>vertical</u> lineages in rural Afghanistan (strongest among the Pushtun tribes along the Durand Line) have developed a sensitive network of interlocking, reciprocal rights and obligations, not only between kin-units, but between patrons and clients. The segmentary system has various levels of intensity, depending on the situation at any given time. Different types of external and internal stress trigger off different responses. For example, when the British invaded Afghanistan four times in the nineteenth century (1839, 1842, 1878, 1879), the important political (<u>i.e.</u> military) responses came from the tribes, some opposing the British, some actually supporting them.

Pre-1880 tribal and subtribal loyalties were largely territorial, and those regional loyalties are still important in most parts of Afghanistan. Feuds occurred between neighbouring vertical-structured, segmentary groups, but when an <u>external horizontal</u> force intruded and threatened <u>indigenous vertical</u> structures, regional traditional enemies often united and attempted to throw out the invader.

(4) The Pushtunwali in action

In the midst of a twentieth-century mechanised war, the Afghans often follow the dictates of their Pushtunwali (Code of the Hills). The Pushtunwali relates only to the Pushtun, but variations of customary law (<u>rasma ruwag</u>) exist among all the ethnolinguistic groups in Afghanistan (Ahmed, 1980; Steul, 1981).

One example of events which triggered off the Pushtunwali will suffice to illustrate the point. In 1983, the Soviets launched a combined airborne and ground attack in the Jigdalak area about half way between Kabul and Jalalabad. The mujahidin had been very active in attacking outposts, ambushing convoys and cutting the power lines between Sarobi and Kabul. The Soviet tactical plan was to land heliborne troops in the Jigdalak Valley in order to secure the high ground while an armoured column from Kabul broke through to the area. The mujahidin would be destroyed by a pincer movement.

The heliborne troops landed, but were immediately brought under intense small-arms fire from the surrounding hills. Meanwhile, the armoured column was stopped by mines which had been expertly planted in the road. In addition, the tanks and armoured personnel carriers came up against effective rocket attacks, and suffered severe losses in men and material. The armoured column turned back. Meanwhile, the heliborne troops were being decimated. The Soviets had gone one hill too far.

Helicopters flew in from Jalalabad and Kabul to evacuate the dead and wounded. The mujahidin fired at the helicopters until they landed. Then they ceased fire! Why? Because the Pushtunwali forbids firing at known wounded. The helicopters took off with their cargoes of casualties and the mujahidin refrained from firing. However, when the 'choppers' returned empty, the firing commenced and continued until the 'choppers' landed. Honour amidst the horrors of war is a rarity. As the war continued, however, such niceties disappeared.

(5) The Yugoslav model

Many decry the 'lack of unity' among and between the mujahidin groups but, in my opinion, a logical evolution is taking place. National unity has never existed in Afghanistan because of geographic-ecological factors and ethnolinguistic differences encouraged by regional ethnicity.

Of course, many in the urban intelligentsia do feel loyalty to a great Afghan nation-state, but they constitute a distinct minority.

However, as mentioned previously, a new pattern is evolving and neighbouring groups are uniting to fight a common enemy. Eventually, this pattern will probably evolve into a national liberation movement.

The nearest analogue in modern times is the World War II Yugoslav partisan movement. The Yugoslav nation consists of seven ethnolinguistic groups. At first the groups independently resisted the Germans and Italians. As the war progressed, however, they united into two opposing politico-military organisations: the left under Tito, the right under Draza Mihajlovic. These two groups fought each other when

The Mujahidin and Muhajerin

they were not fighting the Germans and Italians.

Given Afghan culture, it will take longer for the Afghans to unite into even two groups. And, in some areas (such as Nuristan and the Hazarajat), Afghan ethnic groups fight each other when the Soviets are not in the region. These internal fights are to establish political pecking orders within ethnic zones, and are possibly a first step toward nationalism.

In addition, the Soviet invasion has forced many Afghans, rural as well as urban, to state that they are fighting to 'drive the Soviets from our country - our homeland', and such attitudes will become more prevalent as the war progresses. The Soviets, therefore, have unwittingly thrust nationalism on top of regionalism.

(6) The warrior-poet

The Afghan not only fights for group honour, but also for individual honour. The ideal male personality type is the warrior-poet, a man who is brave in battle and can articulate well at the village or tribal council. Afghan history, folklore, folksongs and literature are replete with the idealisation of such attitudes. Seldom does a man achieve both statuses, but when he does, he becomes the hero of his age, the prime example being Khushal Khan Khattak (AD 1613-1690).

The persistence of warfare themes in Afghan culture is well documented, and anyone living anywhere in Afghanistan can attest to the violent patterns in the society. The history of Central Asia reeks with warfare, the rise and fall of various Turkic dynasties and empires, i.e. Turkoman, Uzbek, etc. The exploits of brave warriors are extolled. Even the Kirghiz of Hajji Rahman Qul (now settled in the Lake Van region of Turkey) recount such tales of events lived through in recent times. And the Qizilbash, though reduced to being primarily bureaucrats and technocrats for the pre-1978 Mohammadzai, were originally founded as a warrior class.

Therefore, the non-Pushtun peoples of northern Afghanistan have a long tradition of being warrior-poets. They fought not only Pushtun, but Russians,

The Mujahidin and Muhajerin

Persians, Moghul Indians and the British, and are now fighting as hard - or harder - than the Pushtun to the south and south-east.

The current Russo-Afghan War has given the Afghans a chance to achieve warrior-poet status, and, on the whole, they welcome the opportunity, which partly accounts for the tenacity and longevity of the resistance. With minimal support from the outside, the mujahidin have been fighting for eight years as of 24 December 1979. Which means the freedom fighters have fought the Soviets for longer than the Soviets fought in World War II (four years, three months): the Perfidious Polish Campaign (17 September - c. 1 January 1940); the Great Patriotic War (22 June 1941- 7 May 1945); the Japanese Coda (9-11 August 1945).

The Muhajerin in Pakistan

It is impossible to separate the mujahidin from the muhajerin. A constant flow exists across the border. Men go to battle and return. Young boys reach the age of 17 or 18 and go to fight. An unlimited pool of recruits comes of age annually in the camps.

The refugees were first forced to live in tents, and the camps are still referred to as Refugee Tented Villages (RTVs) to indicate their status in Pakistan: i.e. they are 'temporarily' out of their homeland and will return when the situation permits.

However, most camps have evolved into the same type of mud-brick villages which the Afghans left behind. The refugees have 'cloned' their former villages on Pakistani soil. A major problem, however, is that technically the refugee cannot own land, or farm, except as hired labour.

In addition, the re-creation of the 'Bronze Age' is occurring in the commercial sense. Bazaars spring up to satisfy the needs of the RTVs, and shopkeepers have links with nearby towns to obtain the necessary goods. These links are widening all the time.

Other problems complicate the scene, however, and some are psychocultural. It is the women who suffer the most. Afghan villages are space-orientated. Within walled family compounds, space for physical and psychological movement pervades the cultural atmosphere and there is much movement between compounds.

The Mujahidin and Muhajerin

When the men are in the field, women dominate the villages (N.H. Dupree, 1984).

A positive note must be briefly sounded. Most refugees in Pakistan are Pushtun, but other Afghan ethnic groups are also represented. At times hostile to one another, at times tolerant, a major pattern is the evolution of a feeling that 'we are all Afghans - at last'. This attitude has a long way to go, however, before it expresses itself as a genuine nationalism.

Politically, the structure is also changing. In most rural areas of Afghanistan (there are exceptions) no single malik (or whatever regional term means 'chief' or 'headman') governs a village or other rural groups. The ideal is collective leadership of the elders, activated by the jirgah (Pashto) or majlis (Dari), the institutionalised village council. Each member of the council has a speciality, i.e. water and land rights; marital relations; pasturage problems; feuds (the malik or war chief). The most visible elder to the outside world is the man who is the go-between between his people and the government. He is the individual called the malik by outsiders.

During the first prime ministership of Mohammad Daoud (1953-63), a new, informal power group began to develop in the countryside. The unfair conscription of the past was substituted by a fair (using Afghan standards) method of drafting men to serve in the army, air force, police, gendarmerie, and labour corps.

After two years of service, usually far from their home villages, these young drafters returned with a common experience outside the traditional village culture. Back home, in most cases they came together as informal power groups. As time went by, the groups grew in size. They did not openly challenge the traditional elders, but their influence and opinions often had an impact on the decision-making process.

Currently, three types of maliks exist in the approximately 350 RTVs in Pakistan. The classic 'white beards' or elders basically perform the same functions they did in Afghanistan. However, unique economic, political and social strains have arisen in the new condition. The traditional maliks represent

The Mujahidin and Muhajerin

the past, and new maliks have evolved to meet the requirements of the RTVs and the war across the border.

The second type of malik is the <u>rupiyah malik</u>, or the man with the rupees. He has returned from a job in the oil-rich Gulf States, Iran, or elsewhere in West Asia and North Africa. Now wealthy, he may or may not have been a member of the traditional power elite, but comes to his new position of power by virtue of his money, which he often uses to construct guest houses, mosques (complete with loudspeakers), shops, etc., in order to enhance his prestige. Also, he often functions as the go-between between the RTVs and the Pakistani government officials, representatives of the United Nations High Commissioner for Refugees (UNHCR), and professional members of bilateral and international volunteer agencies. In his role as go-between, the rupiyah malik is in a position to increase his wealth through collusion with Pakistani officials responsible for the distribution of refugee aid supplies. Of course, not <u>all</u> rupiyah maliks engage in such activities.

The rupiyah malik is now widening his coterie of followers, but it is questionable how many will be supported if and when the refugees return home.

The third type of malik is a different breed: <u>those who command the freedom fighters</u> inside Afghanistan. Some are religious leaders, others are from the families with traditional power, still others are in the same genre as the young men who returned home from military service in pre-1978 Afghanistan. These leaders are listened to respectfully, although most still defer to the traditional maliks. But the impact and power of these mostly young field commanders increases with time. A major effort of the KHAD (Afghan KGB) is currently geared to the assassination of these military commanders (L. Dupree, 1984).

In addition to the <u>'normal' refugee migration</u> from Afghanistan to Pakistan and Iran, other types of migrations have developed. For the past two years or so, a type of <u>seasonal trans-border migration</u> has evolved. Farmers, particularly those with lands near the Durand Line, go back into Afghanistan to plant crops. Most return to the camps in Pakistan, but some remain behind to tend the crops. Also, the mujahidin encourage farmers to stay on the land in order to ensure a constant food supply. Forced retention of farmers on the land is rare, but not unknown.

A re-migration pattern has emerged because of the war. The descendants of several Pushtun groups sent north by Amir Abdur Rahman in the late nineteenth century have returned to the lands of their grandfathers and great-grandfathers. The northern non-Pushtun ethnic groups (such as the Turkoman, Uzbek, Tajik and Hazara) often 'encourage' such departures. In any event, the re-migrated Pushtun usually deposit their families in the relative safety of the RTVs in Pakistan, and then return to Afghanistan to fight in their homelands of origin. They have said that no matter what happens, they will remain in the south, and not return to the north.

Therefore (and inadvertently), the Soviets have forced at least a partial redistribution of ethnic groups inside Afghanistan, roughly recreating the regional groupings of pre-1880. But adjustments have been painful, and loss of property severe. Any readjustment after the war will be just as painful, as the 'northern' Pushtun try to integrate with their southern cousins.

However, the post-war creation of a federal Afghanistan based on primary ethnolinguistic units will be easier.

Afghan cultural patterns as we knew them before 1978 are being altered by external and internal forces. Whatever happens, Afghan culture will be recognised as distinctively Afghan in general, and superficially distinctive within regions. This is neither an encouraging nor pejorative statement, but this is what cultural processes are all about.

Meanwhile, there is no light at the end of the Salang Tunnel.

References

Ahmed, Akbar (1980) Pukhtun Economy and Society, Routledge & Kegan Paul, London
Allchin, F.R and N. Hammond (eds.) (1978) The Archaeology of Afghanistan, Academic Press, London

Bosworth, C. (1963) The Ghaznavids, University of Edinburgh Press, Edinburgh
Dupree, Louis (1980) Afghanistan, Princeton University Press, Princeton
--- (1984) 'Afghanistan in 1983. And Still No Solution', Asian Survey Vol. XXXIV No. 2 pp. 229-39
--- and L. Albert (1974) Afghanistan in the 1970s, Praeger, New York
Dupree, Nancy Hatch (1983) 'Afghanistan: Archaeology', Encyclopaedia Iranica, Ehsan Yashater (ed.), vol. 1, Fasc. 5, pp 525-544, Routledge & Kegan Paul, London
--- (1984) 'Revolutionary rhetoric and Afghan women', in Revolutions and Rebellions in Afghanistan, Nazif Shahrani and Robert Canfield (eds.), University of California Press, Berkeley
Kakar, Hasan Kawun (1979) Government and Society in Afghanistan: The Reign of Amir Abd al-Rahman Khan, University of Texas Press, Austin and London
Rowland Benjamin (1970) Zentralasien, Holle Verlag, Baden-Baden
Steul, Willi (1981) Hilfe fur Afghanistan, Aktuell, Bonn

A Select Bibliography of Recent Books on Afghanistan

Arnold, Anthony (1981, 1985) Afghanistan: The Soviet Invasion in Perspective, Hoover Institution, Stanford University
--- (1983) Afghanistan's Two Party Communism - Parcham and Khalq, Hoover Institution, Stanford University
de Beaurecueil, Serge (1983) Mes Enfants de Kaboul, Editions J.-C. Lattes, Paris
Bennigsen, Alexandre and Marie Broxup (1983) The Islamic Threat to the Soviet State, St Martin's Press, New York
Bhargava, G.S. (1983) South Asian Security after Afghanistan, Lexington Books, New York
Bradsher, Henry S. (1983, 1985) Afghanistan and the Soviet Union, Duke University Press, Durham
Chaffetz, David (1981) A Journey through Afghanistan, Regnery Gateway, Chicago

The Mujahidin and Muhajerin

Chaliand, Gerard (1982) (trans. by Tamar Jacoby), Report from Afghanistan, Viking/Penguin, New York

Cleveland, Ray L. (1983) The Middle East and South Asia 1983, Stryker-Post Publications, Washington

Collins, Joseph T (1985) The Soviet Invasion of Afghanistan, Lexington Books, New York

Dupree, Louis (1980a) Afghanistan, Princeton University Press (1st paperback ed.)

———— (1980b) Red Flag Over the Hindu Kush, Parts I-VI, American Universities Field Staff Reports, Asia, Nos. 44-45, 1979; Nos. 23, 27-29, 37

Fullerton, John (1983) The Soviet Occupation of Afghanistan, South China Morning Post, Hong Kong

Gall, Sandy (1983) Behind Russian Lines: An Afghan Journal, Sidgwick & Jackson, London

Girardet, Edward (1985) Afghanistan: The Soviet War, St Martin's Press, New York

Griffiths, John (1981) Afghanistan: Key to a Continent, Westview Press, Boulder

Haliday, Fred (1983) Threat from the East? Soviet Policy from Afghanistan and Iran to the Horn of Africa, Penguin, Harmondsworth

Hammond, Thomas T. (1973) Red Flag over Afghanistan, Westview Press, Boulder

Harrison, Selig (1981) In Afghanistan's Shadow: Baluch Nationalism and Soviet Temptations, Carnegie Endowment for International Peace, Washington

Hyman, Anthony (1982, 1985) Afghanistan under Soviet Domination, Macmillan, London

Khalilzad, Zalmay (1980) The Return of the Great Game, California Seminar on International Security and Foreign Policy, Santa Monica

Magnus, Ralph (ed.) (1985) Afghan Alternatives: Issues, Options, and Policies, Transaction, Inc., New Brunswick, New Jersey

Male, Beverly (1982) Revolutionary Afghanistan, St Martin's Press, New York

Manzar, A.M. (1980) Red Clouds over Afghanistan, Institute of Policy Studies, Islamabad

Monks, Alfred (1981) The Soviet Intervention in Afghanistan, American Enterprise Institute for Public Policy Research, Washington and London

Nayar, Kuldip (1981) Report on Afghanistan, Allied Publishers, New Delhi

Newell, Nancy Peabody and Richard S. (1981) *The Struggle for Afghanistan*, Cornell University Press

Reeves, Richard (1984) *Passage to Peshawar*, Simon & Schuster, New York

Roy, Olivier (1985) *L'Afghanistan: Islam et Modernite Politique*, Editions du Seuil, Paris

Rubinstein, Alvin Z. (1982) *Soviet Policy Toward Turkey, Iran, and Afghanistan*, Praeger, New York

Ryan, Nigel (1983) *A Hitch or Two in Afghanistan*, Weidenfeld & Nicolson, London

Shahrami, M. Nazif and Robert L. Canfield (eds.) (1984) *Revolutions and Rebellions in Afghanistan: An Anthropological View*, Institute of International Studies, University of California Press, Berkeley

Siddiq, Mr A.F. (1983) *Afghanistan: The Economic Impact of the Soviet Invasion*, Paper No. 1, Research Institute for Inner Asian Studies, Indiana University

Steul, Willi (1981) *Hilfe fur Afghanistan*, Aktuell, Bonn

Tapper, Richard (ed.) (1983) *The Conflict of Time and State in Iran and Afghanistan*, St Martin's Press, London

Van Dyk, Jere (1983) *In Afghanistan: An American Odyssey*, Coward-McCann, New York

Victor, Jean Christophe (1983) *La Cite des Murmures*, J.C. Lattes, Paris

Vogel, Heinrich (ed.) (1980) *Die Sowjetische Intervention in Afghanistan*, Nomos Verlagsgesellschaft, Baden-Baden

Wolpert, Stanley (1982) *Roots of Confrontation in South Asia: Afghanistan, Pakistan, India and the Superpowers*, Oxford University Press, Oxford

Ziring, Lawrence (1981) *Iran, Turkey and Afghanistan: A Political Chronology*, Praeger, New York

--- (1982) *The Subcontinent in World Politics*, Revised ed., Praeger, New York

3

CONCEPTS OF PERSONAL, MORAL AND SOCIAL DISORDER AMONG DURRANI PASHTUNS IN NORTHERN AFGHANISTAN

Nancy Tapper and Richard Tapper

This chapter discusses the Durrani Pashtun response to disorder and affliction in terms of their notions of the self, personhood, moral responsibility and social order.(1) The Durrani material seems to present two kinds of problems: first, how does the classification of components of the person relate to the classification of causes of affliction and, second, how do these two systems of classification relate to ideas of social roles and responsibilities?

Our approach to these problems is threefold. First, we look at how Durrani relate aspects of the physical body to personality and concepts of the person. Second, we consider the way they define and distinguish good/correct/responsible behaviour from that which they consider bad/improper/irresponsible. In other words, our second focus is their system of morality. Third, we are concerned with Durrani ways of dealing with random afflictions such as ill health and personal accidents on the one hand, and large-scale changes in social organisation and natural disasters on the other. The two most striking features of the system of causality and explanation we describe are the extent to which gender distinctions dominate other perceptions and categories relating to the person and how these gender distinctions themselves are subsumed by abstract and comprehensive notions of the subordination of all living things to the will of God.

Durrani attribute personal afflictions such as injury or ill-health either to God acting directly but for unknowable reasons or in response to human sin or to intermediate supernatural agencies such as spirits or the evil eye, in which case the victim is not usually held morally responsible for the affliction. Many of our observations on Durrani responses to disorder and personal affliction lend themselves to interpretation and explanation in the light of current ideas in the anthropological literature on spirit possession and gender relations,(2) but these do not account for all the features of the system we describe.

Disorders resulting from breaches of moral rules on authority, sexual behaviour and social relations generally are attributed to individuals' 'insanity', lack of 'reason' and inability to control themselves and their dependants. Here too gender distinctions are of central importance, for such failures of moral responsibility are discussed in the idiom of honour and shame and are dealt with actively and collectively in terms of this ideology of control. Durrani have also experienced disorder and change on a wider scale. Historical events and processes (such as their migration to the north of the country, the Saqawi rebellion of 1929 and the intermittent conflict with other ethnic groups) are perceived by Durrani as affecting society at large and over long periods of time, and are treated as essentially non-social and as outside the control of individuals or social groups. In so far as such processes and events are considered a threat to Durrani culture, they are seen as part of an inexorable movement towards the total social collapse which will herald the end of the world. Durrani take a similar view of what we would call 'natural' disasters such as drought, flood or famine, which are not areas open to question or explanation, however much individuals or groups have suffered. Rather, such disasters, like political disorder and radical social change, are stoically endured and their efforts pragmatically minimised on a day-to-day basis, by the use of whatever resources are available.

Taken together, the ways Durrani view and respond to personal, moral and political disorder suggest sources of cultural flexibility and resilience as well as an active, pragmatic resistance to outside threats. But, before we tackle these issues further, we need

Concepts of Disorder among Durrani Pashtuns

some background information on the community studied.

Durrani Pashtun Society in Northern Afghanistan

Around two million Durrani Pashtun, all claiming common descent, are scattered around Afghanistan, particularly in the south-west of the country. In the Saripul region of north-central Afghanistan, at the time of fieldwork, there were some 15,000 Durrani, mainly from the Ishaqzai tribe, living in 15 localised sub-tribes. They formed 10 per cent of an ethnically and linguistically varied regional population among which they compete for resources (see R. Tapper, 1984).

Though there is considerable and increasing economic and political inequality in any sub-tribe, Durrani maintain a strong ideology of equality. They see themselves as an undifferentiated ethnic group, ideally an endogamous patrilineage of Pashtu-speaking Sunni Muslims, superior by all these criteria to all other groups. Within Durrani groups, the household is ideally independent, a self-sufficient unit under a single male leader who controls its productive and reproductive resources (land, flocks, labour, women). Durrani should never interfere in another household's affairs, except in the extremely rare cases where there is a threat to the absolute rule that Durrani women must marry within the ethnic group. Durrani cosmology and religious beliefs are not unlike those found in other parts of the Muslim world. Briefly, Allah is the only and supreme God, omnipotent but directing only the forces of good (the angels and Muslims), while the forces of evil, represented by devils (sheytan) and jinns (pirey) and people who have lost their humanity by denying God and his laws, are independent of his immediate, though not his ultimate concern.

Durrani Ideas of the Self and the Causes of Personal Affliction

Durrani ideas of the constitution of the self, of the nature of the body and its organs, of health and illness, and of soul, spirit and intelligence, are related to the Islamic-Galenic system described elsewhere (see, e.g., Good, 1977; also R. Tapper & N. Tapper, 1986 and n.d.).

For Durrani, physical and spiritual dimensions of the self are intimately connected. One of the main terms Durrani use is dzan, whose meaning is 'self', but also both 'body' and 'soul'. Another term, surat, refers primarily to the physical body, while ruh and nafas (also 'breath') are the interchangeable main terms for both 'soul' and 'spirit' (which leave the body on death and are taken by angels to God's presence). And there is a further term, sa, which can mean 'breath', 'spirit', 'life-force', and 'blood'.

At this general level women's and men's bodies are similarly constituted. However, when Durrani consider the self in more detail, they focus first on the head and its associated gender differences. The head (sar) is the location of the brain (maghza) in which resides the supreme human faculty of 'aql, 'reason' - that is, the ability to make rational, sensible decisions, but also connoting self-control and discipline. As elsewhere in the Muslim world, men are thought to have greater 'aql than women and, for this reason, they also have more privileges, and more responsibilities, than women who are, conversely, expected to be more emotional and also more susceptible to disease.

The relation between 'reason', the physical body, gender categories and morality can be seen clearly in the three following examples. First, although devils (sheytan) exist independently of the self, and are sometimes said to be a type of jinn, they do not come from outside but are thought to live more or less permanently inside every body. Sheytan can be controlled by 'aql and religious purity (e.g. washing before prayer). Women, who have less 'aql and are more emotional than men, are also said to have more sheytan. The sheytan's object is devilry (sheytani): to cause quarrels and divert thought and emotions from the path of haqq (the right and just) to nahaqq (wrong) and from rawa (permitted) to narawa (forbidden). For this reason all women are excluded from the mosque.

Second, Durrani associate 'aql, 'thought' (pikr) and 'far-sighted(ness)' (durandish) with their own tribal identity and compare themselves favourably in

Concepts of Disorder among Durrani Pashtuns

these respects with members of other ethnic groups whom they scorn as 'witless' (bi-'aql), 'short-sighted' (kota-pikr), or 'shallow' (spak), characterisations both women and men sometimes also use of women. To Durrani, all non-Durrani fail to conform to their notions about the rationality of adults. Indeed the Durrani stereotypes of the Russians are simply an extreme expression of this notion. The Durrani regard the Russians, the only infidel group with whom they have had any contact, as fundamentally lacking all those personal characteristics which determine moral responsibility. The Durrani associate the godless Russians with pork-eating, drunkenness, nakedness, cannibalism and mother and sister incest: their stereotype of the Soviet way of life is antithetical to every value Durrani hold dear.

Third, the head and face (makh) are closely associated, physically and metaphorically with the maintenance of honour. The cut and grooming of hair on the head and the style of head coverings are important idioms for expressing the honorable status of individuals - child or adult, man or woman - and groups.

The head (sar) is often opposed to the body (surat). The main organ of the latter is zra (heart) which is the location not only of the ruh and nafas but also of the main human emotions such as courage, anger, fear, sorrow, love, hate and happiness. As with zra, the characterisation of other bodily organs is also complex. Of these the dzigar or ina (liver) is the most important for it transforms food into blood and (like zra) is associated with powerful emotions such as humiliation and eagerness for revenge. Blood (wina) itself is channelled in reg (veins) which are associated with lineage and descent (see N. Tapper and R. Tapper, 1982), while the blood of childbirth is linked with the key Pashtun notion of homeland (watan) round which all concepts of identity focus.

In sum, the local expression of this system of body symbolism offers Durrani one way of defining their entire social universe - of distinguishing women from men, Durrani from non-Durrani and Muslims from the godless Russians who are less than human because they deny the spiritual dimension of the self. Our discussion also shows how roles Durrani define in physical terms are nonetheless intimately associated with specific rights and duties. All adult Durrani, for instance, are expected to be humane and well-mannered. But men's behaviour is expected to be more serious (drund) or mature (pakha) as well as wise and honourable. A man should display courage in the measured defence of right against wrong. Such responsibility focuses crucially on the men's obligation to protect the weaker members of their households and household resources against all threats. Women, by contrast, are expected to be honourable but passive. A woman's key responsibilities concern child-bearing and raising children. The qualities of reason, courage and piety are not expected in women, but one who displays them is said to be 'like a man' and is admired, but considered eccentric.

Both men and women recognise these definitions of their respective roles and responsibilities and both consider that by far the greater burden falls on men who must act in a wide range of public contexts. Men who show blatant inability to control and use resources effectively are liable to oppression by neighbours and relatives and to lose possession of their resources completely. Such incompetence, and other breaches of convention, may be held to be the work of sheytan, but these should be under the control of 'aql, and specific anti-social acts are never so excused. More often, incompetence and lack of 'aql are attributed to 'insanity' (lewantop), though this does not by itself cancel a person's jural/moral responsibility in this life nor the retribution which may be due on the Day of Judgement. The only possible condition (other than an act of God) which exempts a person from responsibility for failure and for the consequences of his actions, is being possessed by a jinn.

Jinns are supernatural, usually evil creatures that attack or possess people (or animals), causing illness or death. Suffering of all kinds may be attributed to them ad hoc, when other explanations fail. Indeed, possession by jinns is interpreted in amoral terms: that is, the victim of such possession is usually reckoned to be inculpable.

The condition of a person's eyes and mouth may

indicate the first signs of jinn attack and possession, so the eyes and the mouth are also the source of two further possible causes of affliction, the evil eye and curse. The evil eye (nazar, sterga) resembles the phenomenon reported elsewhere (see Maloney 1976). The evil eye is not cast consciously or voluntarily, nor are its victims held responsible for their affliction. Curses fall within the larger category of du'a, written or spoken prayers, which operate by invoking God's power to change events or affect human decisions, and are the main means of preventing the evil eye or countering curses and possession by jinns. When the symptoms of illness do not respond immediately to dietary or herbal treatments, victims may be taken for diagnosis to local mullahs. Broadly, afflictions of any kind may be caused either directly by an act of God, in which case they are a matter for the victim's personal relations with God, or indirectly by some intermediate supernatural force, such as jinn or the evil eye.

An act of God is the usual diagnosis for accidents, obvious physical illness such as measles, smallpox, etc. These are said to be qismati, fated or predestined, and to have occurred for reasons which are unknowable and indeed unquestionable. Indeed, such questions are strongly disapproved, indicating an impudence incompatible with piety: a good person presumes nothing about God's mysterious ways. By contrast, the inability of men and/or women to fulfil their social and moral responsibilities is explained differently. Typically, in the case of men in terms of 'insanity' and, in the case of women, in terms of possession by jinn. People who are so labelled (and it is important to realise that the categories of 'the insane' and 'the possessed' may include social rebels as well as, for example, handicapped men or barren women) lose full adult status and their rights and duties vis-a-vis resources of all kinds.

The complexities of this system of explanation will be described elsewhere (R. Tapper & N. Tapper, n.d.). Of importance here is the way in which an individual's personal characteristics can be related to the good or bad fortune he or she experiences in a subtle, nuanced way. The dual emphasis on the individual and on gender relations both creates and confirms social forms in other areas of Durrani life. This theodicy forms a closed, self-validating system. Ultimately everything comes from God and both the causes of affliction and their cure via exorcism, prayer or charitable acts, are also in the hands of God.

Honour and Shame

The gender distinction is further developed as a way of justifying and explaining, through the idiom of honour and shame, the control of resources of all kinds, whether people, land, animals or other property. As Pitt-Rivers has clearly shown for Mediterranean societies (1977: 1-17), this ideology of control is so structured that the outsider can distinguish two quite opposed notions which meet and are confounded in the actor's concepts. One is honour in a competitive sense which is relevant to this-worldly relations and is based on a recognition of inequality. The other is honour in a religious sense in which altruism and generosity are central and where relations are based on an ideal of equality, seen ultimately as equality before God. No relationship is ever seen exclusively in one sense or the other and the ideology is compelling because it appears to resolve a fundamental contradiction between the ideals of equality and the inequalities inherent in the control and exploitation of resources. As elsewhere, among Durrani concepts of honour and shame are elaborated in an extensive vocabulary, though often they are subsumed under the notion of num (reputation, literally name, the big name or good name of a big man) and Pashtu (a synonym for all or any facet of honour as it relates to women and men). Clearly the latter term suggests explicitly the intimate connection between honour and personal and tribal identity. The same intimate association is implicit in the concept of namus which is that aspect of a man's honour derived from the morality of his womenfolk. Meeker's discussion of namus and the place of women in Turkey fits Durrani data well and provides a neat summary of the central issues concerning the idiom of honour and shame and its relations to ideas of social order and social responsibility. Meeker writes,

Concepts of Disorder among Durrani Pashtuns

> Namus ... implies a common measure which applies to all men and reflects a state of each man. Male 'control' of a woman's sexuality is appropriate for such a universal measure ... [and the] customs concerning the control of women can become almost the very definition of community and a means of differentiation of one community from another (1976: 267, 268).

Among Durrani, aspects of the institution of marriage most clearly show the nature and extent of men's control of women (see N. Tapper, 1981). It is notable that such control coincides with the definition of community in one of the few rigid rules Durrani express. They say that Durrani women should never have sexual contact or marry members of ethnic groups inferior to themselves. Normally such an ideal is never tested but is used as a way of stating Durrani ethnic identity. However, exceptionally, men have risked ostracism from Durrani groups by breaking this rule and marrying a sister or daughter out (see N. Tapper & R. Tapper, 1982), and women too have the power to subvert the social order. As we have seen women who conform to social expectations of female passivity are held, by women and men alike, to be socially responsible. Those few, however, who act in terms of their own personal interests rather than those of their household, perpetuate both the biological stereotypes of women's weaker nature and the dire consequences of moral turpitude. An extreme example, the case of Kaftar, a Durrani girl who eloped with a Shi'ite Hazara, clearly reveals the energy and scope of a community's response to such radical subversion.

Kaftar eloped with a young Hazara who had been a servant in her father's household. When her father discovered what had occurred, he spent two days searching unsuccessfully for the runaways. Only then, in shame and despair, did he ask for help, and at once the Khan of the sub-tribe mobilised fourteen armed and mounted men who went off in pairs in search of the girl. These men spent over a month combing mountainous central Afghanistan for the couple but they failed to recover the girl from the Hazara who realised what a blow had been dealt the Durrani. The men then went to Kabul, and the leaders of the sub-tribe, including the Khan, stayed in the capital throughout the winter trying to negotiate government action to secure the girl's return. Meanwhile financial and other support was organised. The Khan obliged each household of the lineage and their clients to contribute money to the effort to recover Kaftar. When we left the field at the end of the second summer people still hoped to capture the girl, when, they said, they would make an example of her and shoot her in front of all the women of the sub-tribe. The dishonour of Kaftar's elopement, which in this case was shared by all members of the sub-tribe, lay in both the father's and the daughter's betrayal of that most basic of Durrani ideals. The Kaftar scandal confirmed all the Saripul Durrani's worst fears about both the nature of women and about the Hazara, the most despised of ethnic groups. The reaction of the sub-tribe community was as swift and forceful as they could make it.

Historical Change and Responsibility

For many Durrani in Saripul their ability to approximate the ideals of honour has changed dramatically in recent decades. Settlement and the increasing importance of new kinds of political control in the region have forced ordinary Durrani to become ruthless in the defence of the interests of their households. The confusion engendered by changes in the wider environment has been more fully described elsewhere (see R. Tapper, 1984). Such confusion was particularly felt by peasant landowners. For many of them the weakening of ethnic loyalties paralleled a breakup of family ties and a general decline in religiosity and seemed to forecast the end of the world. As one Durrani village headman said in the summer of 1972:

> In our history books it says we shall not reach the year 1400 (A.H.). Shortly before it is due, the end of time will arrive. The mullahs can't agree ... they are of no use, and we have no sheikhs or prophets now to guide us. Those we do have are not straight; they say one thing but

have another in their hearts. God knows what is in their hearts. The world is coming to an end ... Our books say that at the end of time, truth will be lies, people will abandon right and do wrong, brothers and fathers and sons will fight together. That is the way things will be, they say - but look around now: not one person in ten prays. The world is coming to an end.

The year 1400 A.H. began in late 1979 - shortly before the Soviet invasion of Afghanistan.

The Durrani reaction to what they see as deleterious social change has two main dimensions. On the one hand, they see themselves forced to increase their efforts to control the fortunes of their households by means of the agonistic competitions couched in the language of honour and shame, but, on the other, they are aware of the inexorable pace and direction of such changes and consider that however hard a household struggles, without God's blessing, it is doomed to failure. In so far as radical, long-term changes are associated with the unknowable ways of God, then resignation tempers the household's efforts towards control.

These same two dimensions are evident in Durrani responses to radical changes in their physical environment - 'natural' disasters such as drought and famine. They are able to greatly intensify their practical efforts to cater for the needs of their household and are willing to exhaust themselves physically and mentally to lessen the effects of a disaster, or avert its further consequences. Such pragmatic activity is taken for granted as the obvious reaction of all responsible adults - women and men. But it is also associated with resignation, not of an eschatological kind as is the case with changes in the wider social environment, but of a physical kind. For instance, in 1971-2, after a summer of drought (cf. Barry, 1974: 175 ff.), the Durrani of Saripul experienced the most severe winter in living memory. Their accounts of the weather were striking in three quite different ways. First, there was a complete absence of comments treating the winter disaster in a wider metaphysical context.(3) Our friends offered no theodicy, or indeed any explanation for the harshness of the winter and their experiences during it. It was indeed as if questions about such events were simply unthinkable. Second, they described their troubles, their bitterness and misery almost wholly in terms of physical exhaustion and pain. Third, all the accounts focus on the efforts individuals made to help their households survive the ordeal. One young man talked of the end of the winter thus:

> But finally there was nothing left for the sheep to eat. I went to Juma Khan and took off my turban. I bared my head and pleaded with him to give my sheep some straw. He swore he would not give them any, but I said 'I'll kill myself, or break you in little pieces; they will be dead by morning' and he put down a little straw for them - the merest handful. Then I told my wife, 'Cook up all the flour we have into bread and give one piece to each sheep', but the sheep were finished. I killed 25 sheep hallal that one night. And then they all died. We could not even kill them. We just threw them out of the room; we didn't even cut off their wool; they were just piled up. Every night 20, 30, 15 died. This year Hajji and I, we were so tired and unhappy about the sheep, we just cried.

Conclusions

Parkin has recently written that evil

> is not *anything*: it denotes rather an area of discourse concerning human suffering, human existential predicaments and the attempted resolution of these through other humans and through non-human agencies, including a God or gods (1985: 10-11).

and he suggests that the problem for anthropologists is how acknowledged suffering can be discussed.

The Durrani Pashtun reaction to acknowledged suffering forms a system of beliefs and practices which may be discussed at two separate but related levels. The Durrani definitions of the self and the person provide a key to this system.

Concepts of Disorder among Durrani Pashtuns

As we have seen, Durrani define their relation to the world of things and animals in terms of qualities, like 'reason', and spiritual notions like the 'soul', which also define the relationship they should seek with God. And, of course, all social relationships can also be understood in these terms and indeed further defined in terms of people's responsibilities as established in God's law. In other words, in the Durrani view of the world the individual is the measure of all relations while the measurements themselves are ultimately always made in terms of the supernatural.

In effect, the Durrani ideas of the self and personhood constitute a single frame of reference and a standard which may be used to guide behaviour and emotional responses in virtually all situations. Clearly the simplicity of such a system of moral responsibility is itself a source of its strength and plausibility. Moreover the force of the system is increased by the heavy emotional and aesthetic load its limited and highly condensed concepts and symbols carry. Durrani ideas of the person subsume, via the idiom of honour and shame, virtually all other social classifications and are central to the Durrani understanding of the relation between suffering and responsibility. The comprehensive Durrani philosophy of the person, which is a key to their version of practised Islam, shares many characteristics of the implicit belief systems of closed societies described by Horton (1967), among them stability and resilience in the face of change.

To Durrani, it is men's nature to protect and defend their weaker women and children from both privation and temptation even unto death, while a failure to offer such defence will almost certainly result in a man and his household losing their Durrani identity and leaving the area in shame and poverty. In the history of the sub-tribe there are many precedents for men's deaths in such contexts. Moreover, as we have seen, Durrani ideas of the person and gender stereotypes also define men's wider social commitment to lineage and community. And, as was clear from the Kaftar example, social responsibilities of this kind can, in extreme cases, lead to collective military action. The deaths of men who die in the defence of household or community can always be interpreted as honourable and sometimes such men may also be considered martyrs. In either case Durrani believe that such good deaths will be rewarded in the afterlife.

The primacy of the household in Durrani social organisation and its management in terms of honour and shame, give Durrani the energy and determination to actively defend their honour and control household resources in whatever circumstances. In doing so, Durrani see themselves as acting according to God's laws. And yet Durrani also know that the efforts of individuals cannot ensure the wellbeing of a household in the face of events and processes which are outside Durrani society.

The parameters of human responsibility are defined by the single, comprehensive system of Durrani notions of the person and the related ideology of honour and shame. All that is outside the area of human responsibility can also be explained in a simple, monolithic way: God's ultimate control of the world is complete, unknowable and unquestionable. However, there is a broad area of ambiguity between these two areas of control, the one within the ambit of human responsibility and the other in which all explanations must be in terms of God's unalterable will. Virtually any action or event may be explained in either or both ways, according to context and the perspective of the interpreter. Victims often favour explanations in terms of acts of God, while spectators are more willing to attribute affliction to irresponsibility on the part of the sufferer. Here we may see a constant tension in the Durrani practice of Islam. To the extent that people may themselves be held responsible for an affliction, they are likely to seek remedies to control it and reorder their lives. Conversely, in so far as they are content to accept suffering passively, they are also exonerated from personal responsibility.

Our aim in this chapter is to make the Durrani responses to disorder and affliction comprehensible by examining the conceptual systems of which they are a part. Our interest in the topic has been spurred by the Soviet invasion of Afghanistan and our approach offers insights into the sources and nature of the

Concepts of Disorder among Durrani Pashtuns

Durrani, and perhaps more general Pashtun, reaction to it. We have seen that Durrani define the self and the person in explicitly religious terms and, in this respect, infidels are automatically seen as less than human. Soviet atheism encouraged Durrani traditionally to see all Russians as inverting all that Durrani value. Durrani religiosity is then an obvious and effective vehicle for their resistance. And, as we have seen in the apocalyptic scenario sketched by the village headman, the Soviet invasion itself is easily explained in religious terms, while Durrani resistance to it becomes a moral responsibility. The dual response to acknowledged suffering we have described for Durrani may, in a general way, typify the reaction of many different peoples to radical social change; however the detailed structure and meaning of the response must be different in each case. Pashtuns have reacted to the Soviet invasion in two quite different ways simultaneously: by showing great resilience and pragmatism in protecting their households and ultimately their humanity, while at the same time accepting that even if their efforts should fail, they are acting in accordance with God's will -- our Durrani study suggests why this might be so.

Notes

1. This paper was prepared for the seminar, 'Afghanistan - A Threatened Culture', held in Stockholm in December 1985. It was also read at the University of Uppsala. We are very grateful for all the useful comments we received on those occasions.

    Fieldwork was done jointly as a Social Science Research Council Project, Richard Tapper also being supported by the School of Oriental and African Studies, University of London. The present tense in the paper refers to the fieldwork period of 1970-72. We have had no information since the Soviet invasion about the Saripul Durranis with whom we worked, but we have every reason to hope that whatever changes, losses and suffering they may have experienced, their quick practical responses, as with earlier disasters, will guard their basic cultural

integrity and allow them a degree of self-determination.
2. Compare the range of interpretations of possession as providing explanations of misfortune and expressing emotional and/or intellectual responses, from Lewis's early formulation in terms of 'relative deprivation' (1971) to Whyte's more recent account of possession as an expression of women's muted or counterpart models (1981).
3. The only disaster accounts we heard which had a specifically religious dimension were the stories Durrani told of flashfloods in which the waters had been parted and the camps protected when a woman or man held a Koran in front of them.

References

Barry, M. (1974) Afghanistan, Seuil, Petite Planete, Paris
Good, B.J. (1977) The heart of what's the matter: the structure of medical discourse in a provincial Iranian town, University Microfilms, Thesis, University of Chicago
Horton, R. (1967) 'African traditional thought and western science', Africa 37, 50-71, 155-87
Lewis, I.M. (1971) Ecstatic Religion, Penguin, Harmondsworth
Maloney, C. (1976) The evil eye, Columbia UP, New York
Meeker, M.E. (1976) 'Meaning and society in the Near East: examples from the Black Sea Turks and the Levantine Arabs', International Journal of Middle East Studies 7, 243-70
Parkin, D. (1985) 'Introduction', in The anthropology of evil, D. Parkin (ed.), Blackwell, Oxford
Pitt-Rivers, J. (1977) The fate of Shechem or the politics of sex, Cambridge UP, Cambridge
Tapper, N. (1981) 'Direct exchange and brideprice: alternative forms in a complex marriage system', Man (N.S.) 16, 387-407
--- and R. Tapper (1982) 'Marriage preferences and ethnic relations among Durrani Pashtuns of Afghan Turkestan', Folk, 24, 157-77
Tapper, R. (1984) 'Ethnicity and class: dimensions of intergroup conflict in north-central Afghanistan', in Revolutions and rebellions in

Afghanistan, (eds.) M.N. Shahrani and R.L. Canfield, Berkeley: University of California
—— and N. Tapper (1986) '"Eat this, it'll do you a power of good": food and commensality among Durrani Pashtuns', *American Ethnologist*, 13/1
—— and N. Tapper (n.d.) 'Possession, insanity and responsibility in northern Afghanistan'
Whyte, S.R. (1981) 'Men, women and misfortune in Bunyole', *Man* (N.S.) 16/3, 350-66

4

THE KUSHANS - AN AFGHAN SEARCH FOR ROOTS

Richard N. Frye

Sometimes the origins of ideologies, movements or even events in recent times are shrouded in obscurity, or the genesis of the matter is forgotten. In the present instance, since I was personally involved in the prehistory of the creation of a centre of Kushan Studies in Kabul, Afghanistan, in 1968, it may be of interest to report the events as remembered and to discuss the significance of the centre.

In the early spring of 1965 Bobojan Gafurov, the Tajik director of the Institute of Oriental Studies in Moscow, and recognised head of Oriental studies in the USSR, as well as former chairman of the Tajik Communist Party, sent Rustam Aliyev, an Azerbaijani research associate in his institute, to Harvard University at my request to aid in our Persian teaching programme. The following fall and winter I spent in the Soviet Union as an exchange scholar, and it was then that Gafurov first discussed with me his idea of creating a UNESCO international centre for the study of the civilisations of Central Asia. He was not averse to having an international committee under the auspices of UNESCO, but the idea of having branches of this organisation of Tehran, Kabul, New Delhi, Islamabad and later in Ulan Bator was in his mind. He asked me about persons in Iran and Afghanistan who were working on Central Asian problems, who could promote the idea of such branches in their respective countries, and I remember telling him that, although Ahmad Ali Kohzad, a historian and archaeologist, would be the logical candidate, he was too old and had retired; but Abdul-

The Kushans

Hayy Habibi had just written about the Kushan inscription of Surkh Kotal (<u>Madar-e zaban-e dari</u>) and even though he was known as a specialist on Pashto literature, he was active and interested in the entire history of Afghanistan and an active person.

The result of Gafurov's deliberations was an international conference under UNESCO auspices on the history, archaeology and culture of Central Asia in the Kushan period, held from 27 September through 6 October 1968 in Dushanbe, Tajikistan.(1) Habibi was named one of the vice-chairmen of the conference and was entrusted with the project of establishing a centre of Kushan Studies in Kabul, but the Afghan Institute of Archaeology, formed in June 1967 under the direction of Shaibai Mustamindi, took over the task of what was called 'the regional centre for Kushan history' (<u>da kushaniyano da tarikh mantiqoi merkez</u>). In May 1970 an international congress under the auspices of the Institute of Archaeology and the Historical Society of the Academy of Afghanistan was held in Kabul which resulted in the publication of two volumes there. In July 1973 when Mustamindi and others were attending the International Congress of Orientalists in Paris, and Zahir Shah was in Italy, Daud Khan overthrew the monarchy and established a republic. Mustamindi did not return to Afghanistan. The period from the fall of the monarchy to the overthrow of Daud in the spring of 1978 saw a decline in interest in Kushans among Afghan intellectuals and, if anything, an increase in activities in the Islamic part of Afghanistan's past. Archaeological work, of course, continued with Zemaryalai Tarzi taking the place of Mustamindi, but conferences on Amir Khusrau, Bayezid Roshani, Ansari, Sanai, and others seemed to take the spotlight away from the Kushans.(2)

The Kushans returned in strength in 1978, the same year as the Saur revolution. Even before the country had recovered from the overthrow of Daud an international seminar on Kushan studies was planned for the end of November 1978 under the auspices of a new Academy of Sciences with its new president Gul Mohammad Noorzai. The seminar, from the viewpoint of the government, was intended to rouse support among foreign scholars for the new regime and to legitimise its activities in adhering to UNESCO expectations by promoting scholarship in Kushan studies. Whatever one may say about their motives, the Kushans certainly had returned in force, as seen from publications about them, and this activity did not cease with the coming of Babrak Karmal and the Soviets in December 1979. A second international congress was called in Kabul in the fall of 1982 but only a few scholars from abroad attended. Because of the war, future activities related to the Kushans are limited.

Such, in brief, is the story of the development of Kushan studies in Afghanistan, but what is the meaning of Afghan interest in the Kushans? The rest of this chapter is mainly devoted to speculation about this matter.

Since the founding of the journal <u>Aryana</u> in 1942, at a time when I was in Kabul, interest in the pre-Islamic past of the country had found a vehicle of expression. It is true that there was no university or centre at that time in which ancient history, archaeology or the study of ancient languages could develop. Nonetheless, a few persons, such as Kohzad, who had been a guide and interpreter for French archaeologists of DAFA, kept ancient history before the educated Afghan public. Interest in the Islamic past, however, in the form of poets, writers, collectors of manuscripts, etc., was much more developed than any concern for antiquities. As far as I know, in the years during and after World War II there was no movement or policy to reconcile Pashto and Dari speakers, not to mention Uzbeks, Turkomens, or others, in a common history, seeking by this means to bring about unity, at least in a common view of a common history. On the contrary, the intellectuals among Pashto speakers exalted Khushhal Khan as well as the exploits of Ahmad Shah Baba, and the Afghans in India, while the Dari speakers considered Jami, Ansari and other Persian poets to be their literary heroes, while general Muslim conquerors, such as the Ghaznavids and Ghurids, were their political heroes. Although it would not be easy to prove, it seems that the elevation of the Kushans to the position of prime heroes of Afghanistan's past can be traced to two roots: Iran and the USSR. During the 1960s and early 1970s the Shah of Iran promoted the idea that the Achaemenids, and especially Cyrus, should be the national heroes of

The Kushans

Iran, real Iranian rather than general Islamic heroes. This tendency, greeted by liberals (roshan-fikran) in Iran as a weapon against conservative, traditional Islamic leaders, had a resonance in Afghanistan, especially with the influx of Persian books, printed in Iran, which became the largest component in all booksellers and libraries in Afghanistan. One should not exaggerate the Iranian influences, however, because differences between the two countries (in religion, speech, history, etc.) are not minimal. At this time, however, the wealth and cultural predominance of Iran in the region did influence her neighbours.

More important, of course, and providing a model, was the USSR. The direct influence of Gafurov, and members of the Institute of the Peoples of Asia and Africa, has been mentioned, but what is not known is the role of the Soviet embassy in Kabul or direct governmental contacts. In any case, a model for the 'national roots' of the Afghans existed, such as the place of Tigranes the Great in Armenian history, and the Kushans admirably suited the Afghan situation. First, the Kushans lived in a pre-Islamic period, which was important in shifting emphasis away from the Islamic past of the country. Second, the Kushans occupied all of Afghanistan, as well as the Pashto speaking areas of Pakistan (Gandhara of antiquity); other areas of Kushan expansion into India or Soviet Central Asia were either short-lived in time or not directly ruled. Third, as in the Kushan empire itself, so modern Afghanistan was composed of various peoples and tribes. The Kushan empire fitted very well into the picture of contemporary Afghanistan, and all of its peoples could look back and proudly say 'we are descendants of the Kushans'. Finally, little was known about the Kushans, so, as in the case of all heroes, many stories could accumulate about them. For example, from the many and varied deities portrayed on the coins of the Kushans, one could assert that the Kushans were most tolerant in their religious predilections, even to the extent of the assertion that the Kushans were non-religious, certainly not fanatics. From all of the points above it is clear that the Kushans were the obvious candidates for all Afghans to exalt as their ancestors and in the current search for 'roots' everywhere the Kushans were excellent examples.

From all of the above what may be the future consequences of the policy of emphasis on the Kushans as the ancestors of all Afghans? First, the relation to the present problem of Pashtonistan is obvious. Both Gandhara and Bactria (hodie Balk and Mazar-e Sharif) were the two centres of Kushan rule and of Kushan culture, and the Pashtons could well accept the Kushans as their illustrious forebears. Second, for the USSR, the Pashtons in the south and the Uzbeks in Central Asia are the most dangerous people in a possible anti-Russian movement. At present the Uzbeks and any sentiments of 'Turkestan' or 'pan-Turanism' probably present the greatest challenge to the concept of 'Soviet man' in Russian thinking. After this threat, the greatest problem for the Soviet Union is Islam, although it is considered more of a threat as a competitor to Communism, in its social, political and economic dimensions than as a religion. In other words, Islam as a religion can be used by other ideologies, governments or movements, by the USSR as well, but as an independent religious philosophy Islam belongs to the past, to the Middle Ages, in Soviet eyes. Nonetheless, it is important to detach the Afghans from their Islamic culture and focus any ideas of past glory on the pre-Islamic past. So from the Soviet viewpoint anything which weakens the Islamic heritage of the Afghans, and which supports the unity of the Afghan state, should be fostered and stressed.

If Western governments considered Afghanistan at all, they presumably would support the Soviet position in arguing that Islam is an anti-progressive ideology as well as a religion, and anything which would reduce the influence of Muslim fanatics anywhere should be applauded. At the same time many feel that only Islam can provide a counter to communism in the Islamic world, and, in their eyes, an Islamic totalitarianism would be better than a communist totalitarianism. Since Islam can also be used by anti-Soviet governments and movements in the eastern world, obviously the Soviets must be conciliatory towards Islam while at the same time robbing it of its influence. In the case of Afghanistan, promotion of the pre-Islamic Kushans as a rallying point of national pride for all

The Kushans

Afghans is a step towards detracting from Islam. One reason why the mujahidin in Afghanistan, as well as Muslims in Iran, are mistrustful of the United States and the Western world is their conviction that the West as well as the Soviet Union is basically anti-Islamic and one should not rely on any Western government for support and sympathy in the cause of Islam.

Finally, a policy of emphasis on the Kushans would separate the Afghans from Uzbeks, Turkomens, and even the Tajiks (although they are unimportant in Russian eyes except as a counterinfluence to Turkic pretensions of unity), and feelings of Islamic unity would thereby be countered in some measure. If the Kushans were emphasised in school books and elsewhere perhaps after several generations the Afghans could easily fit into the Soviet scheme of ethnicity and nationalities.

Any prediction of the success or failure of such a policy is hazardous, but even though many peoples such as the Uighurs in Xinjiang, the Uzbeks in Soviet Central Asia, and elsewhere hide their 'national' sentiments behind an Islamic curtain, nonetheless Islam is, and probably will remain, a dominant force in the lives of Afghans. The power and influence of religion everywhere may have waned or even vanished, but the feelings of cultural and social unity in Islam for even nominal Muslims is certainly much more powerful than any recourse to Achaemenids, Kushans, ancient Sogdians or whatever. Anywhere in the world it is difficult to change we-they oppositions or antagonisms, and for Islamic peoples, in spite of intense propaganda and efforts to make men into angels, differences will persist. The Islamic past of Afghanistan is more of a factor of unity and pride than the Kushans ever can be.

Notes

1. UNESCO at its fourteenth session, held at the end of 1966, officially initiated a four-year project, beginning in 1967-8, concerning the civilisations of the peoples of Central Asia. But then only Afghanistan, the USSR, Pakistan, India and Iran were covered by the project, and in April 1967 it was decided that the Kushan

period would be the first priority of the project, and Afghanistan appropriately should be the main centre of such studies. Later the People's Republic of Mongolia and much later the PR China were added.
2. It is not intended here to list the various conferences and symposia held in Kabul during the Daud regime, but the emphasis on prominent Islamic writers and thinkers of the past, such as Biruni, Jamal-ad-Din Afghani and others, including those mentioned in the text, is apparent.

5

ETHNIC FACTORS IN AFGHANISTAN'S FUTURE

Eden Naby

Tribal and ethnic problems have always plagued Afghan state formation. With the events since 1978, many problems of Afghan society have become magnified as have the strengths of the society. Looking under and beyond the current events, I would like to examine the historical and regional elements that affected and may in the future affect Afghanistan's ethnic realities and, further, examine possible ways that the ethnic factor may affect the future of the country and the region.

From 1880, the beginning of the period from Abdur Rahman (r. 1880-1901) onward, internal consolidation became the chief concern with which Kabul grappled. As part of the consolidation process, Kabul administrators and rulers have, since that time, attempted to neutralise ethnic and regional bases for rebellion. Except for events during the rule of Habibullah II (pejoratively called Bacha Saqao - 1929), no serious ethnic rebellion has occurred. Instead there have been several important instances of Kabul expansion into semi-autonomous ethnic areas when ethnicity and religion were used to arouse enthusiasm for Kabul's military campaigns.(1) On the other hand various ruling Pashtun groups have attempted to use ethnic discontent to stir up a given region in order to contest rule in Kabul with other Pushtuns.(2) In other words, despite the playing of the ethnic game in Soviet Central Asia, and despite ethnic stirrings in neighbouring Iran and Pakistan, Afghanistan's non-

Ethnic Factors in the Future

Pashtuns have been surprisingly apolitical.(3) How can we explain this seeming lack of political ambition? How has the coup of 1978 affected these ethnic groups? Given a set of possible variables in the future, how will Afghan government and society be affected by changes in ethnic group perceptions? Will Afghanistan, for example, continue to remain relatively free of ethnic tensions (when compared with Pakistan and Iran)? Or may we expect that,whatever the outcome of the current struggle, a future Afghanistan's ethnic diversity will play a more pronounced political part in decision-making, resource allocation and national character, to name only a few of the issues that ethnic heterogeneity evokes.

The Political Role of Pashtuns and Other Afghan Ethnic Groups

Much attention has been directed at the inter-state position of the Pashtuns, not the least by the Afghans themselves and definitely by outside evaluators.(4) The Pashtunistan issue, from the perspective of successive Kabul regimes, has been the main source of conflict with Pakistan. With about equal numbers on either side of the border (about fourteen million altogether) the Pashtuns have been viewed as being potentially troublesome to Pakistan and possibly the source of alternative political leadership in that country. Within Afghanistan, Pashtuns have exercised virtually absolute political control at the cost of alienating large segments of the non-Pashtun population.(5) Ever since the overthrow of Habibullah II, it has become a political axiom in Afghanistan that the rule of the country must remain among Pashtuns. Indeed in studies and accounts of the resistance, one sees a concentration on the Pashtun fighting tribes with only a relatively recent focus on the steady domestic resistance waged by non-tribal, and/or non-Pashtun elements.(6)

Although the paramount leaders of the coup of 1978, Nur Mohammad Taraki, Hafizulah Amin and Babrak Karmal came mainly from Pashtun backgrounds, nevertheless from 1978 onward the question of political and cultural development of Afghanistan's non-Pashtun ethnic groups has been pressed to serve a variety of

Ethnic Factors in the Future

political ends. Among these have been the attempt to win the allegiance of key elements among the minorities (the educated youth and intellectuals) and to use minorities to fragment opposition to the Pashtun resistance to socio-political change.(7) The increasing military and political role of non-Pashtuns in the resistance grows out of the reasons which the Soviet/Kabul groups originally pressed for nationality (a Soviet term) rights: i.e. the fact that non-Pashtuns form a significant portion of the Afghan population, that although their grievances against Kabul have been muted, they have existed, and that the religious link throughout Afghan communities (at least among large segments of these communities) has sufficed to provide a basis of resistance despite the blandishments of cultural autonomy offered by Kabul. As Kabul has seen the resistance grow among non-Pashtuns, it has switched to new tactics to build groupings that would support the pro-Moscow regime in Kabul. These new groupings concentrate on traditional leadership such as regional and tribal leaders, religious leaders as well as ethnic leaders. The National Fatherland Front is a good example of the kind of overall Afghan rather than ethnic support that is being sought. That the experiment with the National Fatherland Front has failed to yield the desired results is due to the unpalatibility of the Kabul regime rather than to the diminished importance of ethnicity, religion or tribes.

The Non-Pashtun Groups and the Resistance

Pashtun participation in the resistance to Kabul has been relatively easy to document due to the physical proximity of the Pashtun areas to Peshawar, the Pakistani city to which most journalists and students of Afghan affairs journey. This town, traditionally the major market area for Pashtuns of the North-West Frontier Province and once part of the Afghan kingdom, provides a familiar setting for Afghan refugees and fighters from across the border. For non-Pashtuns however, its low-altitude Pashtun culture can be forbidding. Moreover, whereas the trip from neighbouring Afghan areas to Peshawar is relatively easy, for those living in non-adjacent areas, the long trek

Ethnic Factors in the Future

can be hazardous. Thus the preponderance of refugees and fighters met within the Peshawar area are Pashtuns. This is also true for the political side of the resistance which is centred in Peshawar. Most groups are run by, and include, chiefly if not exclusively Pashtuns.

For non-Pashtuns the closest areas of refuge outside Afghanistan would have been Soviet areas inhabited by co-ethnics (the Uzbek SSR, the Tajik SSR and the Turkmen SSR) and Iran. Soviet areas are obviously inaccessible, while Iran's internal turmoil and external embroilments have made it a difficult if not inhospitable place of refuge. Thus the non-Pashtun resistance has limited choices. It can remain in the country, it can risk the long trip and strange atmosphere in the North-West Frontier Province or it can take similar and less certain refuge in Iran. Not surprisingly, the non-Pashtun groups have used all three options. From refugee reports, however, it would appear that the choice of remaining in the country to fight was widely made until the Soviet tactic of wholesale destruction of villages in the northern part of the country was adopted in 1984. The adoption of this tactic was motivated by two main factors: first, the continued strength of the resistance among areas with non-Pashtun inhabitants, particularly the Uzbeks, and second, the proximity of unfriendly natives to Soviet Muslim areas and to the supply routes necessary for sustaining the Kabul regime and the invasion forces. It has resulted in large numbers of Uzbeks and Tajiks leaving their homes for Pakistan. As yet it does not appear to have resulted in diminished resistance in northern areas.

Apart from northern Afghanistan, the other important non-Pashtun area in Afghanistan has been the Hazarajat, the central highlands of the country along the spine formed by the Hindu-Kush mountains where the Hazara people have lived in relative isolation. Among the first to assert their independence of the Taraki regime in Kabul, the Hazaras have been most affected by co-religionists in Shi'ite Iran. The Iranian influences, both Islamic and revolutionary, have rent the traditional structure of Hazara leadership without having succeeded fully in organising resistance to the Soviet/Kabul forces. Direct appeals to the Hazaras as

Ethnic Factors in the Future

a recognised nationality appear not to have been envisioned in 1978. But high rank has been attained by several Hazaras in Soviet Kabul, particularly in the person of Sultan Ali Kheshtmand, who together with Najibullah (Ahmadzai) succeeded to high office following the demotion of Babrak Karmal in the spring of 1986.

The part of the country most difficult to assess, and the ethnic groups that hold the key to the future of the ethnic situation in Afghanistan, however, may not be the Pashtuns, the Tajiks or the Hazaras, or indeed even the much-discussed Baluch.(8) The key to the ethnic future of the country may in fact rest with the Turkic people of the northern plains. In many respects, these are the people most intimately aware of their difference from the culture of the rest of Afghanistan, the achievements and aspirations of their co-ethnics within the Soviet Union, the devastations of war, and the promise or lack of it for them in a future Afghan state.(9)

The Uzbek Community of Northern Afghanistan

Initially, in the period immediately following the coup in 1978, the Uzbek community of Afghanistan appears not to have had cause to resist.(10) The reasons for this may be two-fold: first, events in Kabul may in fact have appeared remote to the community who infrequently participated in central government activity, except in rare cases where they filled slots as technocrats. Therefore, their lack of interest in Kabul events, which may be how the coup was viewed, would have precluded their participation in the early period of resistance. Second, very shortly after the coup, the Taraki regime launched its Soviet-style nationality policy, introduced initially into the Central Asian region during the 1920s. The Kabul nationality policy appeared most active and successful among the Uzbeks, a fact that may have caused the community to regard the coup as boding well.(11)

Whatever their reasons, the Uzbek community of Afghanistan found itself feted and nurtured by incoming Soviet experts, in particular by Soviet Uzbeks who earnestly and sincerely saw the coup as an opportunity to come to the aid of their oppressed co-ethnics in Afghanistan. And there are indications too that segments of the Afghan Uzbek population regarded the opportunity to develop their own culture, to benefit from the brotherly advice of 'successful' Soviet Uzbeks, and to finally be able to express themselves in ethno-cultural terms openly as a welcome change from decades of Pashtun domination. It would be a mistake to regard those who co-operated during the fall of 1978 in the production of Uzbek schoolbooks, the Uzbek newspaper (Yulduz - star), and radio productions in Uzbek as Khalqi or Parchami sympathisers. Several of these persons now reside in the West and we know their motives to be ethnic and not political. Thus it is plausible to assume that in the early stages of the new regime, its appeal to the several ethnic groups, Uzbeks, Turkmens, Baluchis and Nuristanis prevented the Uzbeks at least, the most numerous of the selected ethnic groups, from actively engaging in resistance.

No doubt different parts of the Uzbek community were affected by different factors to differing degrees. For as Audrey Shalinsky has demonstrated, the community is not homogeneous but rather divided, in particular, among those who have lived in Afghanistan for centuries, and those who have come as a result of the establishment of Soviet rule in their original homeland.(12) The presence of these refugee families may eventually be the key determinant of Uzbek action in the future.

Russo-Soviet Interest in Afghan Turkestan

Ever since Abdur Rahman defeated his Russian-backed rival Eshaq Khan and his Uzbek associates, and settled Pashtuns, especially members of the troublesome Ghilzai confederation, in Afghan Turkestan, there has existed among some Afghans the notion that the Pashtun presence has interwoven that area into the fabric of the country irrevocably. In fact, we see that as the Afghan crisis unfolded, these Pashtun settlers were among the first to leave the region for their original homes.(13) We see from other evidence too that the settlement of Pashtuns in the area did not necessarily integrate the area into Afghan life. For example, in the 1930s, yet another figure opposing the Kabul regime based himself in just this area, gathered supporters with the aid of Kabul's neighbour to the north and posed a threat to Kabul. These two major incidents demonstrate that Afghan Turkestan has been, and may continue to be, an area where loyalty and allegiance to Kabul are tempered by other factors. Not the least of these factors is the Russian control of the areas directly to the north since the 1860s.

Leaving aside the rivalries of the Great Game, the period when the British and the Tsarist empires vied for power in Central Asia in particular, one must nonetheless take cognisance of the natural affinity of Afghan Turkestan with large parts of Soviet Central Asia. Just as the various Amirs of Bukhara considered Balkh part of their domain, so too is it regarded by many Uzbeks of Tashkent. While these Uzbeks do not hold the reins of power to move the Afghan plain into the Soviet orbit, they can act as the magnet to attract the Afghan Uzbeks away from Kabul, depending on other circumstances.

In analysing this issue, one must remain aware that the pre-Soviet and Soviet experience of Uzbeks and Turkmens has differed significantly and that one cannot judge Uzbeks inside and outside Afghanistan by the Turkmen example. Working from the present backwards one need only point out that the demographic and cultural strength of Soviet Uzbeks has obtained considerable political clout for them within the Soviet Union but particularly within Soviet Central Asia.(14) Moreover, the Tsarist conquest of Uzbek areas held little of the trauma associated with Goeg Tepe and the wholesale massacre of the Teke Turkmens by Tsarist soldiers. Although it would be inaccurate to term the Uzbeks masters of their own Soviet Socialist Republic, nevertheless, they wield greater power, from an earlier date, in their own affairs than any of the other Central Asian peoples. In part this may be explained by their sociological background as being relatively urbanised and detribalised in contrast with the Turkmens and other Turkic peoples of the region. Within the Soviet context, one may view the Uzbeks as a relatively 'successful' Soviet nationality.

This 'success' of the Soviet Uzbeks has not been lost on the Afghan Uzbeks and its most recent demon-

Ethnic Factors in the Future

stration may be in the initial quiescence of the Afghan Uzbeks in 1978/9. It would be too far-fetched to conclude from these factors that the Uzbeks of Afghanistan will opt for, or co-operate in, the separation of the Afghan north from Kabul. However, to eliminate the possibility, one must examine the options that the future may hold.

Future Options

Settlement of the Afghan war, even under the most ideal of circumstances, raises significant questions about the future. The withdrawal of Soviet troops would raise questions about the replacement of the Kabul regime, the return of refugees and power sharing not only with Moscow-designated Afghans, but also within the resistance itself. If, as authoritative reports confirm, the chief refugee population consists of Pashtuns and that inside Afghanistan the regions of mono-ethnicity have increased due to Pashtun departure, one may wonder how readily the Pashtuns would be welcomed back, particularly once more as the dominant ethnic group. In the resistance, the success of the Pashtuns has not matched their numbers; nor have Pashtun-orientated groups included the mosaic of Afghan ethnic backgrounds. For example, groups such as that of Yunus Khalis, Gailani, and even Mojaddidi remain bound by tribe and/or by region whereas the groups led by non-Pashtuns such as Jamiat-e Islami represent a greater tribal and regional cross-section as does the Harakat-e Islami. Here lie the seeds for conflict on an ethnic level, in addition to the other fractionalisation that would emerge given present circumstances.

Faced with the possibility of returning to a Pashtun-run and Persian culture dominated society, what would the Uzbeks do? What are their choices? They could bargain for the preservation of the nationality system which in principle was established in 1978. However, no country in the Middle East has to date adopted a nationality system, with the exception of Iraq, a poor model since it has continually flaunted its disregard of the nationality principle. Moreover, there are indications that, like Iran, the revolutionary Islamic movements of Afghani-

Ethnic Factors in the Future

stan would shroud multi-ethnicity in the cloak of Islamic homogeneity as would the traditional groups. This leaves the one non-Pashtun oriented group, the Jami'at-e Islami, led by Burhanuddin Rabbani, as an acceptable alternative. Recalling the Bacha Saqoa episode in Afghan history, however, one finds it difficult to imagine the survival of a non-Pashtun leader for the entire country. The installation of a regime that recognises the major role of the non-Pashtuns and the rewarding of this role seems to be the sole means of keeping the Uzbeks in particular from seeking a friendlier ethnic clime.

If the other side of the spectrum of possibilities is examined, one sees emerging among the Afghans a growing sense of nationhood forged by the common resistance. Though drawing on Islam for sustenance, this new identity is also closely allied to the breakdown of ethnic barriers, particularly among the non-Pashtuns and possibly also among the detribalised Pashtuns. The continuation of the resistance at present or increased levels of support could give the members of the resistance a greater sense of identity with an overall Afghan fate. More significantly, the continuance of the resistance would offer circumstances for the incubation and the emergence of real national leaders who could provide a viable replacement for a Soviet puppet. These two elements, then, the development of Afghan national solidarity under the pressure of resistance and the emergence of tried and accepted leadership could overcome the ethnic factionalism that other circumstances associated with Afghan events since 1978 have engendered. Without these two elements, the chances of major portions of the Afghan population, especially the Uzbeks, becoming disaffected with the Afghan state remain strong.

Conclusions

Afghanistan's ethnic heterogeneity has remained a problem throughout its history causing the disaffection to Kabul of important parts of large ethnic groups. The Pashtun ruling elites have been reluctant to share political power outside their own ethnic group, indeed outside the major confederacy. Partially for this reason, the formation of an Afghan

Ethnic Factors in the Future

identity has been slow to emerge. The politicisation of the Afghan people as a result of the 1978 coup and the subsequent invasion of the country has aroused not only national consciousness, but it has also raised questions about the future power-sharing with ethnic minorities who share heavily in the resistance. The Soviet-installed regime has attempted to prevent ethnic minorities' participation in the resistance by wooing them with a culturally attractive nationalities policy based on the policy applied among Soviet Muslims. However, the main target group for this policy has generally not succumbed to such blandishments, choosing instead to send families into refugee exile and to join the resistance. Whatever the outcome of the fighting, these ethnic groups will demand (and deserve) a political role. Without such political compromise, the possibility of northern Afghanistan being drawn into the Soviet Central Asian orbit in the future remains a distinct possibility.

Notes

1. The definitive study of the Abdur Rahman period has been made by Hasan Kawun Kakar, a political prisoner in Kabul since 21 March 1982 (he was released in March 1987. Ed note). See his book Government and Society in Afghanistan: The reign of Amir Abd Al-Rahman Khan (Austin, University of Texas Press, 1978).
2. Eden Naby, 'The Uzbeks in Afghanistan', Central Asian Survey, vol. 3, no. 1, p. 9.
3. Among the many writings on ethnic relations in the region, see Michael Rywkin, Moscow's Muslim Challenge (Montauk, NY, Sharpe & Co., 1983) and Eden Naby, 'The Iranian Frontier Nationalities: The Kurds, the Assyrians, the Baluchis and the Turkmens', in Soviet Ethnic Frontiers, ed. William O'Cagg and Brian Silver (New York, Pergamon Press, 1979), pp. 83-118.
4. For examples, see J.W. Spain The Way of the Pathans (Karachi, 1975), and Erland Jansson, India, Pakistan or Pakhtunistan? The Nationalist Movements in the North-West Frontier Province 1937-47 (Stockholm, Almqvist & Wiksell International, 1981).

5. Naby, p.6.
6. See especially Olivier Roy, *L'Afghanistan: Islam et Modernite Politique* (Paris, Editions du Seuil, 1985).
7. Eden Naby, 'The Ethnic Factor in Soviet-Afghan Relations', *Asian Survey* (1980), Vol. 20, no. 2, pp. 237-56.
8. Selig Harrison has sensationalised the Baluch potentials for disruption in several articles and in his *In Afghanistan's Shadow: Baluch Nationalism and Soviet Temptations* (New York, Carnegie Endowment for International Peace, 1981).
9. For an analysis of the Uzbek situation in Afghanistan see my article cited above.
10. Roy, p. 136.
11. Naby, 1980. A third reason for Uzbek calm in the face of change has been suggested by Olivier Roy: that due to the breakdown in traditional structure among the Uzbeks, there exists a greater fascination with modernity and thus with the promise that the Taraki *coup* held at first. Roy, p. 136.
12. Audrey Shalinsky, *Central Asian Emigrees in Afghanistan: Social Dynamics of Identity Creation*, Ph.D. dissertation, Harvard University, 1979.
13. Roy, p. 228 f.
14. Since 1980 the Uzbek party leadership in Tashkent has suffered several reverses and charges of corruption that have resulted in a tightening of Moscow's hold on the republic and the replacement of local cadres with outside ones.

PART II

AFGHAN LEARNING AND EDUCATION

6

PAST AND PRESENT EDUCATION IN AFGHANISTAN — A PROBLEM FOR THE FUTURE

Sayd Bahaouddin Majrooh

Afghanistan is today under the impact of two Soviet offensives, one military and one ideological. The devastating military invasion is still going on, but a strong, popular, resistance against it continues unabated. Here, only problems related to the ideological offensive, more specifically to education, will be discussed.

In Afghanistan Marxist ideology has had no impact on two sorts of people: (1) the village farmers (forming the overwhelming majority of the population) who are deeply rooted in their popular and religious traditions; and (2) the highly educated (few in numbers) who have a good knowledge of the West and are also aware of their spiritual roots in the country's past and present. Those vulnerable to the ideological offensive are to be found among the urban youth who attend modern schools and university colleges.

Modern education of the Western style is fairly new in Afghanistan. The first modern school opened under the reign of Amir Habibullah at the beginning of this century. But the new system was promoted in a state of discontinuity with the old kind of teaching.

Traditional Learning: Frozen Knowledge

The creativity of the past

In the past there were many well-known centres of learning in Afghanistan. Madrassas or traditional schools flourished in Herat, Ghazni, Kandahar, Kabul and other places. Attached to a mosque, the madrassa was a private institution supported by the local population, rich and poor. The central figure of the madrassa was the scholar or the master teacher, who was provided with a living, and the students, who gathered around him, were also supported by the community. The students attached themselves to the master as his pupils. Depending on the reputation of the former, young people seeking knowledge might travel from distant regions in order to join the better-known school circles. The teaching was carried out on an individual basis. Each student, one after another, would come with his book and receive his lesson for the day, the students being on different levels of study or following different branches of knowledge. The sociological background of the students was usually that of the poor landless family, weakly integrated in the tribal or local communities, which meant that if they wished to rise to a respected position in local society there was no other way open to them than to become priests in mosques or religious scholars. Farmers, tribal chiefs and local maleks did not send their children to madrassas. Rich or aristocratic urban or rural families had private tutors for their children, both boys and girls. Women were not admitted to the madrassas.

The master-teacher of the madrassa was supposed to have encyclopaedic knowledge and to be capable of teaching any branch of the sciences as well as the arts. The traditionally recognised fields of learning were Islamic jurisprudence, Koranic interpretation and the traditions of the Prophet (Tafsir and Hadith), philosophy - including metaphysics, logic and grammar - theology, literary studies covering the Persian classics, and natural sciences, which focused on ancient Greek medicine. The best master-teacher was a type of theologian-alchemist-astrologist.

During the earlier periods of Islamic civilisation important teaching centres were created. Open to new ideas, they made valuable contributions in various branches of sciences and the arts. Outstanding scholars such as Albiruni, Ibn Sina and many others emerged who made the highest contribution to the advancement of human knowledge. Studies of philosophy, astronomy and other natural sciences were

Past and Present Education

encouraged. However, the central element of teaching in madrassas consisted of law and theology. In the course of time a distinction was made between the religious and rational sciences. But gradually the ulema or religious scholars adopted an increasingly hostile attitude towards science and philosophy. Attention was mainly paid to the traditional studies which included theology, law and literature. But even in the favoured traditional fields of studies, genuine research and creativity declined. Original texts of theology, philosophy, jurisprudence, etc, were replaced by commentaries and by commentaries upon commentaries. Time was spent on refutation and counter-refutation and never on basic problems and research. Learning was no longer an active pursuit nor a creative effort of the mind but a passive acquisition of already established knowledge.

The sterility of the present

The traditional education in Afghanistan was influenced mainly by the Islamic teaching centres in the Indian sub-continent. Islam was brought to India by and through Afghanistan, but when, during the thirteenth and fourteenth centuries Islamic madrassas were established in India, these became the main centres of learning for scholars from Afghanistan. However by the time these madrassas were started in India, the creative period of Islamic teaching was already over; second and third-hand commentaries became the basis of teaching. The subjects taught were: law, theology, rhetoric, Arabic grammar, medicine, astronomy, geometry, Hadith and Koranic interpretation. The basic trend of the madrassas was to eliminate the intellectual and rational sciences and to emphasise the purely orthodox religious disciplines. One influential Indian madrassa which trained Afghan religious scholars was in Deoband in northern India, established in the second half of the nineteenth century. The progressively narrowing view of Deoband contributed further to the decline of traditional teaching in Afghanistan. When, from the beginning of the twentieth century, the country slowly started opening up to the outside world and modern schools were being established, traditional education was at its lowest intellectual level. Strictly religious subjects, such as Fiqh, Hadith and Koranic interpretation, were retained, but only studied in second and third-hand commentaries, never in the original texts, while other branches of the sciences and arts were ignored. Among the non-religious subjects, Arabic grammar was favoured, but the way it was studied illustrates the degree of sterility and absurdity of the present-day traditional teaching.

The student had to learn by heart all the grammatical rules, but was never taught how to apply them; he would recite the conjugation of a large number of Arabic verbs in all tenses, always starting with the verb 'zaraba' (to beat: I beat, you beat, he beats, I have beaten, etc.), but he was never able to make an Arabic sentence or understand an Arabic text. Grammar was considered as sacred knowledge having its own intrinsic value.

Another example of the sterility and absurdity of traditional teaching was in the 'art of disputation'. The student was not taught any method of discussion or argumentation. All possible questions were listed and the answers given and the student had simply to learn them by heart (if someone objects so and so, you answer so and so ...). Opponents would come face to face and people would gather around them enjoying the confrontation as at a cock fight. The defeated party was the one who failed to remember the right answer to the objection or faced a new objection not mentioned in his references. The best contest was a disputation between two well-known maulawis (religious scholars). Each one would come with a large following of his students and donkey-loads of commentary books in Arabic. Arguments against arguments, objections against objections, books against books were produced. The disputation, interrupted by prayers, meals and sleep, was resumed the following morning and would continue for days. Strong emotional shows of anger, exchange of insults and occasional physical fighting among the rival students were integral parts of the art of disputation. In the end, the opponent would depart without having won a clear-cut victory, promising to come again soon for the next round. The expenses for meals and housing of the disputing parties and their numerous followers were paid by the local population who enjoyed the occasion and were proud of their own maulawi if he was the strongest. However, even if clearly defeated, he was never dismissed; a religious scholar is always a religious scholar even in defeat. In Afghanistan, men of knowledge of any kind had the respect of the common people.

Traditional teaching was represented by three different religious types: the mollah, the maulawi and the pir.

The mollah

The mollah or the local priest of a mosque had a very narrow educational background. He only knew how to perform the five daily prayers, how to preside over marriage, birth and funeral ceremonies. He did not know how to write, and could only read the Holy Koran without understanding its meaning. His teaching activities were confined to the most elementary aspects of religious practice. The children would learn from him the physical motions and the texts of prayers and other short verses of the holy Koran in daily use. He also taught the rules of fasting, ablution and other basic Islamic rules and regulations. The mollah and his family were supported by the community of believers; he was not involved in local socio-political affairs; he did not participate in the deliberations of the council of village elders - his only function on those occasions was to perform the opening and the concluding prayers of the Jirgah session. While well respected, he still remained the favourite target of popular jokes. There were abundant anecdotes about his gluttony, his hypocrisy and his supposed perverse sexual relations with his male assistant-pupil.

Maulawi (religious scholar) and qadi (judge)

These were trained at Islamic madrassas, could read and write and were well-versed in Islamic law and jurisprudence. Often the same person was both scholar and judge at the same time. As scholar he was a teacher training young students, who, for the greater part became mollahs while the selected few would complete the cycle of learning by becoming qadis or maulawis themselves. As qadi he was a judge presiding over an Islamic court. However, some parts of civil affairs remained outside the scope of religious courts and were dealt with according to popular custom and the tribal code (even crimes). The scholar-judge was highly respected and his advice and judgement strictly followed. As regards the judges, since the end of the nineteenth century (during the reign of Amir Abdurrahaman), a gradual change has occurred and two types of qadis have emerged: the official one, appointed and paid by the central administration in Kabul and an unofficial one in the countryside supported by the local population. But in the fifties and sixties the latter type slowly disappeared from the picture. The mollah, the maulawi and the qadi adhered strictly to the orthodox line of Islamic law.

The pir or spiritual guide

The pir was the leader of a Sufi brotherhood and was the most popular among all the religious figures. He was of saintly descent, he himself, his ancestors and his progeny being considered saints. He was in charge of initiating disciples into the process of inner perfection and was supposed to lead them along the mystic path. He was expected to keep a school of his own in which Sufi doctrines and works of literature should be studied. He was believed to have supernatural powers (especially healing powers). If the mollah and the maulawi were respected, the pir was venerated and the tomb of his ancestors worshipped.

In the past, religious scholars, such as Al Ghazali, attracted to the rational sciences were also deeply influenced by the Sufis. A great Sufi leader such as Abdullah Ansari of Herat was also a great scholar of orthodox religious sciences. Shahabuddin Sohrawardi, the well-known mystic, was also a great philosopher. In modern Afghanistan almost nothing from the high intellectual level of the past remains. All three of the representatives of traditional education have two basic points in common: ignorance and intolerance.

The mollah, with his limited intellectual capacities, knew nothing beyond the horizon of the village or the tribal area. In the past though, he was a little better educated – he could read and write Arabic, but nevertheless his intellectual capacity was rather limited. The religious scholar, on the other hand, lived entirely confined to the text of his commentary books. Although he may have travelled and stayed in India or made the required pilgrimage to Mecca, he had no idea of what was happening socially and politically in the subcontinent or in the Arabic and other Islamic countries. The pir, with the daily worship of his person and the increasing number of worshippers, had no time and did not feel the need to enquire about the rest of the world and convinced by the superiority of intuitive communication with the Truth, he despised rational knowledge. With the generous donations and the blind obedience of his followers, the pir became increasingly powerful financially and socially. Some of them became big landlords, rich businessmen and influential in the government and at the ruler's court. All three had one thing in common: they were neither prepared nor willing to face the modern world; they had no answer for the new problems, and their common attitude was the systematic rejection of anything new. Their dogmatism and intolerance pushed many members of the rising generation towards the opposite extreme: rejecting everything native and old and blindly accepting everything foreign and new.

The tradition of secular education or 'worldly sciences' was more or less maintained. It was carried out in Persian with private tutors whom only rich families could afford. These were literate people who became public letter-writers or clerks and secretaries in the government administration. The few outstanding intellectuals who were able to produce creative work belonged to this category. They were the ones who became instrumental in opening the country to modern trends.

Modern Education: The Magico-Scientific Appeal

For over a century, the Western type of education has been spreading all over the non-Western world. A large proportion of at least two generations received their education in modern schools. Two aspects of

Past and Present Education

this important phenomenon will be considered here.

A man, stranger to himself

Generally in non-Western countries the new educational system had no roots or foundations in the local culture. Except in Japan and in some other countries, no bridge was thrown between the new and the old, between past and present. In Afghanistan modern education did not come as a continuation of the madrassas or the traditional schools; there was a wide gap between past and present. And the decline of the traditional education described above made it difficult to bridge the gap. Neither the traditionalists nor the modernists had the ability or the will to face the problem and offer a solution. The modern schools started with new buildings and a new type of teacher who ignored the traditional teaching. The modernisation of education was promoted by people privately educated in Persian literary subjects. A second generation, having started in the private traditional schools, switched to the new government institutions. The third generation followed the new education from the primary school to graduation. Our best scholars, poets and writers were among the first generation. The second generation also produced some good literary figures. The third generation was much less productive.

An individual who was educated in the new system and who also had the chance of completing his studies in an institution for higher education in the West, became a strange animal. He was neither a complete Westerner nor a genuine Easterner. He became a stranger: a stranger to his own society and even worse, a stranger to himself. A deeply split personality, he was constantly at war with himself. Suppressing his Eastern-conditioned subconscious drives with his Western-trained consciousness, he remained a prisoner of his foggy subjectivity and his own overevaluated self-image. He would despise the villagers whom he considered as 'backward and ignorant'. With his Western outlook, he would deprecate his own culture and society about which he knew little. Nor did the people consider him one of their own; he was received as a stranger, as 'a government official from the city', who did not speak the same language, did not pray and was suspected of drinking wine. Thus the modern-educated man was separated from the common people physically by his manners and Western clothes and morally by his judgement of values and Western outlook; with the difference that the villager preserved his identity as a human being well integrated in his community, while the educated one had lost his own cultural and social substance. This weakness made him vulnerable to the ideological offensive.

The main result of modern education was that the new Western-type schools opened the eyes of the people to the social, political and economic conditions in the industrialised countries and at the same time showed them what a gap was separating their countries from the developed world. The alternatives for an educated man from this underdeveloped country were either to go to the West and live under humanly decent conditions, or to make his own country worth living in, economically and politically. As not all the educated people had an opportunity to live in the West, only the second possibility was left open to them.

The myth of revolution

Having learned the new ideas about time, history and rapid changes, the educated men became impatient. In their countries the remnants of colonialism were still to be found: tyrants and dictators, oppression, and the vast misery of the local population. They did not believe that a process of evolution would achieve anything - anyway it would have been too slow a process for them. They wished to see changes in their own lifetime. For this reason the Myth of Revolution took on in their eyes the form of a magical means able to fulfil all their dreams. Revolution became the magical solution for all evil.

In this respect 'Marxism-Leninism' presented the most attractive prospect: it was magic with a scientific and rational appearance, a logical dream destined to become true, with Marx presenting theoretical coherence and Lenin showing the practical ways to seize power in order to build the dreamland.

Some aspects of Marxism-Leninism attractive to

people in the Third World would appear to be the following:

- The fact that it was predicated on historical arguments was something new and exciting for the already educated.

- The non-historical nature of the ideology as a dogma valid for all places and time. This must be especially reassuring to people used to living under strong timeless dogmas.

- Its messianic appeal could be expected to help mobilise magical-prone backward peoples into action.

- Its scientific terminology has a special appeal to the modern-educated sections of the people.

- Its 'dialectical materialism' with a two-fold thrust, one aimed at the educated class impressed by its 'revolutionary' logical system with a supposedly scientific basis; the other, offering the illiterate masses scientific justification for the contradictions in their mythical-prone minds.

In my view, thanks to the Soviet system in general and the Soviet military invasion of Afghanistan in particular, Marxism-Leninism is in the process of demystification. But the most serious side of the development up to 1985 is the stubborn persistence of the magical appeal of the Myth of Revolution. Other modernist trends for fast changes are trapped in it: a nationalist movement wanting a modern type of nation-building speaks in terms of 'National Revolution', and Islamic movements bent on renovating the old message of Islam, propagates the 'Islamic revolution'.

Afghanistan Under Soviet Occupation: A Threatened Culture

Since the beginning of the twentieth century, the modern system of education has become widely spread throughout the country. Despite the hostile attitude of the traditional religious leaders, ordinary people slowly adopted the system and at the end of the period became strongly in favour of it; delegations from the countryside came to Kabul pressing the Ministry of Education to open primary and secondary schools for the villages. Two universities (in Kabul and Jelalabad), lycees and professional high schools existed in the capital and in the major provincial cities. Secondary and primary schools, including schools for girls, were created in the remote corners of the country, and an extensive literacy programme for adults (both male and female) was launched. Increasingly large numbers of Afghans were regularly sent to Western countries for higher education. In 1960 coeducation was introduced at Kabul University; women were no longer forced to be veiled, and a growing number of them, upon graduation from Kabul colleges, started working in the government administration. For the first time in the history of Afghanistan, women were elected as members of Parliament, becoming ministers and diplomats.

With the Communist coup of April 1978 this development was interrupted and the Soviet invasion in December 1979 set the modernisation movement in education back to its state of about 70 years ago. Presently, Afghan culture is threatened from two sides: there is a process of destruction inside Afghanistan and a rapid degradation outside, in the refugee camps.

Cultural Destruction Inside the Country

As the Marxist trend was an entirely urban phenomenon and the party recruited its members mainly among city students and teachers, the population blamed the whole modern educational system for it. The favourable attitude of the people towards the modern schools reversed and changed overnight. People stopped sending their children to schools. In the countryside the school buildings converted into Communist Party headquarters, became the target for resistance attacks. Only in Soviet-controlled cities, especially Kabul, did schools continue to function but at less than half their normal capacity, and under a heavy

Past and Present Education

Sovietisation process.

Generally speaking, the majority of the urban population living under the direct control of the occupation forces have the same negative attitude towards the regime and its educational methods as the rural population. Only a small number of party members, their families and some affiliated opportunists are at the service of the enemy. The Russians, having lost confidence even in them, no longer think that the present old and young generations of Afghans can be 're-educated' according to their will. Their hopes are now focused on children between six and twelve. How much those young Afghans will actually be Sovietised, only the future can tell. The Sovietisation programme inside Afghanistan is confined to the cities, in particular to Kabul: in the capital to some high schools, the University and the 'Fatherland Orphanage', where the children of party activists killed in the fighting against the resistance are educated. The main aspects of the Sovietisation programme are:

- The extensive teaching of the Russian language, which began in the University and high schools, has now expanded to the secondary and primary schools, replacing English and French.

- 'Principles of Marxism-Leninism', 'Political Economy', 'Dialectical Materialism', 'the History of the Party' are taught in all college departments. As well, the project to rewrite the history of Afghanistan is in progress.

- Radio and TV programmes about life in Russia, documentary films about social and technical progress in the different social republics.

- Films about World War II and the so-called 'Patriotic War' against Nazi Germany.

- Regular propaganda and indoctrination meetings, conferences, film shows, dissemination of printed materials by the huge Soviet 'Friendship House' in Kabul.

Past and Present Education

- Organisation of Soviet-style women's, young people's, workers', writers', etc. unions.

- Special institutions for higher education in economics and politics for party members.

- Over ten thousand students between the ages of 12 and 20 are sent to Russia and other East European countries for military, political and intelligence training. In addition, boys between six and twelve simply taken in the streets without the knowledge and the permission of their parents, are sent in increasing numbers to the Soviet Union.

At present there is not much left of either traditional or modern education. The good mollahs and maulawis have either joined the resistance or are living in the refugee camps in Pakistan. The ones who have decided to serve the Marxist regime are well paid, performing the daily prayers and religious sermons on the radio and TV in favour of the regime but are not allowed to teach religious subjects. Over 90 per cent of the Afghans with a higher education from Western or other non-Communist universities have either been killed or have disappeared into prisons or else have fled to Western countries. The majority of the young non-party students at Kabul University and other colleges have either been arrested, or have left the country in order to avoid military service under the Russians. They have joined the resistance, or are living in foreign countries without having completed their studies. In the Afghan countryside, for over six years there have been no government schools, the children are not going to school. A young generation of illiterates will be added to the old one. At the moment some efforts are underway for opening primary schools in the villages. But the war situation and the constant threat of Russian military operations have made the task extremely difficult.

Cultural Degradation Among the Afghan Refugees Outside Afghanistan

Afghan refugees who have settled in Western countries

such as the United States, Germany, France, etc., are using the educational facilities of their host countries. Their children speak English, German or French, even with their parents; they do not have the means of learning to read and write their mother tongue, be it Pashtu or Dari. They are in the process of being assimilated into Western society.

The situation among the five million refugees from Afghanistan in the neighbouring countries is quite different: in the refugee camps in Pakistan containing over three million refugees, the circumstances are tragic. In Iran with more than a million refugees, the position is reportedly worse.

In the first two years after the Soviet invasion (1980-1) the refugees did not think much about education for their children; the urgent problems were food, shelter, medical care and fighting. In some camps a few good mollahs started elementary religious and Koranic teaching for children. Later, international humanitarian organisations encouraged the Pakistani Commissioner for Afghan refugees to build schools. In addition, the Afghan political organisations became aware of the importance of having educational institutions.

A small number of Afghan refugees living in cities such as Peshawar, Rawalpindi, Islamabad or Karachi send their children to local private or government schools, in which Urdu is the medium of teaching with English as the second language. The Afghan children hear about the Qaede Azam (The Great Leader) Mohammad Ali Jinnah, 'the founding father of the nation', but never about Afghanistan or a nation called by that name. The national languages, Pashtu or Persian Dari, are used by Afghan children at home or with other Afghans, becoming thus only an oral means of communication separated from the old literary tradition.

In the refugee camps, primary schools for Afghan children have been opened (but not yet covering one quarter of the refugee population). Teaching is carried out in Pashtu or Dari, reading and writing are added to the religious subjects. A few secondary schools have also been opened by the Afghan political organisations in Peshawar. But some strong negative factors are at work which prevent them from becoming a

Past and Present Education

normal modern system of education. All the Afghan political leaders in exile have two basic attitudes in common: they emphasise the religious dimension of the struggle and ignore (even in some cases reject) the national character. Both the revolutionaries (or the modernists) and the moderates (or the traditionalists) have the same negative attitude towards the secular social and natural sciences, considering them to be too Western. None of the new political leaders who have emerged in the resistance period have been able to build a reputation for themselves on a national scale. The reason is that because of their past and present social and political background (which is the subject of a separate study), they do not seem to have developed a clear national consciousness and awareness of a national interest transcending party lines or local and regional considerations. Consequently education, for the traditionalists, is to re-open the old religious madrassas, and for the revolutionaries, it is to build an institution in order to train militants for 'revolutionary Islam'. In their eyes, skills in medical, engineering sciences or in other secular fields are of secondary importance, one can live without them.

Their attitude to the teaching of Afghan history is most significant. The traditionalists consider it a secular subject, even an un-Islamic one as far as the pre-Islamic period is concerned. The revolutionaries are in principle against popular tradition which in their view has corrupted the purity of Islam. Thus both despise the study of Afghan history. In the few secondary schools for refugees, history is not taught at all. Mathematics and some physics are more or less tolerated. Geography is avoided as much as possible. A teacher who talked about the earth being spherical and turning around the sun, was expelled by the religious school headmaster. Some Western well-wishers have given thought to the prospect of an Afghan university in exile. The project stumbled on the main obstacle: will it be an Islamic revolutionary university or a traditional one?

The host country, Pakistan, having been founded in the name of Islam, is officially undergoing a process of Islamisation. Pakistan has since independence in 1947 had trouble with Afghanistan, and is

Past and Present Education

therefore not much inclined to promote Afghan national education and thus strengthen the national feeling of future Afghan generations, and the present Afghan religious leadership is helping the host country in this policy.

If the situation remains as it is, Afghan children born in the refugee camps will not know who they are. They will have no knowledge about their country, which they will not have seen, they will have no feeling for their past nor their culture about which they will not have learned anything.

One example, among many others, of cultural deterioration is the changing pattern and quality of Afghan carpets. Uzbek and Turkomen families of northern Afghanistan are coming out in increasing numbers. The women are the ones who made the well-known beautiful carpets. Now in the refugee camps around Peshawar, special workshops are being built. Women work there like slaves. In their native land they were used to their family workshops, and weaving carpets at home was part of the family daily work. In the past, inside Afghanistan, carpet weaving was entirely women's work. In the refugee camps in Pakistan, under the influence of local religious feeling, refugee women are more and more confined to their tents, as a workshop outside the home is not a place for women. Now Afghan refugee men are trained by Pakistani carpet-makers to make Afghan carpets. A Pakistani trader who has no idea of Afghan history and tradition and no feeling for genuine works of art, is showing the refugee workers how to change their traditional patterns and, using artificial dies and cheap materials, produce new types of carpets in large numbers for the market. The same process of degradation is going on in other branches of traditional handicraft such as embroidery, styles of dress, carpentry, etc.

Concluding Remarks

The intention of the Soviet system concerning Afghan culture and history is clear. The aim is to destroy the collective memory, to make the Afghans forget their social history and their cultural identity. Thus up-rooted, free from the socio-cultural ties with

Past and Present Education

the past, a new man capable of being re-educated, will be created. Men of the older generations, having too strong a memory to be easily erased, are in the process of physical elimination. Attention is now focused on the younger generations, especially the children.

From the past only events such as 'the struggle of the Afghans against British Imperialism' in the nineteenth century, and King Amanullah's exchange of messages with Lenin and the establishment of friendly relations with the Bolshevik regime (1919) are retained. In their eyes, the proper history of Afghanistan begins with the Communist coup in April 1978, before that everything is pre-history which does not extend further than to 1964, the foundation year of the Khalq party. The new subject introduced in the teaching programme, is 'the history of the Party' which is supposed to cover this pre-historic period.

At the present time, what is going on in Afghanistan is simply the physical devastation of a country and the cultural destruction of a nation. Still worse, the political leadership of the resistance does not seem capable of launching an appropriate counter-offensive in the cultural front.

An Afghan farmer, a refugee from Logar, said one day with deep sorrow:

> The Russians, in order to deprive the freedom fighters of shelter, destroy the vegetation and even cut centuries-old plane trees down. If we could replant them now, it would take them at least a hundred years to reach the size of the old one.

This picture describes the whole economic, social and cultural situation of Afghanistan under the Soviet military invasion.

Our concluding remarks are therefore in the form of three questions:

1. When Afghanistan is liberated, will all the educated Afghans come back in order to take active part in the reconstruction of their country?

Past and Present Education

2. Will a genuine revival of traditional scholarship be possible?
3. Could a modern system of education, better adapted to the national character and in harmony with our tradition and history, be implemented?

In any case, the present destruction and the future liberation of the country will give us the chance to make a new start. It will be worth trying.

7

SCHOLARS, SAINTS AND SUFIS IN MODERN AFGHANISTAN

Bo Utas

Some 15 years ago, there appeared an excellent book entitled Scholars, Saints, and Sufis: Muslim Religious Institutions in the Middle East since 1500 (edited by Nikki R. Keddie, University of California press, 1972). Unfortunately, it had no contribution on Afghanistan. On the whole, the religious and cultural elite of contemporary Afghanistan has received much less scholarly attention than, for example, that of its neighbour Iran. The following is in no way a general description or analysis that could fill that lacuna. It is merely a few observations that have a bearing on the difficult situation of Afghan culture today. They are offered from the point of view of a cultural historian and not from that of a social scientist.

In the above-mentioned work, the terms 'Scholars', 'Saints' and 'Sufis' refer to various forms of religious leadership. In the present study I shall, however, use the word 'scholar' in a broader sense, including not only the so-called 'doctors of religion' (i.e. 'ulama) but also more or less secular scholars and intellectuals, such as the type of general literary-cultural personality or polyhistor that has been of great importance in Afghanistan - as well as academics of a more narrow, modern description.

In his contribution to the present volume on 'Past and Present Education in Afghanistan', Sayd B. Majrooh characterises the traditional theological education as sterile or even absurd, and he gives a lucid description of the teaching that leads to such results. The learned theologians of Afghanistan, often referred to as maulavis, used to receive their basic education in Koran schools (madrasas) in the main Afghan cities. For more advanced studies a few turned to foreign centres of Islamic learning, especially to the Indian theological school in Deoband, founded in 1867 and known to be quite conservative within its Indian context. Before the Russian Revolution, Central Asian theological schools, especially in Tashkent, Bukhara and Samarqand, also played a certain role. In later years some theologians have ventured as far as the famous al-Azhar in Cairo, where they could have come under both modernist and 'fundamentalist' (e.g. Ikhwani) influence. Finally, there is the Theological Faculty of Kabul University (founded in 1950), the graduates of which (qadhis, etc.) had to compete, generally with little success as regards jobs, with graduates of the Faculty of (secular) Law at the same university (already founded in 1938).(1) The Faculty of Law (and Political Sciences) had about 400 students in 1976-7, a hundred of whom graduated that year, while the Faculty of Theology probably had only half that number.(2)

The traditional theological education could, without doubt, be described as scholastic and sterile, but constructive criticism of this should, perhaps, rather come from the inside. It is far too facile a standpoint for us Westerners to regard the 'backwardness' of contemporary Muslim theology and education as something axiomatic. As a result of such an approach, much of our attention has been attracted by modernist ('liberal') and, lately, so called 'fundamentalist' or 'islamist' tendencies. This has probably led to a serious underestimation of the influence and potential vitality of traditional or orthodox Islam. The abovementioned work Scholars, Saints, and Sufis was important in turning our attention to this distortion in Western perspectives. Subsequent political development has underlined this. Even if we tend to regard the present Islamic Republic of Iran as some kind of 'fundamentalist' (i.e. pseudo-theological) polity, it becomes more and more clear that traditional Shi'i

Scholars, Saints and Sufis

theology constitutes much of its mainstay. Similarly, I think, one may conclude that traditional 'ulama are getting the better of 'Mawdudism' in Pakistan.

The general tendency of Sunni 'ulama in most parts of the Muslim world, through most of Islamic history, has been to endorse the regime in power. As regards Afghanistan, this may be demonstrated by the 'Assembly of Theologians' (Jam'iyat-i 'ulama) that was founded in 1929 by Nadir Shah.(3) This organisation first of all served the purpose of controlling the 'ulama and of integrating them in the centralised state. While the leading 'ulama and maulavis were made part of the new establishment, also by means of marriage and other alliances, as a group they gradually lost their influence. This development was further underlined by the incipient secularisation of the administration of justice and by the introduction of a westernised school system. Traces of this tradition of subservience to the government in power may still be seen today when a somewhat shadowy Jam'iyat-i 'ulama expresses continual support of the present regime in Kabul.(4)

The traditional standpoint of the Sunni 'ulama is thus that as long as the government guarantees the preservation of the Muslim faith they support it, even if it acts against the shari'a. The present regime has made many declarations in support of Islam and of Muslim institutions. Its official standpoint is summed up in Article 5 of the 'Constitution' or 'Fundamental Principles':

> Respect, observance and preservation of Islam as a sacred religion will be ensured by the Democratic Republic of Afghanistan, and freedom of religious rights guaranteed for Moslems ... The government will help the clergy and religious scholars in carrying out their patriotic activities, duties and obligations.(5)

However, the majority of the leading theologians clearly have little confidence in such professions, for they have withdrawn their support from the regime and many have joined the resistance. Those religious leaders promoted by the government, and who support it, are little-known personalities of no previous standing among the public. A good example of this are the antecedents of the newly appointed Minister of Islamic Affairs, 'Abd ul-Vali Hujjat, who has been described as a 60-year-old Tajik from Takhar province, educated in a madrasa in Kabul, later a mullah in a mosque and a teacher in a madrasa; then an official in the Ministry of Justice and after the 1978 coup President of the Provincial Court in Herat.(6) The actual outcome of the theological opposition to the regime has been described by many observers, for example, by Olivier Roy in his article 'Intellectuels et ulema dans la resistance afghane'(7) and in his recent book L'Afghanistan: Islam et modernite politique (Paris, Editions du Seuil, 1985). Olivier Roy advances the interesting theory that in the resistance movement a new balance of functions has been reached between the 'ulama, the 'islamists' and the emerging secular and military leaders.

There is a strong dominance of Arabic in the syllabus of traditional theological education, including Arabic rhetoric, grammar and logic. In contrast to this stands the traditional literary or secular education which, in the words of Professor Majrooh (this volume, Chapter 6), was 'carried out in Persian with private tutors which only rich families could afford'. There is, in fact, a marked dichotomy in traditional Afghan education between the heavily Arabicised theological learning and the basically Persian literary culture. The dichotomy between these two cultures goes back through a thousand years of history, and it is still far from resolved. This is perhaps more obvious in present-day Iran than in Afghanistan. The New Persian language is a very special medium. It incorporates, or even personifies, both a literary-cultural and an administrative-political tradition that has been playing a dominant role not only within the confines of present-day Iran and Afghanistan but also in the whole region, including Central Asia and India.

The secularly educated elite of Afghanistan was less bound by religious conservatism than other groups of society. It dominated not only the literary culture but also the upper strata of administration. The literary culture was to a great extent also a political culture. In those circles new ideas and modern trends could get a foothold. In this context it suffices to mention Mahmud Tarzi and his journal Siraj ul-akhbar, which appeared between 1911 and 1919. That type of modernist or liberal personalities are often referred to as raushanfikran, 'the enlightened', and the introduction of a westernised educational system, beginning with the Habibiya school in 1903, was certainly due to their influence.

My suggestion that this type of education was based on a Persian literary culture needs some modification. The ruling establishment of Afghanistan was, after all, Pashtun, and since 1936 Pashto is the national language together with Dari (i.e. Afghan Persian).(8) The Persian influence on Pashto as a literary language was, however, so great that, for the purposes of the present argument, both can be regarded as one entity. Furthermore, the position of Persian (be it called Farsi, Dari or Kabuli) was traditionally so strong in the cities and in the administration that Pashto had little chance of competing. Not without reason has Kabul been called pashto-khor, i.e. 'the Pashto-eater'. On the other hand, many central literary personalities made great efforts to develop Pashto literary culture, too. As an illustration one may mention the parallel institutions Anjuman-i tarikh, 'The Historical Society' (established in 1942), and Pashto Tolana, 'The Pashto Academy' (established in 1935), and their impressive programmes of publication.(9)

Many of these cultural personalities were veritable polyhistors. They wrote on history, languages, folklore, society, etc., but above all they were literary men, poets more often than not. My argument here is that they expressed (and express) much of what is central in Afghan or Pashto-Persian culture and that people of this category - and their less prolific heirs - are now locked in a very difficult situation. It is striking that, in contrast to the religious leadership, they have to a certain extent stayed on in Kabul. Senior scholars often appear as mushavir, i.e. 'consultants', to the ministries, and their younger colleagues fill the staff of the Faculty of Letters of Kabul University. As a matter of fact, that faculty is the only one to function in more or less unimpaired form. It is true that a number of scholars of the older generation, notably Khalilu'llah Khalili, and people like Sayd Bahaouddin Majrooh of the generation after have left Kabul, but many chose to stay. It may suffice to mention the late 'Abd ul-Hayy Habibi. The question remains: what is the reason for this?

On the personal level, there might be dozens of reasons, of course, but I shall try to point out some more general or structural factors. Persian urban culture may be regarded as an age-old apparatus, not only for producing and enjoying literature but also for administration and execution of power and business. During more than a millennium the urban Persian-speaking elites have succeeded in surviving a great number of changes in political dominance and influences of foreign languages and cultures. This has not been an ethnic but a cultural process. The Persian language is the dominating medium but many of its users have a different linguistic background (Turkic, Pashto, Balochi, etc.) and often retain their mother tongue as a token of their ethnic identity in a narrower sense. In a historic perspective, this Persian establishment has generally succeeded in coming out on top. The intruders have quickly become Persianised. The main method of achieving this has been, I think, co-operation with the new masters. The urban Persians (including Persianised Pashtuns, Turks, etc.) have put their cultural and executive apparatus at the disposal of the victors, and they have triumphed in the long run, not individually, perhaps, but as a class. Now, the question is: will the trick work once more?

During an on-going process there are no certain answers to such questions, but there are signs that may be interpreted. Some observers and scholars suggest that a Soviet type of 'nationality policy' is being implemented in the parts of Afghanistan that can be run from Kabul.(10) In the long run this could lead to a 'Sovietisation', meaning, among other things, that the Russian language substitutes Persian as the means of communication, i.e. the lingua franca, between the various ethnic groups of Afghanistan.(11) If Soviet influence can be maintained on a high level during an extended period of time, this is not an unlikely development. In such a process too, the tens of thousands of Afghan boys and girls that are currently being trained in the Soviet Union may play a crucial role.(12) In her contribution to this volume (Chapter 5), Eden Naby especially stresses the ambiguity in the position of the Turkic peoples of northern Afghanistan. The situation of other non-Pashtun 'nationalities' (Tajik, Hazara, Baloch, etc.) is in many respects different, but a successful policy of cultural-linguistic particularisation would change all ethnic relations in a decisive way. That would not only mean the end of Pashtun political dominance but probably also of the importance of the Persian-speaking establishment. The example of Soviet Central Asia is telling. In Central Asian cities like Samarqand and Bukhara there were once Persian-speaking urban elites, too, that are now at the point of losing their cultural identity.

If a Soviet type of ethnic policy becomes effective in Afghanistan, these traditional men of letters run the risk of being gradually forced into small niches assigned to suitable representatives of ethnic folklore. This threat may look nebulous in Kabul today, but nevertheless I think it is quite serious. Unfortunately, the alternatives for these scholars are not much more promising. If they leave for Pakistan, they are sure to face great difficulties. The parties of the resistance movement have little room, or even tolerance, for this type of intellectual. The academic world of Pakistan obviously has none. Those who manage to go to Europe or the United States may have a slight chance to continue working in their own field, but their cultural identity will be at peril in the foreign surroundings and they are easily lost to the collective cause of shaping the future of Afghan culture.

In this study, 'scholars' have been divided into two categories, religious and secular. On the other hand, 'Saints and Sufis' may be fused into one category. If we leave the rather awkward English translation 'Saint' for the religious leader called <u>shaikh</u>, <u>pir</u>, <u>murshid</u>, <u>aqa</u>, <u>miyan</u>, <u>ishan</u>, etc. aside and notice that the word 'Sufi' covers both the leader and his adherents, this complex could instead be called <u>tariqas</u>, i.e. the Sufi orders or mystical 'brotherhoods'. Western scholarship has tended to distinguish between two forms of contemporary Sufism. This has, perhaps, more a historical than a factual explanation. The classical Islamic mysticism (Sufism) has mainly been studied by specialists of religion and literature, i.e. so-called 'high' religion and 'high' literature. They have elucidated advanced philosophical, literary and artistic aspects of esoteric religion, but that is no complete description of the Sufi orders, neither of those of the twelfth and thirteenth centuries, nor of those of today. Muslim scholars have adopted a similar approach. Thus the contemporary Afghan writer 'Abd ul-Hakim Tabibi, in a book entitled Sufism in Afghanistan (Sair-i tasvvuf dar Afghanistan, Kabul, 1357/1977), treats the great classical poets, basing himself partly on secondary Western sources, but says nothing about living Sufism in his own country today. Contemporary Sufi activities have mainly been studied by social anthropologists and other social scientists. They have described organisational forms and social roles, but the more esoteric aspects of modern Sufism have, naturally, been less accessible to them. On the other hand, ramifications of Sufi orders have reached the West and gained adherents there. Here, once more, the religious and esoteric contents have attracted attention. A common conclusion has been that there must exist two kinds of contemporary Sufism: one esoteric and one belonging to a mainly superstitious 'folk Islam'. This may be a delusion. The few studies that trace the history of a Sufi order from the Middle Ages to our day tend to underline the continuity in its development, for example, B.G. Martin's 'A Short History of the Khalwati Order'(13) and Hamid Algar's 'The Naqsbandi order: a preliminary survey of its history and significance'.(14)

B.G. Martin (op.cit., p. 276) gives an enlightening definition:

> Roughly, a tariqa or brotherhood may be defined as a hierarchical Muslim institution with a multiplicity of functional levels. Its leaders may use it at different times and places for varying purposes; its adherents use it for other ends ... It has a useful social role to play besides its purely spiritual or quietistic mystical functions. An order may become involved

in politics; it may provide medical or psychiatric help for its members, or it may become concerned with magic or astrology. For these purposes, it may include within its ranks remarkable magic-makers or miracle-mongers...

The 'two forms' analysis of modern Sufism has recently been applied to Afghanistan by Olivier Roy in an article entitled 'Sufism in Afghan Resistance'(15) and again, in a modified and elaborated version, in his above-mentioned book L'Afghanistan: Islam et modernite politique (esp. pp. 53-62). Roy neatly distinguishes between a 'spiritualist Sufism' (i.e. the esoteric type) and, with a loan from a North African context, a 'maraboutic Sufism' (i.e. the folk Islam type). In the autumn of 1977 and the spring of 1978, I visited twelve major khanaqahs, that is, Sufi convents or lodges, in Kabul and in western and northern Afghanistan and interviewed the same number of leading pirs. In a preliminary report, 'Notes on Afghan Sufi Orders and Khanaqahs'(16), I gave a brief sketch of the functions of the pirs and khanaqahs I studied at that time (7 Naqshbandi, 3 Qadiri and 2 Chishti). Taking all levels of activity (cf. the definition by Martin above) into consideration, it was nowhere possible to distinguish between a 'spiritualist' and a 'maraboutic' type. The situation is obviously different in the tribal areas of southeastern Afghanistan,(17) but it is possible that in-depth studies will reveal a close relation between the spiritual master, the vaguely charismatic 'saint' and the 'magic-maker' even there. The case of the Mujaddidi and Gailani families, on whom Roy bases much of his argument, is very special, since they are quite recent newcomers to this region (the beginning of this century).

In general, the position of a Sufi pir, or master, is determined by his silsila, in other words, his spiritual genealogy. This genealogy defines his affiliation to one or more of the main tariqas and, in some respects, also to other masters. Although this genealogy in principle is a purely spiritual matter, in practice it is nowadays generally physical in its later links. This means that the pir-ship tends to be inherited in regular dynasties. The charismatic quality which is thus inherited, spiritually or physically, is popularly called barakat (originally 'Divine blessing') or karamat (originally 'generosity'). Now, barakat is one thing and learning is another, and pirs who inherit their barakat tend to lose interest in acquiring a wider learning and they generally employ a maulavi to look after such matters and even to run the customary Koran school.

The following, and thus the influence, of a pir can be of many kinds. Adherence is commonly inherited (meaning both in the pir's family and in that of the adherent). Of course, the popularity of a pir will also depend on the reputation of his barakat and/or learning. There is no quantitative data on this but there is reason to suspect that until recently, say one generation back, most Afghans had some relation to a pir, in particular as someone to turn to at various times of distress. Female Afghans may also turn to female members of the pir's family. That would be the most general type of adherence. The next degree of relationship is to belong to the circle around the pir or to one of his khalifas or 'deputies' performing the special rites of the order in question. The most central of these rites is the meditative prayer exercise called zikr. This is generally a vocal, collective exercise, called jahr but it may also be a silent, individual meditation, called khafi (practised by some but not all of the Naqshbandis). For participation in the zikr the express permission (ijaza) of the pir is necessary, and this is the main criterion for calling someone a Sufi (also murid). Finally, there are higher degrees of initiation that vary from order to order and master to master.

A Sufi master can fill all or only a few of these functions, but the fact that he, for instance, appears as a charismatic healer with a wide popular following does not mean that he has no more advanced disciples nor that he could not also be the spiritual leader of prominent members of the society. I have seen pirs who at one moment give saintly blessings to nomad herdsmen passing on their bi-annual migration, bringing a gift of a lamb or two, and the next receive a judge, an officer or some other high official in confidential conversation. The influence of the pirs is thus based on a variety of roles, but most widely

Scholars, Saints and Sufis

on their popularity as charismatic leaders, at times on their wealth and general standing in society, and at times also on their ability to solve conflicts. The latter is a natural role, as pirs by definition stand outside both the tribal system and official society and because they are often held to be persons of special integrity. Over their direct disciples they can wield even greater influence, because they are supposed to be perfect spiritual examples, models for systematic imitation (taqlid) of their murids.

The relations between Sufi leaders and the orthodox clergy are generally more friendly in Afghanistan than in most other Muslim countries. There is at times even a kind of symbiosis between pirs and maulavis, and leading pirs may occasionally be considered as 'ulama.(18) This is especially feasible in the Naqshbandi order, which all through its history has stressed both the necessity of strict adherence to the rules of the shari'a and all Sunni rites as well as the integration of the Sufi in an active social life.(19)

In the face of the communist take-over and the Soviet military intervention, the Sufi leaders have reacted very much like the 'ulama. Many of the old pirs have fled the country and the younger ones have often joined the resistance movement.(20) Thus, of the twelve khanaqahs that I visited in 1977 and '78 none seems to be functioning today. Some of the pirs I met then have been killed or have died a natural death, while others are in exile or have joined the resistance inside the country. It is difficult to estimate how far the pirs can mobilise their followers for the struggle, but in some instances at least their influence must be considerable. More important in the long perspective are probably the spiritual and moral resources that are vested in these brotherhoods, capable of combining a wide, popular appeal with advanced concepts for a minority. Besides which, their more or less covert form of organisation make them well suited for work under political pressure.

From a general point of view, Sufism constitutes a bridge between Islamic-Arabic and literary-Persian culture. In Sufism, Arabic and Persian are equally important, the Arabic sources of Islam (the Koran and the hadith) as much as the Persian poetry and the tracts written by many generations of Sufis. On one level of Sufism, the gap between Pashto-Persian and Turco-Persian literary culture, on the one hand, and Arabic religious and legal culture, on the other, somehow becomes negligible. This may prove to be an important asset in the future development of Afghan culture.

Notes

1. Sovremennyj Afghanistan, Moscow 1960, p. 294.
2. Cf. Republic of Afghanistan Annual, 1978, Ministry of Education and Culture, Kabul, pp. 550-3.4. Cf. Sovremennyj Afghanistan, p. 488.
4. Cf. BBC Summary of World Broadcasts, SU/6635/C/1 29 Jan. 81.
5. Kabul New Times, 20/21 April 1980; quoted from Gerhard Moltmann, Die Verfassungsentwicklung Afghanistans 1901-1981 (= Mitteilungen des Deutschen Orient-Instituts, 18), Hamburg 1982, p. 170.
6. Afghan Information Centre Monthly Bulletin, Peshwar, No. 49, April 1985, p. 2.
7. Peuples Mediterraneens, No. 21, 1982, pp. 129-51.
8. Article 3 of the Constitution of 1964 and Article 23 of the Constitution of 1977; cf. Moltmann, op.cit., pp. 106, 128.
9. Cf. Sovremennyj Afghanistan, pp. 297, 306.
10. E.g. Sauri Bhattacharya, 'Soviet Nationality Policy in Afghanistan', Asian Affairs, 15 (1984): 2, pp. 125-37.
11. Cf. Rasul Amin, 'A General Reflection on the Stealthy Sovietisation of Afghanistan', Central Asian Survey, 1984, pp. 47-61.
12. The size of the editions of certain Soviet school books may give an unintended hint on the numbers of Afghan students trained in the Soviet Union. Thus the Russian weekly book catalogue Novye Knigi 1984:15 announced the publication of a series of elementary books in Dari (Afghan Persian) on Leninism in editions of 25-40,000 copies each (pp. 30-31). The same and similar titles to be published in Pashto were announced in editions of 12-15,000 copies (ibid., p. 68). These books are, or course, also intended for

circulation inside Afghanistan. Note the difference in numbers of copies between Dari and Pashto books!
13. N. Keddie (ed.), Scholars, Saints and Sufis, pp. 275-305.
14. Studia Islamica 42 (1976), pp. 123-53.
15. Central Asian Survey 4 (1983), 2, pp. 61-79.
16. Afghanistan Journal 7 (1980), 2, pp. 60-67.
17. Cf. also Jon W. Anderson, 'How Afghans define themselves in relation to Islam', in M.N. Shahrani and R.L. Canfield (eds.), Revolutions and Rebellions in Afghanistan, Berkeley, University of California, 1984, pp. 266-87.
18. This is repeatedly stressed by Olivier Roy in the works quoted above; cf. n. 15.
19. As already expressed in the original precepts of the order, for instance in the rule khalvat dar anjuman, i.e. 'solitude in company'.
20. Olivier Roy (cf. n. 15 and his book l'Afghanistan) describes their activities and party preferences.

8

MODERN POLITICAL CULTURE AND TRADITIONAL RESISTANCE

Olivier Roy

Modern Education

Previously, there existed in Afghanistan two educational systems: the government's and the Koranic. The former was of recent origin, having been established mainly in the 1950s. It had several different levels: a state faculty in Kabul, training schools for teachers in Kabul and in some provincial capitals, high schools (called 'lycees') in Kabul, all provincial capitals and in some other cities, middle schools (sixth to ninth grades) and elementary schools in every town, in bazaars and even in small villages. This system was quite comprehensive. In the 1968 budget, the expenditure on education amounted to 19.1 per cent of the total expenditures. The sixties saw the first generations of students in the modern sense of the word. There were in all about 4,000 students enrolled in the university. The subjects taught in government schools were history, geography, physics, mathematics, Persian language and literature, Pashto and religion, i.e. basically, a normal modern curriculum. The books, too, were modern. Even religion was taught by government teachers. Since religion was a compulsory subject, one cannot say that it was a really secular system, but most of the manuals (reading-books, literature and history books) emphasised modern aspects of life rather than traditional patterns. In history, Afghanistan was depicted as an ancient state, whose past went back to the Indo-Europeans, while the impact of Islam was largely discarded.

The teaching at the university was entirely modern. First of all, most faculties were established with foreign assistance and were simply replicas of Western originals. Philosophy, sociology and political science were introduced without any reference to traditional knowledge. So a new intelligentsia was created whose members were no longer the sons of the political establishment. In this context it could be mentioned that at the end of the sixties most of the students living on Kabul's campuses had a rural background. When they were politicised, they became the core of various extremist parties. Among these were, of course, the Communists. Another party which should be mentioned here was the 'Muslim Youth Organisation' (Sazman-e jawanan-e mosalman). The young militants of this organisation were not traditionalists. Most of them belonged to the science faculties. Their aim was to develop a modern political ideology based on Islam, which they saw as the only way of coming to terms with the modern world and the best means of confronting foreign imperialism. They wanted to retain the educational system of the government and the modern curriculum. Some of them became teachers in village schools. They became suspect in the eyes of the traditional mullahs who were struck by the propensity of these young men to emphasise modernity rather than referring to Islam. And for a foreigner like me, it was sometimes difficult to tell a Maoist teacher in a village school from his Muslim colleague. For reasons of political expediency, the former emphasised his Muslim credentials as much as the latter.

The young Muslim militants, that is, those who have survived, now figure prominently as leaders of the resistance movement, above all in Jamiat-i Islami and the two parties which are both called Hezb-Islami. They are influential mainly in the north. All of them favour the reopening of modern schools. The only difference as compared to the old government schools is the stress they put on Islam, not only as a religion but also as a political ideology. In their view, however, the study of political science should not be confined exclusively to Islam. They also wish to include Western ideologies and even think that the students should know about Marxism. The science curriculum, in their opinion should be extended.

The reopening of this kind of school would, however, be fraught with many difficulties. First there is the lack of text-books and teachers and, on top of that, there is the security problem. In the first few years of the war it was still possible to start schools in places where the Soviets never came. But now, because of the escalation of the war, there is no safe place in Afghanistan.

Yet another problem is that the resistance has very few teachers. All former students who have remained inside Afghanistan are now in charge of the war and have no time for teaching. So very few modern schools are now functioning inside Afghanistan. I have seen a few in Hazarajat, where there is no actual fighting. They were run by former students belonging to the Nasr and Nehzat parties. There have also been some attempts by non-fundamentalist groups to start schools, by Ittihadia in Hazarajat, and in Wardak. These schools are usually supported by foreigners and the teachers are salaried. This may create problems with other schools that are established without foreign money. I am also a bit sceptical about training Afghan teachers outside and then sending them inside and paying them a salary. Because of the war, the main motivation has to be political - not financial.

Traditional Education

Everyone has heard about the village Koran school, the maktab, led by the local mullah, where young children get a basic training in reading, writing and religion. This system is prevalent throughout Afghanistan, but in the big cities, where the government-run primary schools were well established, it was fading away. However, in the countryside many began their education in these schools and were then sent to government schools. There is also, however, another educational system, which has often been overlooked. I am referring to the private madrasa.

This system functions in the following manner. The alim (singular for ulema) is called mawlawi in Afghanistan. Upon finishing the village Koranic school (maktab), the religious student (taleb) spends several years with a local mawlawi who instructs some dozen students in an ordinary mosque turned into an 'upper' religious school (madrasa). The school's standing depends on the prestige of the master. Instruction is carried out individually and consists in learning twenty didactic books in a fixed order. Upon receipt of a diploma from his master (ijaza), the graduate can open his own madrasa, or continue his studies in a school of higher learning.

In Afghanistan, however, despite the efforts of the Amirs (including the royal madrasa set up by Abdurrahman and the dar ol-olum-e arabiya opened in Pul-i Charkhi in 1940), there has never been a madrasa capable of offering a first-class education.

The most gifted Afghan ulema pursued their studies in India, particularly at the famed Deoband madrasa. After the partition in 1947 Peshawar replaced Deoband as the centre of advanced studies for traditionalist ulema. Until 1917, the ulema from the north of Afghanistan went to Bukhara, to the madrasa Diwan Begi.

The ulema are scholars, not intellectuals. They adhere to the age-old curriculum common to the whole Muslim world, i.e. classical Arabic, kalam or theology, tafsir or interpretation of the Koran, hadith or traditions of the Prophet, fiqh or Muslim law. The ulema feel that they belong to the Muslim community, the umma, rather than to any particular nation. Admittedly, what the ulema transmit is a culture based on commentaries inculcated by repetition, but it should also be recognised that it is a culture which escapes the confines of parochialism. Even so, this culture is ill-equipped to provide an ideology capable of making sense of the modern secular world. As in all Muslim countries, the ulema appear to have been incapable of adapting to the modern world and have allowed power to slip into the hands of new elites.

Nevertheless, the cultural tradition represented by the mawlawi remains very strong in Afghanistan, even beyond religious matters. For example, I had the opportunity of visiting the library of mawlawi Mirajuddin in Astana, Panjshir Valley, in 1981. It housed 400 books, mainly lithographs or manuscripts. I found the opus of Galien, Jalinos in Arabic-Persian, the Greek doctor used by Mirajuddin to prepare medicines.

Modern Culture and Traditional Resistance

There was also a manuscript in Arabic by Euclides, used by the mawlawi to teach geometry to his maktab pupils and other, more modern manuals, especially in astronomy. The mawlawi had constructed an astrolabe and a celestial sphere, calculated the proper position of his village, and accordingly informed the government that the official map was not accurate in this regard. Of course, all the best-known books of hadith, Koran commentaries, and books on religious law were also to be found in the library.

Generally the mawlawi specialise in one of the three following areas: religious law, theology, or philosophy. Sufism is also widely studied. And one should not forget classical Persian literature (Saadi, Hafez), which is used to teach classical Persian, as well as morality and history to young children.

Has this culture become sterile, as it has been claimed (cf. Professor Majrooh's Chapter 6 in this volume)? Certainly, very few new works have been created, and access to it is more a matter of memory than of creativity. Yet the aim of Afghan Islamic culture, as a traditional culture, is not in the first place to develop a critical attitude, but rather to give access to literacy, knowledge, and Weltanschauung. It is a collective memory, a sense of identity, and a set of ethical principles embedded in a corpus of literary and theological works to last forever. Naturally, no Westernised intellectual, liberal or Marxist, can feel at ease in this culture. Hence the sometimes strange convergence of Westernised aristocratic and Communist viewpoints on the mollahs.

However, if most mawlawi remained at ease in this traditional culture, some nevertheless became aware of the challenges posed by Western education and did their best to come to terms with it. This was the aim of the professors who staffed the government Faculty of Religious Law. The majority of them had a traditional background (Koranic schools) coupled with a modern education (studies in the government educational system). The Faculty of Religious Law was at the crossroads of both systems: it was fully integrated in the modern university and its teaching staff was in close contact with other faculty members teaching Western philosophy and political science. At the same time fiqh and theology were absolutely ortho-

Modern Culture and Traditional Resistance

dox, and the foremost teachers completed their studies in Cairo at the University of Al-Azhar. A few of these professors launched Islamic political parties, and their survivors, for example, Professor Rabbani, now head a part of the resistance bridging the gap between traditionalist ulema and young intellectuals.

Today, inside Afghanistan, the network of Koranic schools in those villages still left standing, remains intact. But without the madrasa, these schools are not enough to perpetuate traditional Islamic culture. What has happened to the madrasa? Kabul's state university of Islamic law is under Communist control, and only partially open. Other state madrasa have been closed. Urban private madrasa have been shut down with many of their teachers already killed under Taraki and Amin. Most of the rural madrasa are either closed or turned into a jabha-ye toleba: the whole madrasa has become a military unit. The teachers function as officers and the pupils (toleba) as soldiers. This reminds one of the robat in Morocco at the time of the Spanish crusades. Basic teaching is still carried on, but the main activity is war. These units, mainly affiliated with the harakt-e-engelab, are to be found in Pashtun areas, from Kandahar to Badghis province. They are generally linked to a Sufi order, mainly naqshbandi, and the local mawlawi is usually a murid. Some examples of this development are Mizan in Zabul province, Kilimbaf in Jawzjan and Jawand in Badghis. In fact, very few madrasa are still carrying on the full range of traditional teaching inside Afghanistan.

Today we can say that young intellectuals and traditional clerics are no longer opposed to one another. Most of the former have spent some time in Koranic schools, either before entering or during the very long winter vacations. This is the typical pattern in Hazarajat and Nuristan. For example, Mawlawi Afzal, who was educated in the traditional madrasa of Pakistan and now is the head of an 'Islamic government' in Nuristan, taught during the winter young students from government schools which had been closed. (A similar case is that of Wazir Shah, a former civil servant and now Minister of Culture in this 'government'.)

In conclusion, both traditional clerics and

modern Muslim intellectuals are still active inside Afghanistan but are confronted with difficulties in perpetuating themselves. What is done in Peshawar for them? Modern education is mostly accessible through Western-backed schools that recruit from among the urban-educated. These schools train teachers who are to be sent into Afghanistan with a salary. This is a mistake on three counts. Firstly, young Kabulis who have never been involved in the fighting do not generally adapt themselves well to conditions in the free areas. The education which these young men receive is entirely secular. This increases the suspicion which most fighters harbour towards the newcomers as belonging to leftist organisations. Thirdly, to pay somebody for taking part in this war has vicious side-effects: why not pay the mujahedin?

The prospects for the traditional clerics are also dim. Most of the new madrasa built in Peshawar are wahhabi-sponsored. wahhabis generally despise traditional Afghan Islamic culture, considering it to be full of ignorance and superstition. The following quote from Arab News (14 September 1985, p.9) is illuminating: 'The Muslim scholars in the world have a great role to play in enlightening the ignorant Afghans. Un-Islamic customs and traditions have found their way into their lives.' The fact that the author makes no reference to Afghan clerics shows that he is ignorant himself; the target of his attack is really Sufism and traditional Persian literature. In this context it should be mentioned that wahhabism is found mainly in Nuristan and West Badakhshan but is otherwise strongly opposed even by fundamentalist Afghans, who stick to the traditional culture.

The way to Hell is paved with good intentions. Before trying to establish any educational network in Peshawar or inside Afghanistan, we should consider the variety and resources of what already exists and functions. We should not repeat the mistakes that were made under the King, i.e. to place two unconnected systems side by side, one traditional, the other Western. This will produce exactly the schizophrenic society which gave rise to the Afghan communist - and most of the emigres in the West.

9

AFGHAN EDUCATION DURING THE WAR

Batinshah Safi

My description of Afghan education during the war is divided into two parts: education inside Afghanistan and education for the refugees outside Afghanistan. The first part is divided into two sections: education in the countryside (under the control of the resistance) and education in the cities (under the control of the Kabul government).

But first I will give a short description of the education conditions in Afghanistan before the war. In 1977 about 10,000 students attended the courses at Kabul University and the teachers' training colleges. Eight hundred thousand pupils in 4,000 schools were being taught by 23,000 teachers. Eighty-five per cent of the population of Afghanistan (17 million) were living in the countryside and were mostly occupied with farming and animal husbandry. The majority of the primary and the secondary schools were situated in the countryside.

Between 1979 and 1981 most of the school buildings in the countryside were destroyed. The reason is simple: these buildings were transformed by the Karmal government into propaganda and administration centres for the government. Communist teachers were often killed if they had not fled away. Many teachers were abroad as refugees and those who remained joined the resistance.

As a result, almost all the schools stopped functioning and thereby education in the whole country came to a standstill.

Education During the War

Education inside Afghanistan

During the first years of the war the Afghan resistance expected to be able to get rid of the Soviet occupation forces and their puppet regime in Kabul. Gradually realising that the war would be long they became more and more interested in education and started some schools sporadically (in mosques, destroyed buildings, etc.). But there was a lack of books and other education materials. The people were too poor to pay the teachers' salaries and the parties could not help them.

The Afghanistan Education Committee

The Swedish committee for Afghanistan, which has been working in Peshawar, Pakistan, giving humanitarian aid to the Afghan people in the liberated areas of Afghanistan since 1982, was visited by a great number of Afghans asking for help to establish schools inside Afghanistan. As a result, the Afghanistan Education Committee was established in December 1983 by Afghans and Europeans and with the financial support of the Swedish Committee.

The Afghanistan Education Committee (AEC) is an impartial organisation which is not related to any specific country or party. At the end of November 1985 the AEC had eight Afghan and foreign staff-members and employees. The office is situated in Peshawar.

The aim of the AEC is to make the Afghan children in the liberated areas familiar with reading and writing in accordance with Afghan culture, and to employ Afghan teachers who are living in the countryside and the liberated areas without any other means of teaching the children. The project also prevents people from fleeing to other countries in order to educate their children.

In 1984 AEC had received applications from 35,000 students and 1,400 teachers. By November 1985 the AEC supported 18 projects in 14 different Afghan provinces with 78 primary schools up to grade 23, with a total number of 8,327 pupils and 206 teachers. Applications have come in from almost all the provinces of Afghanistan (about 50,000 pupils).

Education During the War

The AEC provides the representatives of the schools with books and other material for the students and the teachers, including salaries for the teachers and money for the transportation costs of the educational supplies. The AEC also provides cameras, film rolls and cassettes for the schools. The AEC has supplied a curriculum for grades 1-4. In 1984 and 1985 approximately 100,000 books were printed by the committee. The curriculum has been discussed and accepted by the resistance groups in Pakistan and inside Afghanistan. The monthly salary is 420 Pak. Rps (3200 Afs) for the headmasters and 400 Pak. Rps (3000 Afs) for the teachers.

The war in Afghanistan has not only affected education in the countryside. It has also seriously affected education in the cities under the control of the Kabul government. Between the years 1979 and 1984, 355 teachers have disappeared from Kabul University alone. Thousands of students have left. Some of them have joined the mujahideen, others have fled as refugees to foreign countries. The number of pupils in the lycees of Kabul and other bigger cities has been drastically reduced. Most of the students are children of members of the communist party. Some are of working-class origin. In 1984, the number of male and female students was 6,000, and 600 students graduated from different faculties. Out of these 600 graduates, half are said to have joined the mujahideen. At present, the majority of the students at Kabul University are girls. The Faculty of Engineering and the Technical Secondary Schools, equipped with workshops and machines, which had been set up by the United States, are now closed. The Engineering Faculty has merged into the Polytechnical Faculty. The Technical Secondary School has been transformed into an art school.

The lecturers from the Federal Republic of Germany have been dismissed from the faculties of Science and Economy and have been replaced by lecturers from the German Democratic Republic. Lecturers from other countries at the faculties of Engineering and Agriculture in Kabul and at the University of Nangrahar have also been dismissed and replaced by teachers from the Soviet Union.

A new Faculty for Social Sciences has been set

Education During the War

up. Only children of communist party members are admitted.

A new Department for the Russian language has been organised at the Faculty of Literature. Russian is taught up to the M.A. degree.

The education policy of the Soviet Union in Afghanistan

Afghan children from the age of 7 to 14 years are being sent to the Soviet Union. A former member of the planning department of the Ministry of Education in Kabul (now a refugee in Pakistan) told me in March 1985 that 10,000 Afghan children had been sent during the autumn of 1984 to the Soviet Union. The children are to stay in the Soviet Union for between five to ten years. Most of them are sent without the knowledge of their parents, many of them are picked up in villages destroyed by the Soviet forces.

People from other strata of Afghan society are also invited to visit the Soviet Union. In October 1984, 15,965 Afghans visited the USSR. Of these, 177 belonged to the youth organisations, 11,600 to the Democratic People's Party, and 824 persons were related to party members killed during the war. Two thousand were party members from the different provinces, 24 were committee secretaries and 740 were employees of the Department of Information.

The army and the police departments have sent the biggest contingents to the 'sister nation'. Some of them are sent to the German Democratic Republic.

Common workers and employees of the city administration are also sent to the Soviet Union for training. More then 1,000 employees of the state radio and television network have been sent for further training in propaganda methods.

All these facts show that the Soviet Union is deeply engaged in the Sovietisation of Afghan education.

The lack of professional teachers at the schools and in the universities has created a lot of problems. The students are now being taught that lessons are of minor importance. The most important thing is to defend the revolution and maintain a durable friendship with the Soviet Union.

Education During the War

Education Outside Afghanistan

There are two different types of schools for the refugees in Pakistan: private schools run by the parties in Peshawar and schools run by the Commission for Afghan Refugees.

Private schools run in the North West Frontier Province by the old seven-party alliance and the three-party alliance have all told 473,653 pupils and 1,748 teachers. Six per cent of the pupils are girls.

The seven-party coalition has compiled and printed books from the first to the sixth grade. The seven-party curriculum has 60 per cent religion and 40 per cent modern science. The teachers in the secondary schools are paid a monthly salary of 800 Rupees, the teachers in the primary school 550 Rupees.

The education curriculum sponsored by the Commissioner for Afghan Refugees is divided into two parts, science and art. After primary school, education in the arts is mainly based on the Pakistani education system. It does not pay any attention to Afghan culture and the present situation in Afghanistan. For instance, the children have to learn about the old Pakistan-India wars and famous Pakistani commanders.

The Commissioner for Afghan Refugees has set up the following schools:

<u>One secondary school</u> with 225 pupils, 6 Pakistani and 65 Afghan teachers.
<u>Primary schools</u>. About 406, attended by 57,141 boys and 5,268 girls, and with 394 Pakistani and 1,064 Afghan male teachers and 144 female teachers.
<u>Middle schools</u>. 68 schools with 19,395 boys taught by 199 Pakistani and 416 Afghan teachers.

The total is 528 primary, middle and secondary schools, 82,029 pupils (boys and girls) and 2,229 teachers. Of the pupils, 6.4 per cent are girls. A teacher in these primary schools has a salary of 560 Rupees, a teacher in the secondary school gets 1,000 Rupees. As regards the age of the pupils, it is worth mentioning that most of the pupils from the third grade and above are already advanced in age. Many pupils of the fifth grade are more than 16 years old.

Education During the War

In addition to these schools, the Wahabis have started four schools in Peshawar with 400 pupils in all. Maulawi Jamil Rahman is the leader of the Wahabis. Their organisation is supported by Saudi Arabia.

Most of the professional teachers are also engaged in non-professional occupations. Most of them do physical work in order to provide for their children. In the refugees and Commissary schools the majority of the teachers are non-professionals. When the old seven-party coalition fell apart most of the teachers lost their jobs because the parties started running their own schools again and the teachers from other parties who had been employed by the seven-party coalition were fired.

Finally, about 60 Afghan students have been admitted to Peshawar University. There are more than 20 lycees for the refugees. The graduates from these lycees and the lycees inside Afghanistan and from Kabul University want to continue their studies, but conditions are not favourable. They have no chance of getting higher education. I would like, therefore, to end my paper with a hadith from the Holy Prophet: Seek knowledge even if in China.

PART III

THE WAR

10

MODERNISATION FROM BELOW: THE AFGHAN RESISTANCE BETWEEN THE FIGHT FOR LIBERATION AND SOCIAL EMANCIPATION

Jan-Heeren Grevemeyer

Introduction

The war in Afghanistan has now been going on for nearly eight years; for six years a large portion of the population has been fighting the Soviet invading forces. Occasionally reports of negotiations in Geneva or of talks between Russia and America indicate the possibility of a political solution to the Afghanistan conflict. One of these potential solutions was outlined in a commentary in the highly renowned Frankfurter Rundschau: namely that Moscow should withdraw its troops and, in co-operation with the USA, guarantee the non-alignment of the country situated on its southern borders; Pakistan should close its borders with Afghanistan with the approval of the USA. The resistance groups thus cut off from their supply bases would eventually disperse and, under a general amnesty, the refugees would be able to return to their home villages. In addition - and this is in effect the quintessence of the article - the great powers involved in the conflict had only to win one ally: 'Time which heals all wounds' (FR: 2.9.1985).

This proposed solution, or indeed any similar one, reveals an essential defect - it does not take the Afghan resistance movement into account. This negligence of the Afghan resistance movement is a reflection of the cynicism of the great powers who strive to settle national or international conflicts in the Third World above the heads of the parties directly concerned. It is also an indication of the fact that the politically conscious and articulate classes in the West think in the same terms - at least in the case of Afghanistan - and regard the Afghan resistance movement, its aims and social contents, as quantites negligeables. This attitude, so common among liberal and politically active people, has a logic of its own: if liberation movements use - at least verbally - slogans and concepts derived from the European workers' movement, i.e. terms such as 'proletariat', 'bourgeoisie', 'class struggle', 'alliance of workers and peasants' and similar modernisation stereotypes - then support is readily given. But if such concepts are not part of a social movement, the same intellectuals, who can normally explain each and every contradiction in any liberation movement of the Third World, have trouble in finding their bearings. The Afghan resistance movement is a case in point.

From the very beginning groups and parties from all over the country took up arms with slogans and concepts which reflected the values of a traditional society, that is of a 'feudal', a 'peasant' or an 'inward-looking' society. Indeed, it was principally an 'introverted' revolt. Its main aims were the restoration of an ancient way of life, the abolition of a regime seeking to interfere with the traditional social conditions, and the repulsion of arrogant modernisers. How is it possible to show solidarity with a resistance movement where 'medieval' Islamic views on the world serve to mobilise a narrow-minded male society's struggle for traditional privileges?

The Eurocentric world view underlying this attitude need not be further elaborated. Yet the fact remains that for a large section of the politically conscious intellectuals in the West, the solution to the Afghan question is a strictly political affair which should be left to the governments concerned. For them, it is not a social modernisation movement, even though in the course of the now more than seven-year-long war dramatic changes have, in fact, occurred in this respect.

These changes are basically due to the changing character of the Afghan resistance movement. While, in the beginning, a general uprising against the socio-political reforms of the central government took place, after the Russian invasion it took on the quality of a modern guerrilla war against an 'infidel' foreign aggressor. The war had set into motion a chain of events causing general social change which has left no aspect of the socio-political and cultural life untouched; almost unnoticed by Western observers a process of modernisation from below has developed on the lee side of the war. This process is reflected in the change of military tactics, in the infrastructure of the resistance, in the emergence of new elites and in the growing importance of ideology in determining new sets of social and political relations. But as the success of the resistance hitherto is due to these changes, the same changes have also contributed to creating new internal conflicts, stemming from political, religious and ethnic differences transformed into ideologies of nationalism and Islamic government. In an interview which I had in October 1984 in Quetta with representatives of the Nasr-Party, they frankly admitted that there were two wars raging in Afghanistan – one against the Soviet invaders and one between the various resistance parties or groups themselves, the latter being almost more important as it must now be decided how the future Afghanistan is to look politically and socially.

This statement, or indeed any similar one, reveals a growing consciousness among the new elites and their followers about the function of the war as a vehicle for social emancipation and national awakening. In this way a change which all governments since 1919 have been attempting to bring about is indeed taking place, but emanating from the grass root level and not being forced down from above. As a reaction to the rapidly escalating war against a superior opponent, society is beginning slowly and painfully to emancipate itself from the traditional values, behaviour patterns and principles of political allegiance – a far-reaching change and an irreversible process.

I will therefore proceed by focusing on the modernisation process against the background of a traditional society. By analysing this issue, I would like to answer two questions: (1) how realistic is a political solution that leaves out the quality and the influence of the resistance movement and (2) what is the meaning of the term 'threatened culture' under the present conditions of social evolution in Afghanistan?

First of all, I shall turn to the significance of this resistance movement for the Afghan society as a whole. For many members of the party and armed forces the Soviet invasion at the turn of the year 1979/80 meant an abrupt end to the 'new model revolution' which was instigated in 1978. The government under Babrak Karmal, whom the Soviets installed, had therefore from the very beginning no legitimacy in their eyes. Starting from mid-1981 onwards ever-increasing numbers of Soviet advisers have entered the central administrative and decision-making bodies, with the result that the function fulfilled by the present government is in fact merely that of a legitimising or propaganda instrument. It is difficult to establish the number of members in the party. While the official claim is that there are 95,000 party members, the truth may be closer to the estimate of 15,000 hardcore activists (Harrison, 1985). The USSR has in the last few years made strenuous efforts to build up a future elite by sending young Afghan men and women to socialist countries - to Russia in particular - in order to educate and train them there. But this strategy does not alter the fact that the military conflict is a war between Russians and Afghans in which Afghanistan is represented politically and militarily by the resistance movement. This historical role of the resistance movement does not necessarily mean that it lives up to what is expected of it. The decisive questions to be asked therefore are: what technical and social resources are available to the resistance, what is the potential which the resistance movement can mobilise, and which processes of consciousness or modernisation are taking place?

Chaliand (1981: 79) stated in a report about the Afghan resistance that it does not indicate 'political or social innovation' and is therefore, 'historically speaking, nearer to the Basmachi movement ... than any modern guerilla movement'. In his analysis of the Afghan resistance three years later, Franceschi (1984: 173 ff) came to the conclusion that, technically speaking, the internal resistance 'is still at the stage of being a people's movement' which has not yet been transformed into 'an organised guerilla movement'; however, 'time and the demands of war have gradually caused a social fermentation, the results of which are becoming increasingly apparent'. In a very detailed analysis edited in 1985 by Olivier Roy the author points out, that 'the prerequisites for a modernisation of the traditional society exist in the resistance' (1985: 216).

These statements indicate that changes are occurring. But attention is principally centred on the deficiencies, i.e. the divisiveness of the resistance, the inadequacy of guerrilla training, the lack of cooperation between the various regions, military amateurism (cf. Franceschi 1984: Ch. 3: Des hommes en armes). In an analysis published in 1985 of the resistance potential in Afghan society in the face of the Soviet invasion, the authors draw similar conclusions; the negative factors mentioned are the lack of unity in the resistance movement, its inability to reach agreement as how best to deal with the 'Russification' campaign, its complete incompetence in organising the rural economy and its difficulties in reacting to Soviet tactics (Kamrany and Poullada 1985: 140 ff).

On the other hand, positive aspects of the resistance mentioned in the same study are courage, persistence, ability to adapt, cunning and faith based firmly on Islamic beliefs, etc.

What is striking with these statements is that they bear a similarity to British opinions in the nineteenth century. The inability of the Afghans to unite, the divisiveness of the resistance groups, the alleged propensity toward self-destruction while at the same time acknowledging the courage and fearlessness of the Mojahedin (this, however, is ultimately yet another expression of Afghan anarchy) are views identical to the ones offered by the British to explain the failure of their policies. The impressions of the British travellers, adventurers, journalists and the military in the last century are still valid, if they are viewed within the framework of Western rationality. If, however, one's point of departure is the context of the historical and social forces that have shaped Afghan society, then an evaluation of today's freedom struggle would be very different indeed.

For example, the much-quoted attribute of courage - the readiness to take up arms against the central power of the state - arises from the traditional system of norms which not only legitimises the use of violent means to protect the individual's existence, but also prescribes it in many cases, for instance when family integrity is offended, when property is violated or when the autonomy of the village community or its authorities is encroached upon. This conception of justice is not equally prominent among all the different peoples in Afghanistan, but everywhere the individual has always been expected to be ready to use violence, if necessary, in pursuit of justice (cf. Barth, 1985: 258; Dupree, 1973: 248 ff.).

Such a system could only develop in a society where fundamental political structures, social values, and cultural patterns distinctly differ from those in European (and other Asiatic) societies. The basic difference centres around the role of the state in a peasant society.

The Rural Society and the Kabul State

In modern historiography there is a tendency to view the rise and fall of Iranian empires as the starting point for an understanding of Afghanistan. These empires, then, would appear to be the basic units upon which the region's history is based. Disintegration, partition and restructuring, internal anarchy, civil wars and vendetta are seen simply as some form of malfunctioning in an overall machinery labelled 'empire' or 'state'. However, instead, it may well be possible to use the terms 'feudal division', 'anarchy' and 'segmentation' as the key concepts of analysis. If such an approach is adopted, effective control of a region and its inhabitants by a supreme ruler would represent the exception, and an atypical form of government. This approach is the natural one, if the political and social conditions of Afghanistan are taken as the starting point.

It was not until the succession to power of Amir Abdorrahman (1880-1901) that Afghanistan, with the help of British money and weapons, became a centralised state. Through military, administrative and tax reforms the Amir was able to lay the foundation for a future government based on a bureaucratic system. His most important achievement, however, concerned the subduing of the segmentary forces, i.e. the local, regional and provincial rulers. The central authorities, always short of manpower to build up an efficient local administration, were compelled to co-operate with the rural upper classes, although they had been defeated militarily and politically. These classes were now eliminated from regional positions of political decision-making but their hold on the villages became correspondingly stronger. Having changed their base to the village level, they gradually realigned themselves and their clientele. Afghanistan became a centralised state based on a segmentarian society.

Following the political and military defeat of the local, regional and provincial upper classes by 'Abdorrahman at the end of the nineteenth century, his son and heir, Habibollah (1901-19), inherited a centralised state unchallenged by segmentarian forces - a 'tacit land' as Ghobar put it (1346/1967: 699). The political prerequisites for a stabilisation and expansion of 'Abdorrahman's reforms were thus favourable. But Habibollah was not interested in an active domestic policy and consequently the centralised administrative system created by his father began to crumble and in the end the centralised state power disintegrated. The provincial governors pursued policies independent of Kabul - above all the tax policy, which began to resume features of the traditional 'plundering and robbery' system.

The reforms introduced by Amanollah (1919-29) signified a turning-point. His reign was also a turning-point for the traditional regional and provincial upper class which was to be obligated to support the modernisation policies to be introduced by the court.

Having lost their power through Abdorrahman at the end of the nineteenth century, the tribal and regional political and military upper strata developed into a class of middlemen in the twentieth century. Their base now being in the villages, they correspondingly had to build up a clientele on the village level. The reforms introduced by Amanollah institutionalised this class of middlemen as 'self-financed public servants' (Anderson, 1978: 170). This is one of the most important changes within the 'traditional' society in Afghanistan during the last 100 years.

Under the new political conditions, this class made the rural population dependent on them by means of rental tenancy and the mechanism of debt. Economic coercion replaced non-economic pressures. At the same time, the peasants received the resources necessary for guaranteeing their continued existence by virtue of these same rents and indebtments. In addition, the clerical and worldly elites of the villages fulfilled important functions as mediators in disputes. Incidentally, the nomadic element had been continuously decreasing since the time of 'Abdorrahman's internal imperialism. Through these political and economic institutions (rental tenancy arrangements, mechanism of debt, formation of a class of middlemen), hierarchical collectives evolved outside (or below) the state administration which functioned as relatively independent units in dealings with the state. The patron-client relationships which determined the social network in the villages, proved to be very flexible and adapted readily to the new economic and political conditions.

The local upper class - principally worldly and clerical landowners and bazaaris - had theoretically, to be sure, various possibilities for strengthening their position, for example, land concentration, cash-crop production, mechanisation of farming methods or investment of the farming surplus in setting up industries - but all this was mostly out of the question in Afghanistan. The consequence of this was an 'envillagement' of the society - the rural upper classes became mediators between the peasantry and the government. In this system, indebtment and rental tenancy arrangements played a crucial role as Janus-headed institutions.

Indebtment (Qarz) originally meant help in cases of need, but it also meant the exchange of manufactured goods for agricultural produce, though not simultaneously, as the production of agricultural and manufactured goods are not coincidental. This system retained its external form during the expansion of trading relations, but changed in quality. The craftsman was replaced by the bazaar merchant or the Khan, who both granted loans which served to tide the peasants over between production cycles and enabled them to buy essential goods. However, while the original Qarz relationship with the craftsman was integrated in a system of equal exchange, the lending of money established a debt which caused lasting dependence on the money-lender. This dependence produced a client relationship which compelled the peasants to enter into a relationship of unequal exchange when buying goods.

The acceptance of the giving of loans does not, however, occur in an arbitrary fashion. The purpose of giving a loan is also to build up a clientele. The creditor for his part has solid obligations towards his clients. This finds expression in the fact that the loans were not time-limited and in the readiness to find work for the clients. This clientele consisted of members of the creditor's family, of already established clientele (farm labourers, tenant farmers on land belonging to the creditor or relatives of the same) or of people not known in the neighbourhood, who could offer securities.

The economic processes which formed the basis of the indebtment are not abstract, but are bound by personalised social relationships. Consequently, the prospect of getting into debt is at the same time regarded by the borrower as the giving of help (Komak). 'Plundering by debt' and 'help through loans' balance each other in Afghanistan. The same can be said for the tenancy system.

Normally, only a proportion of the land is worked by a big landowner's family - that proportion which corresponds to the work capacity of the family and perhaps of some employed farm workers. The remaining land is rented out according to various stipulations, under which the tenants enter into a client relationship with the landowners. The alternative, cultivating all the land with the help of farm labourers, has always been of only peripheral importance. For this reason, the tenancy system can be seen as a Janus-headed institution, in the same way as the Qarz system: on the one hand, it contributes to the exploitation of the peasants as their labour is very poorly paid; on the other hand, it reintegrates those peasants who have lost their land through debt or who live at mere subsistence level into the social framework of the village by offering them the opportunity of renting, or partly renting, additional land.

If economic and social considerations are intermingled in the distribution of the rural surplus within the village, then the same can be said for the function of the middlemen. They are at the top of the economic hierarchy in the village, while at the same time constituting the political link between the village and the higher institutions outside the village. Their function is ambivalent.

As political mediators between the state and their own peasant followers (their relatives and their clientele), the middlemen are, on the one hand, keen to accept positions in the provincial bureaucracy established in the 1920s, and hence, in state power. On the other hand, they are responsible for protecting those dependent on them from state interference or intervention. In the village itself, they have a mediating function in the formal and informal settlement of disputes. Their political and economic functions are linked. Generally speaking, the middlemen are big landowners. Through investments in the bazaar and as creditors, they are associated with the merchants — in many cases the latter are family members. It may therefore, be assumed that the tenant farmers dependent on the big landowners are also bound to some of the bazaar merchants. As a result, peasants are doubly indebted to the middlemen: in a direct manner, by the acceptance of loans, either in kind or in cash, and indirectly, by indebtment to the merchant who is related to the middleman.

The middlemen are thus beneficiaries of both the institutionalised appropriation of surplus and the unequal exchange in the bazaar which results from the peasant's indebtment. If these economic practices had been implemented in their unadulterated form, even for only a short period of time, this would have led to the complete impoverishment of the peasants and to a general expropriation of their land. This has not happened because the middlemen are under the obligation to return a proportion of the acquired surplus.

Not only the middlemen were able to evade the

claims of the central power by having recourse to the village reciprocity institutions, but the regional bureaucracy also tended to make themselves independent of Kabul. The civil servants installed by the state did not direct their loyalties abstractly towards the bureaucracy, but understood their office to be a personal 'tenure' in the wholly traditional manner.

The policies of this class of civil servants are aimed at finding a compromise between the demands of the central administration (Kabul), the claims of the established rural upper classes, and their own desire to enrich themselves. It was this very lack of impartiality among the civil servants towards the 'citizens' (citoyens) and their lack of loyalty towards the state itself - more prosaically: corruption - which many new laws tried to abolish. These laws reveal to what extent the regional bureaucracy had been able to establish itself as a third power between the rural middlemen and the Kabul central administration, and how unsuccessful the state was in trying to deal with it. It is not surprising that reforms initiated by the state were either completely unrealisable, or else only superficially carried out.

This civil servant class - along with the traditional social groups of the rural society - formed the milieu of twentieth century Afghanistan characterised by the tension between the modernisation demands of the centralised state and the opposition to these same claims.

The hopes which governments since Amanollah had pinned on the installation of members of the rural upper class as middlemen were not fulfilled. The state administration remained altogether too weak, so that it could not effectively control them, at the same time as they lacked the financial means to bind this class financially and politically to the state. On the local level, however, below the state administration, these middlemen secured a permanent place for themselves in the social structure - once they had been recognised by the state as local headmen.

From the military point of view, they played no role until the emergence of the nationwide resistance movement in 1978/9. Apart from a few exceptions, there were no anti-centralistic rebellions in the country, as had been usual until the end of the nineteenth century. Politically and socially, however, this class of middlemen was able for the most part to evade the control of the centralised state and to serve as mediators with the help of the regional bureaucracy. It was, therefore, this very flexibility of the village conditions - and not the 'Asiatic' stubbornness or a 'traditional' inflexibility - which time and time again limited the intervention claims of the modern Afghan state. As a consequence, a separate social milieu evolved outside Kabul and a few other towns. This milieu in fact comprised about 90 per cent of the population. Kabul represented the 'state', rural Afghanistan the 'society'.

Over and above its general modernisation attempts the state intervened directly only twice in the social structures of the villages - under King Amanollah and again during the Taraki/Amin government in 1978/9. In the first case, the segmentary collectives, under the leadership of the clergy and with religious slogans, rebelled against the modernisation attempts. In the second case, they rebelled under the leadership of the religious and worldly upper classes against efforts to introduce a radical land reform which was intended to abolish the prevailing patron-client systems.

The governments which followed Amanollah had learned their lessons. By various strategies they endeavoured technically to modernise the country, while not calling into question their relationship with the rural upper strata. Certainly, progress was made in the improvement of the infrastructure and general administration, but the agricultural sector, and hence the social organisation of the peasant society, was for the most part unaffected. Large-scale agricultural projects after World War II tied up huge amounts of the state finances. Progress made, however, was minimal and contributed nothing to a transformation of society.

The antithesis of the countryside to the urban central government remains up to the present day and finds expression in the dichotomy between the Kabul government and the resistance movement. But under the present conditions of a general war against a foreign occupation force which supports the central government, this dichotomy gains a completely new, and for the first time, a dynamic quality; out of the original

Modernisation from Below

attempt to ward off the efforts of arrogant modernisers prepared to use force to introduce social reforms - and thereby to change the living conditions of the rural population, that is the vast majority - grew a socio-political people's movement which in its turn has also become an active force for change.

This process of emancipation can be seen clearly in the socio-political changes which have taken place, making a simple categorisation of the resistance movement as 'traditional' erroneous. The limits within which these changes are taking place are set, for the most part, by the technical and organisational modernisation within the resistance movement itself.

Technical and Organisational Modernisation (1)

When the resistance movement came into existence, its instigators were aware neither of the social dimension of their struggle, nor of the complexity of their opponents. The aim of the resistance movement initially was to retain the relative autonomy of the individual village community. It had its beginnings in a spontaneous peasant revolt under the leadership of the traditional authorities in accordance with the social structures of the land (Puig, 1984: 219; Fullerton, n.d. 51). A partly detailed documentation of the events has also been compiled by Afghan eye-witnesses.(2) The uprising in the Hazarajat for example has been described in several monographic works by Gharjestani:

> As soon as weather conditions in March/April 1979 permitted the inhabitants of one village to communicate with those in the neighbouring one, several peasants united under the leadership of their village chief and attacked the administration building. For the main part they were armed with a few old rifles, with clubs and knives and had no knowledge of what was happening outside their valley or in Kabul; they overpowered the few policemen, drove the official and pro-government representatives of the state (teachers, tax collectors, accountants) out and then went on to the next village in order to incite the inhabitants there to emulate their

example (Gharjestani, 1363/1985: 148 ff).

From the hinterland the uprising spread to the outskirts of the Hazarajat. On May First of 1979 the population of Bamian - a district center and garrison town - started with their rebellion. The usual picture also here: The real fight was carried out by simple peasants under the slogans of 'freedom for the country' and 'in defence of our Koran and Islam'. Within a few days about 4,000 people gathered, armed with 'knives, swords, sickles, shovels, pickaxes and clubs'; their leaders were secular and religious dignitaries (Gharjestani, 1360/1981: 53 f).

Following the Soviet invasion the nature of the new opponents led very quickly to an adaptation process which can be summed up under the following key phrases: transformation of the peasant revolt into guerrilla warfare; procuring and hoarding new weapons; formation of a trained staff; training in guerrilla warfare tactics; formation of regular troops and militia; construction of an information network; reorganisation of the structure of leadership by means of grass root elections of the commanders; collaboration between villages and tactical discussions between commanders; formation of urban guerrilla groups; systematic utilisation of the withdrawal areas to tend the wounded, to protect families and to reorganise the units (Roy, 1985: 233 ff).

This technical-organisational adaptation process differs in degree from area to area and from group to group. This is dependent on the availability of weapons and the number of followers at the group's disposal - both variables are in turn dependent on the association of individual groups and their commanders with the large exile parties. When one considers the initial level of organisation and the general lack of resources, then the process of professionalisation of the war is indeed far advanced, and this is demonstrated not only by the relatively small losses among resistance fighters, but also by their success in maintaining control over wide areas of the country.

Socio-Political Modernisation

The most decisive changes concern the emergence of new

elites and new political ideologies. They go hand in hand with the professionalisation of the war and the organisation of the resistance in various parties.

At the beginning of the revolt 1978/9 the rural population was led mainly by the traditional authorities. The technique used by the invaders since 1981 of completely destroying the supply and retreat bases of the resistance movement has deprived the secular rural upper class of its economic and social foundation (migration of clientele, destruction of crops, dwellings and water resources). In addition, the altered nature of the war made the introduction of trained cadres necessary - this secular class was thereby forced out of its dominant position. The opposite was the case for the religious upper strata: the emergence of new ideologies (which they themselves normally propagate) offered them the opportunity of becoming not only religious but also political leaders. At the same time the professionalisation of the military conflict gave young technicians, engineers, officers, civil servants and teachers the chance to establish themselves on a lower and middle level as commanders.

The need for an ideology to sustain the war effort, together with the need for building an infrastructure in the parties, gave the educated clergy and committed intellectuals an opportunity to gain prominence, since they could articulate people's interests and organise them. They have now become a new military, political and cultural elite which is very different from the old one that consisted of the modern middle and upper classes in Kabul. Most members of the old elite have emigrated to the West. Those who belong to the new elite - and have survived the persecution of the Taraki/Amin government - are now usually also in exile, most of them in Pakistan. The members of this elite are entrusted with decision-making and act voluntarily. They are firmly convinced of their duty and owe their positions principally to their achievements (and are not, as was formerly the case, legitimised by age, descent or financial means).

The resistance groups which are well known abroad operate mostly from exile in Pakistan. But the quality of their leadership and of their propagated ideologies are not fully typical for the resistance movement in Afghanistan itself. The fighting groups have gradually developed their own local leadership and have become increasingly organised; to a considerable extent, they have learned to co-operate with adjoining groups.

For obvious reasons the survival of the resistance movement depends on people with technical and organisational skills moving into leading positions. They have in particular been given political leadership in the internal resistance. As a consequence, the ancient hierarchical relationships in the country have changed. This process is accompanied by the emergence of new ideologies and a new consciousness.

The emergence of new ideologies is one of the most far-reaching consequences of the Soviet invasion and the reorganisation of the resistance movement. Within the bounds of religious, ethnic and nationalistic ideals, society is gradually beginning to move in a new direction away from its parochial orientation. These ideologies are not merely appeals to an Islamic consciousness, which have contributed to a revitalisation of already existing ideas, but they are paired with political programmes which have also allocated a new role for Islam itself. If, formerly, the purpose of Islam was to regulate the affairs of the individual, it has now become a vehicle for political reform which opens prospects for ethnic unity in a province, or for the Afghan nation as a whole.

This development is influenced to a great extent by the emergence of a changed consciousness which has been created by the compulsory geographical mobility, by the broadening of experience and by the violent changes in the circumstances of the individual.

This new consciousness is apparent in the identification with parties or party programmes, in the questioning of ancient and unjust social structures by the lower classes and in the foundation of grass root decision-making bodies. This change in the consciousness of the rural population is slowly and painfully taking place. The decisive factor is that the new elite in the internal Afghan resistance movement is gradually beginning to develop its own ideas on social and political organisation. These can be divided roughly into three categories:

1. Concepts for technical and organisation innovation which include the experiences of guerrilla movements in other Third World countries; this type of concept is for example represented by Ahmad Shah Masud.
2. Ideas for the necessary promotion of self-help organisations among the people which go beyond purely military requirements; associated with this are visions of a future Afghanistan, organised as a federal state, in which the most important basic and human rights are to be guaranteed.
3. Ideas for ethnic emancipation – these concepts are of course mainly articulated by representatives of minorities who have been oppressed up to now, for example, the Hazara.

These changes brought about by the military conflict are undoubtedly recognised by the new elite in the resistance movement. A commander told me in an interview in December 1983:

> We are backward and no one can expect us to unite within the space of four years. That is impossible. We must now become politically-minded and develop a political consciousness. Now we are building a nation – something which we have never been. The Russian invasion has given us a common goal. We have a common enemy and fight side by side. We all have this armed conflict in common. Up to now we have never had a common aim; how could we have learned to understand each other or reach an agreement without a common goal? We now have this common mission and that is the fight for freedom, in which we are getting to know each other and so we can now build up a nation ... under normal circumstances we would perhaps have needed a hundred years to build up a nation – now we may possibly need only 10 or 20 years.

The complexity and vastness of these experiences have eliminated the parochial orientation of society. It

Modernisation from Below

is apparent to all that it is no longer a question of the fate of an individual's village or valley community, but that of the whole society and, above all, of the entire state. However, very serious conflicts are already becoming obvious in the conceptions of the future state order. On the one hand, there are regionally orientated resistance groups whose programme advocates the autonomy of their region in a future federalistic state. Moreover, their general religious orientation contains strong ethnic or communal elements. On the other hand, there are the fundamentalistic parties whose concepts of Islamic rule could only be realised in a centralised state under an authoritarian leadership.

Cultural Modernisation - The New Political Culture

The new consciousness of allegiance beyond one's village, clan or tribe, the political association of the individual to parties, as well as the resistance movement expressing itself in ideological terms are factors leading to the development of a new political culture. By now it is clear to all that without the simultaneous establishment of a revolutionary culture, victory in the military conflict must remain unattainable. The newly-emerged political culture is documented in the creation of a widespread press and publishing system.

In order to understand the general technical and social problems which the resistance movement faces in building up a new political culture, I would like to begin with some facts. In the seventies about 90-95 per cent of all Afghans were illiterate, though every Afghanistan subject since 1923 had had the right to an education at no cost. Because of the strictly centralised publication policy, relaxed only for certain periods (1949-52; 1964-70), there existed at the end of the seventies only 25 newspapers with a circulation of 150,000 and as many specialised magazines with a circulation of about 50,000. Only about 3,000 books were printed from the 1920s until 1978 with a circulation of 500 to 2,000 per edition. For technical and linguistic reasons even the introduction of transistor radios could not solve the problem of spreading information. For these reasons about 90 per cent of the whole population remained more or less untouched by any discussion about development and modernisation aims.

When the reform programme of the Taraki/Amin government (1978/9) slowly drove an ever-increasing number of people into the resistance movement, there were only a few options of publishing anti-government propaganda. This consisted mainly of distributing the so-called 'night letters', which were put on walls or slipped under doors. In the areas which were already liberated in 1979 (Hazarajat, Kunar) there existed neither technical facilities nor skilled workers. However, it was probably in August 1979 that the first newspaper appeared in a liberated area: The 'Voice of Nurestan' (Seda-ye nurestan). The situation was somewhat different among the opposition groups in Pakistan, Iran and some Western countries. The opposition movement abroad consisted at that time of two distinct groups: political organisations such as the 'Hezb-e-eslami', already active during the regime of Daud, and groups of Afghan students who had been politically active since the early seventies (mainly in West Germany). While the student groups had experience in editing magazines before the coup, the opposition groups in Pakistan and Iran began their publishing immediately after 1978. For example in Iran the 'Islamic Party' edited the Rah-e haqq magazine (The Way of Justice); the 'Islamic Union' published the Peiam-e afghanestan magazine (Afghanistan's Message); and the Peiam-e mobares magazine (Message of the Fighters) was written and distributed by a group called the 'Moslems who fight in Afghanistan'.

The Afghan resistance parties in Pakistan, with a few exceptions, started publishing periodicals only after the Russian invasion, for example the Esteqlal magazine, edited in Peshawar. Generally speaking the number of newly-founded periodicals remained limited until 1980. They addressed a small circle of insiders, the contributions were fairly simple and included non-professional war reports as well as unspecified ideological discussions.

The situation changed rapidly after the Soviet invasion. With the increasing number of refugees fleeing to Pakistan and Iran the resistance parties gained an ever greater number of followers and began to organise themselves better while at the same time receiving economic aid.

Systematic purges of the administration, of the military and of the educated modern middle class by Russian advisers and the change of military tactics used by the Soviet occupying forces (destruction of the means of existence, i.e. the harvests, the irrigation systems, villages and cattle) resulted in the emigration to Pakistan or Iran of about one-third of the total population. The stream of refugees did not only contribute more soldiers, but helped to professionalise the resistance movement because more and more experts joined the movement.

Since 1980 more than 100 different magazines have been published and are being published by the Afghan resistance movement. On top of this about 500 brochures, pamphlets and books have been published. Peshawar has become the most important publishing centre. Additional publishing houses are found in Quetta, Lahore and Islamabad. In Iran, Teheran is the centre for publishing activities. Sometimes magazines or brochures are also edited in Qom or Mashhad. In the West, Germany is the centre for publishing and distributing periodicals and books. Possibly some magazines have also been published in India, France, Denmark, England or in the United States. These publications are edited either by the main resistance parties in Pakistan or Iran, small resistance groups or by individuals. The large resistance parties very often publish in different places and in various languages (Arabic, Urdu, English or German). The major part of all writing is done in the two main languages of Afghanistan, Farsi-Dari and Pashtu. The periodicals appear weekly, bi-monthly or monthly; smaller organisations often publish their magazines irregularly or change their names. The editions vary from a few hundred to several thousand.

The contribution in the magazines, brochures and monographs include reports from the front, information on the situation in Afghanistan, among refugees or on the international scene, biographies of martyrs, historical essays on the role of Russia in Afghanistan or the pre-history of the coup of 1978, speeches of leading personalities of the resistance movement and texts from the elite about aims and views of the war, as well as about the future shape of a finally liberated Afghanistan, plus a literary treatment of events in prose or poetry.

With regard to the contents, the themes reflect the changed situation since the Soviet invasion. Two factors are important in this regard: firstly the fact that both the war against the Soviet occupying forces and the internal disputes are a long-lasting, interdependent process of learning, and secondly the idolisation of the resistance movement through religious, ethnic and nationalistic ideas.

Four broad political tendencies can be discerned in these publications: the fundamentalist parties, parties which follow traditional Islam, parties which propagate an enlightened Islam, and democratic ideals influenced by the West and groups in the tradition of Western leftist movements.(3)

Narrowly connected with the emergence of a new political culture is the renewed interest in the value of education and the social position of women. The setting-up of a school system and the numerous attempts to found independent schools where subjects are taught with relevance to the requirements of war, both in the liberated areas and in the sanctuaries, are perhaps the most conspicuous expression of the modernisation of the Afghan society which is taking place.

Conclusions and Perspectives

The war in Afghanistan has been going on now for over seven years and no political solution is in sight. On the contrary, the armed struggle seems to broaden from year to year - as noted by John Fullerton (n.d.: 45) when analysing the dynamics of the resistance movement: 'European underground opposition to Nazi occupation in World War II pales into insignificance when compared to the populist armed resistance to the Soviet occupation of Afghanistan.'

If you consider the price of the readiness to defend Afghanistan's political integrity and right to self-determination, you can well repeat the old question whether it is not better to be red than dead: about one million killed since 1978, one third of the population living as refugees in Pakistan and Iran, two million fugitives in Afghanistan itself, the economy collapsed, the infrastructure of the country (roads, hospitals, schools, administration network) for the main part destroyed, once-flourishing villages and whole regions laid waste, the former charm of the country and its people turned into sadness, despair and hatred. In spite of all these negative sides, the immediate prospect is one of continued stalemate - even if there are breaking points in the various elements of the resistance potential (Kamrany & Poullada, 1985: 185).

This readiness to resist Soviet penetration and domination regardless of cost often irritates Western governments and observers. For some Western governments an overly successful resistance movement threatens the detente between the West and the USSR, while not a few observers view this readiness to resist as a typical Afghan inclination towards self-destruction which should be stopped for human or moral considerations. All of them, however, treat the resistance movement as a freedom fight against the Soviet invader. Regarding the war as an emancipation movement aiming at the creation of a new society, this idea is either not taken seriously or remains unnoticed. Or as Hekmatyar (1361/1982) put it: 'The West tries to explain our Islamic Jehad as a freedom movement. But we began our war and our Jehad in order to create a new society.'

In the final analysis this is a question of how to interpret the resistance movement. Whilst Western journalists normally draw upon empirical observations and rely on reports from the resistance fighters to describe the military quality of the war and the resulting misery, Western experts generally focus on analysing the ability of the Afghan society to stand its ground against Soviet forces by making inquiries into the traditional social and political system of the society. As for the latter, their point of departure is the assumption that the Afghan resistance movement owes its strength to the norms and values of the traditional society. In this respect, the apparent changes are treated as a technical problem. But the process of adaptation and modernisation is not only a technical process which enhances the potential of the traditional society to resist Soviet domination. The transition from a peasant revolt to guerrilla warfare, the rise of new elites, and the growing importance of ideology in moulding new kinds of social and political relations - these changes are not merely reflections of a traditional society's ability to meet a threat of the kind that Afghanistan is faced with today. Rather they reflect the fact that traditional society is changing fundamentally. One might deplore the inability to unite, but it is precisely the divisions existing today which offer the most striking illustration of the general transformation. Formerly a village or <u>qaum</u> marked the boundaries of segmentarian conflicts. The new internal conflicts, which are caused by political, religious and ethnic differences transformed into ideologies of nationalism and Islamic government, transcend the old parochial forms of organisation. It is no longer just a question of resisting an aggressor, but also a violent struggle for a new society. This dynamic process of modernisation from below inevitably not only threatens traditional culture, but also transforms society from its very foundations. In this process, traditions are enlarged with new elements or may simply be invented. They can be redefined, revitalised or put aside. Even though people remain the same, as well as the notions used to explain the changes, the new political culture and the new social organisation have very little in common with the old traditional culture and its values system.

The longer the war continues, the more the resistance movement, and hence also the whole of Afghan society, changes in the direction of a modern society. But as the conflict has taught us: it is not a modernisation process in the usual Western sense of the word. Instead it is a modernisation movement within the framework of the experiences and learning gained in the war. The resistance movement can legitimately bring about these changes because it represents the will and ideals of the society.

Since the beginning of the twentieth century Afghan governments have tried to modernise Afghan society. By issuing decrees, and by passing laws they have hoped to create a developed country and a nation-state, where the government represented the interests and will of the citizens. In the same manner the

Modernisation from Below

present government claims to represent the 'real will and interests of workers, peasants, tradesmen, nomads, the intelligentsia and other toilers and the entire democratic and patriotic forces from all nationalities, tribes and clans' (<u>Fundamental Principles of the Democratic Republic of Afghanistan</u>, 1980). But all attempts have failed and have only deepened the differences between the (rural) society and the (Kabul) government. For the first time in modern Afghan history the resistance movement links both parts of the whole, that is to say 'modernisation' with 'commitment of the entire population'.

It is not yet certain who the winners will be, neither in the war between Afghan society and the Soviet occupying forces, nor in the disputes between the various resistance parties. But any political solution to the Afghan question without consulting the resistance movement appears to be illusory. We may or may not agree with the aims and views of the various resistance parties. We may be impressed by the armed struggle or may call it a typical Afghan urge toward self-destruction; the fact is that the Afghans have their own pride and their own solutions. Our duty should be to assist them morally, practically and politically in their anti-imperialistic liberation fight as well as in their struggle for a new Afghan society.

Notes

1. This chapter is based mainly on three kinds of sources: (1) reports from Western journalists, scholars and travellers who have visited Afghanistan; (2) information collected during my field work in Iran and Pakistan in 1983 and 1984; (3) articles and books published by Afghans. The last category has hitherto by and large been treated as mere propaganda. Properly used, however, the Afghan resistance press furnishes us with quite a number of valuable insights. It is, for example, almost exclusively this press which has documented the aims and views of the different resistance parties as well as their Islamic claims for legitimacy. In addition, many articles and various special publications reveal

the life and work of commanders, and thus they give us an insight into the formation of the new elite. In this connection special mention must be made of the obituary notices, because they often inform us about the education and former positions of the shaheds.
2. Apart from the eyewitness account cited in the text, there are several other reports. One extensive report by Golzarak Zadran and published in Peshawar (1362-63/1983-84) deals with events in Paktia. The first volume covers the history and geography, the social and political structure of Paktia before the uprising in 1978 and an account of the events leading up to March 1979. The second volume deals with the period between March 1979 and March 1980, while the third volume covers events up to March 1982.
3. Quite a number of magazines are edited by the fundamentalist parties (Hezb-e eslami, Jame'at, Nasr); their periodicals are often published in different languages and in different countries. Magazines published by parties who follow a traditional Islam (Harakat-e enqelab-e eslami; Hezb-e nejat-e eslami) are exclusively printed and distributed in Pakistan. About 10-15 different periodicals have appeared so far. Parties or political groups who propagate an enlightened Islam and democratic ideas influenced by the West cover a wide political range and hence offer quite a number of different periodicals. Pressure from the influential parties, financial problems and the limited number of their followers or assistants often result in delays or cessation of the publication. These kind of magazines are published in Pakistan and sometimes in New Delhi. Typical examples are the Monthly Bulletin published by the Afghan Information Center, the Neda-ye khorasan magazine edited in Quetta by the Cultural Council of the Hazara and the Qalb-e asia magazine, edited by Mahmud Farani. Magazines edited by groups in the tradition of Western leftist movements are normally published in the West, specially in West Germany; the two main leftist periodicals are the Reha'i magazine and the Afghanistan Tribune

Modernisation from Below

(Karlsruhe) (Grevemeyer, 1985).

References

Anderson, Jon W. (1978) 'There are no Khans anymore: Economic Development and Social Change in Tribal Afghanistan', Middle East Journal, XXXII, 2, 167-83

Barry, Michael (1984) Le Royaume de l'insolence. La resistance afghane du Grand Moghol a l'invasion sovietique, Paris

Barth, Fredrik (1985) 'Motstandskampens rotter i afghanska kulturer och samhallen', In Afghanistan - en handbok, Stockholm, pp. 55-68

Chaliand, Gerard (1981) Rapport sur la resistance afghane, Paris

Dupree, Louis (1973) Afghanistan, Princeton

Franceschi, Patrice (1984) Guerre en Afghanistan, Paris

Fullerton, John, N.D. The Soviet Occupation of Afghanistan, Hong Kong

Fundamental Principles of the Democratic Republic of Afghanistan (1980)

Gharjestani, Mohammad Essa (1360/1981) Shekast-e rusha dar hazarehjat, Quetta

—— (1363/1985) Rastakhiz-e jang-e afghanestan, Quetta

Ghobar, Mir Gholam Mohammad (1346/1967) Afghanestan dar masir-e tarikh, Kabul

Grevemeyer, Jan-Heeren (1981) 'Im Windschatten des Widerstands. Zentralstaatsbildung und koloniale Intervention in Afghanistan', in Jan-Heeren Grevemeyer (ed.) Traditionale Gesellschaften unter europaischer Kolonialismus, pp. 83-104, Frankfurt a.M.

—— (1982) Herrschaft, Raub und Gegenseitigkeit: Die politische Geschichte Badakhshans 1500-1883, Wiesbaden

——— (1985) 'Im Windschatten des Krieges - Die Entstehung eines neuen Publikationswesens im afghanischen Widerstand', in Blatter des iz3w, Nr. 128, pp. 33-6

Harrison, Selig S. (1985) 'The Afghan Arms Alliance', in South - The Third World Magazine, No 53, pp. 16-21

Hekmetyar, Golbudin (1361/1982) Jang az didgah-e

qoran, Teheran
Kamrany, Nake M. & Poullada, Leon B. (1985) The Potential of Afghanistan's Society and Institutions to Resist Soviet Penetration and Domination, Los Angeles
Puig, Jean-Jose (1984) 'La resistance afghane', in Afghanistan la colonisation impossible, Paris pp-213-45
Roy, Olivier (1985) L'Afghanistan. Islam et modernite politique, Paris
Zadran, Golzarak (1362-3/1983-4) Dar al-jehad afghanestan. Paktia de jehad peh ghalbalu ke, (3 vols.), Peshawar

11

A LOCAL PERSPECTIVE ON THE INCIPIENT RESISTANCE IN AFGHANISTAN

Jan Ovesen

The ambitions of this chapter are as modest as its size might indicate. On the basis of certain observations during my anthropological fieldwork among a group of Pashai-speaking people, from February-September 1978,(1) I offer a few comments, essentially as a supplement to the analysis made earlier by Lincoln Keiser (1984). Keiser had worked in the same valley as I (the Darra-i Nur) ten years earlier and he had the opportunity of talking to Pashai refugees in Pakistan in 1980. My own first-hand observations are confined to the period immediately before and after the 'Saur Revolution' and my few analytical points should be seen as an addition, from that perspective, to those made by Keiser.

Local Political Organisation and National Government

The Pashai are an ethnic group numbering until December 1979 about 100,000 and living in eastern Afghanistan, on the southern slopes of the Hindu Kush. Pashai society is a 'tribal society'. Although the Pashai are culturally and linguistically closer related to their northern neighbours, the Nuristani (Ovesen, 1984), their social structure is in many ways similar to that of the Pakhtuns. Both are examples of what in anthropological literature is known as a 'segmentary lineage system'.(2) Briefly, this means, in the Pashai context, that the people are divided into a number of patrilineages, each of which is

Incipient Resistance

divided into half a dozen sublineages, each of which, again, consists of a varying number of households.

Both the lineages and the sublineages are headed by an older man who in principle has the title of malek (headman). Native ideology puts great emphasis on the equality of all these potential maleks, even though very few of them are acting maleks, i.e. take upon themselves the function of political leader in the society. To function as malek requires, in addition to being elderly, a 'greybeard', that one is committed to spending a great deal of one's time and energy on persuasion and display of generosity, and that one has the ability to take advantage of the position as a go-between in matters concerning the relation between the village population and the local representatives of the national government. The position of an influential malek is thus an achieved one, and it takes a continuous effort to maintain it. For, as a corollary to the ideology of equality, there will always be contenders to such a position who jealously watch each step of an influential malek, ready to hop in and take over, should he falter.

The egalitarian ideology is not restricted to the local community but has as a concomitant a pronounced resistance against any attempt at domination from the outside. The Pashai jealously guard their political and territorial autonomy; there is a long tradition of conflict with their southern neighbours, the Pakhtuns, and the attempts at intervention in community matters by the national government have always been met with resentment and, at times, with open hostility.

The relations between the national government and the local population were, as I have already hinted, taken care of by the maleks. Complaints and petitions by the villagers were presented to the malek whose task it was to convey them to the local sub-district governor (alaqadar); and, conversely, when the government officials wanted to get hold of a particular villager, a messenger (a conscripted soldier, a small 'force' of whom was at the disposal of the alaqadar and the police commandant) was sent to the malek who then had to find the person in question. Since such contacts were often prompted by conflicting interests, the resolutions of the problems were frequently made possible only by handing certain sums of money over to

Incipient Resistance

the officials, and it was understood that the malek was entitled to keep a smaller part of it for himself. Such gifts, which we would perhaps call bribes, were necessary for the whole system to work as relatively smoothly as it did prior to the coup in April 1978.

The 'Saur Revolution'

After the Khalq and Parcham parties had successfully carried out their coup d'etat on 27 April 1978, the new socialist regime was faced with quite a few practical problems. One was administration. Afghanistan is divided into 28 provinces, each headed by a governor. Each province is divided into about a dozen districts (oluswali) and occasionally sub-districts (alaqadari), headed by an oluswal or alaqadar and a police commandant. So it became necessary for the new regime to replace overnight, or at least as soon as possible, most of the over 600 officials with politically reliable people, preferably party members. The socialist parties had their greatest support among members of the urbanised middle class, such as younger schoolteachers and the like. These people had often had very little contact with village life, and many of them had, precisely because of their overt political sympathies, been denied government posts during the Daoud regime and had thus little or no administrative experience.

On the other hand, the traditional village leaders, the maleks, stayed on. Although they were officially recognised as spokesmen for the local population they were not officials. Their position was a function of the traditional socio-political system, for which national political and ideological categories were of little relevance. For the maleks it was always a question of making the most of any political situation. This pragmatic attitude may be illustrated by the example of my host in upper Darra-i Nur, who was the most influential malek in the whole area. He was a Muslim (of course) with fundamentalist inclinations, but had nevertheless found it expedient at a certain point to join President Daoud's party. Immediately after the coup I myself was ordered to return to Kabul to have my research permit reviewed. After about six weeks I obtained a new permit (much to my astonishment) and was allowed to go back to my field. On my way up the valley I met my host who was on his way to Kabul together with half a dozen other maleks from the area. Even though he had immediately removed President Daoud's portrait from his wall and renounced his membership of the Daoud party, he had, he told me, spent a couple of weeks in jail. But now he was on his way, together with the others, to congratulate Chairman Taraki and to swear allegiance to Khalq. He came back a week later, an ardent supporter of the new regime.

The Revolution That Turned Sour

In so far as we can generalise on the basis of this one example at Darra-i Nur, the socialist take-over did not necessarily meet with immediate opposition in the rural areas. Taraki had taken care to publicly demonstrate his allegiance to Islam, and that was in the beginning sufficiently reassuring for people like my host, who were otherwise concerned with Realpolitik on the local level. It was only when the new regime took measures that were blatant violations of traditional norms and values that reactions became unfavourable. And it was when the inflexibility and inexperience of the new local government officials made 'normal' political interaction impossible that open hostility occasionally became inevitable.

An example may illustrate this. Among the Pashai, if a man discovered that his wife was unfaithful, he was obliged to kill the adulterer, otherwise he would lose his honour. (Strictly speaking, he should kill the wife as well, though few went so far; a beating was usually sufficient.) Of course, homicide, for whatever reason, was officially a crime, also in the eyes of the Daoud government. But in such, not uncommon, cases of homicide because of adultery, some solution which did not violate the native code of honour could usually be worked out with the local government representative. Shortly after the new government officials had taken over in Darr-i Nur, a man killed another because of adultery. The killer had taken to the mountains, and the new police commandant sent two soldiers up to bring him in. They got the man, but when they passed through his own village on their way down to the headquarters, a group of five or six armed men blocked their way and threatened the soldiers to release the prisoner. The soldiers had no choice but to let him go and to go down and tell the commandant. Faced with such an act of overt insubordination, indeed 'counter-revolutionary behaviour', the young commandant sent for reinforcements from the oluswali of Shewa, and the next day a contingent of about ten soldiers armed with modern automatic weapons arrived at our house. But since the village of the killer was further up the valley and situated on the hillside, there was little the soldiers could really do. If they approached the village in daytime they would be spotted long before they arrived, and in any subsequent fighting they would be at a disadvantage. After dark they took off, however, and during the night they besieged the village, returning at dawn to our house. This went on for a couple of days. Meanwhile my host and other maleks were engaged in intense diplomatic activity, and apparently with some success in the end. The soldiers were withdrawn after a few days, and we could all breathe freely again. But it was precisely this kind of situation, an uncompromising confrontation between local, traditional norms and actions on the one hand and the literal adherence to the law by government officials on the other, that in less fortunate circumstances had led to further escalation of the conflict. Had the soldiers been less careful (or more 'brave') they might certainly have been shot, and the government's answer would have been helicopter bombardment of the village, as had happened elsewhere.

Apart from such direct confrontations, other measures by the new government also contributed to making it less than popular among the Pashai. Many of the decrees that were issued during the first months following the coup, even if they were well-intentioned, did not go down very well with the villagers. One example was the decree, implemented while I was still in the field, that abolished the system of mortgaging land, known as garavi. According to this system, a man could sell his right of user to a plot of land for money, and he could only reclaim his land by paying back the full amount he had received, all at once. In other parts of Afghanistan, this system had been used by wealthy landowners to acquire more land from poor smallholders in desperate need of cash, whose chances of ever getting back their land were very slim. So the government had decreed that all land acquired under the garavi system was to be given back to the original owners without compensation. But in Darra-i Nur the individual plots of land - irrigated field terraces - were rather small, and the land was fairly equally distributed. Few persons had more land than they could cultivate themselves, and, roughly speaking, only a minority of artisans had no land of their own; they received their income in cash by selling their products. So, in Darra-i Nur, the system often worked the other way round, as it were. Thus, for example, a silversmith in our village had saved up 100,000 Afs, with which he had acquired land from a local landowner who needed cash to finance his malek career. Shortly afterwards the government decree came, and the silversmith had to see the results of years of saving go down the drain.

Faced with that kind of measure by the new regime, it became increasingly obvious to maleks such as my host that they could not count for very long on the support of their people if they kept being apologetic for the government, and they soon about-turned and joined the incipient resistance movement.

Conclusion

In the rural areas there was from the outset very little ideologically dictated opposition to the socialist regime. It was only when the practical measures by the new government were seen to run counter to traditional norms and practices that the villagers started to object. As I have indicated, some of the immediate causes for conflicts were to be found in the regime's insufficient knowledge of and/or lack of consideration for the real economic, social and cultural conditions in the rural areas.(3) Only gradually, but, as we can see by virtue of hindsight, as a matter of course, did the conflict become expressed in general ideological terms. This was a consequence not only of the ideological commitment of the regime, but also of the totalitarian nature of Islam as a social and religious ideology. Because

Incipient Resistance

Islam is not just 'a religion' but is intimately associated with almost every aspect of social and cultural life, it was inevitable that the villagers in their turn would explain and legitimise any traditional norm and practice by reference to an 'Islamic' prescription (whether or not such could actually be found in the official 'theology'). So when the socialist regime attacked some specific local practices, it was perceived as striking at the very foundations of a sacredly constituted social order.

Notes

1. Fieldwork was financed by the Danish Research Council for the Humanities.
2. The anthropological literature on segmentary lineage systems is considerable; here I shall only refer to the classic description by Evans-Pritchard (1940). For an account of the Pashai system, see Ovesen (1981).
3. While the level of industrialisation in Afghanistan is, of course, very low the leaders of the new regime seemed to have imported revolutionary ideas and associated rhetoric mainly geared to industrial conditions. This had occasionally almost amusing results. Thus, for instance, the idea had presumably filtered through that the forces of 'the toiling masses' could be harnessed for the revolutionary cause by the formation of 'trade unions'. So, The Kabul New Times had at some point sent a reporter down to the bazaar to talk to some of the merchants, and as a result a headline on the front page ran: 'Traders now ready to form Unions'.

References

Evans-Pritchard, E.E. (1940) The Nuer, Oxford
Keiser, R. Lincoln (1984) 'The Rebellion in Darra-i Nur. Sharani, in M.N. & R.L. Canfield (eds.) Revolutions and Rebellions in Afghanistan: Anthropological Perspectives, Berkeley
Ovesen, Jan (1981) 'The Continuity of Pashai Society', Folk, vol. 23, Copenhagen
--- (1984) 'The Cultural Heritage of the Pashai', Anthropos, vol. 79, St Augustin

12

THE AFGHAN RESISTANCE: ACHIEVEMENTS AND PROBLEMS

Mohammad Es'haq

Before I begin talking about the achievements and problems of the resistance, let me mention some very important features of the Afghan resistance. Contrary to what some people may think, it is not new; it has its roots in the history of Afghanistan. Brave Afghans have always fought dictatorship, backwardness, foreign influence and corruption. The resistance is not just a reaction against the Soviet invasion; it existed before that invasion and it will not die with the end of this situation.

The resistance is nation-wide and all ethnic groups take an active part in it. This movement is not merely a regional one - its activities cover the whole country.

The aim of the resistance is clear, simple and comprehensible to all Afghan citizens. Its aim is to liberate Afghanistan, and to let the people decide their future according to their cultural heritage and religious beliefs.

Islam is the religion of the people of Afghanistan and religion to them means a way of life. It gives us the energy to fight with empty hands, to unite all the people of different languages and races in our country and it gives us a code of conduct in war and peace. Ninety-nine per cent of our people believe in Islam; it is a powerful force with which to combat the invaders who are waging a total but undeclared war against our country and people.

Islam for us is not a copy of any outside model and we do not feel responsible for what some people do

Resistance – Achievements and Problems

in the name of Islam.

Leadership in any movement plays an important part. When the Soviets invaded, the people of Afghanistan did not have one outstanding leader to guide them in their struggle against the invaders. Old bureaucrats and feudal landlords deserted the people; either they collaborated or they left the country. People chose their own leaders, previously unknown men both inside and outside the country.

The guerrilla war creates its own leaders. After six years of war against the Soviets the resistance is in a considerably better – and steadily improving position. Although we still do not have one single military or political leader, our present situation is in fact much better than it was before. We now have famous commanders and well-known political leaders and with each day these effective leaders gain more authority. God willing, the future will bring further improvements.

The Afghan resistance has some unique characteristics which make it different from other contemporary movements. It is a truly independent movement. Whilst fighting against one superpower it has not become the tool of another superpower or regional powers. It accepts aid but will not compromise its politics for it. It may be true to say that some individuals in the resistance movement show closeness to some foreign powers, but the majority remain totally independent.

It is a moderate type of movement, not warmongering. Even at the height of provocation it remains calm and reasonable, trying to understand the enemy and allowing it every opportunity to correct its mistakes.

The resistance is Islamic and in being so respects people of other religions. In the seven years of our armed struggle no individual or group of Afghans has committed any act of aggression against the Soviet Union outside Afghanistan. This illustrates how the resistance respects international laws. Even when the enemy mercilessly kills their brothers and sisters they treat Russian prisoners like guests.

These are not calculated political moves; they take root from the humane and moderate nature of the Afghan people.

Resistance - Achievements and Problems

The Afghan resistance is not organised homogeneously all over Afghanistan. Even within a party the organisational structure and effectiveness is not homogeneous. This is because of diversities in the social and geographical structure of Afghan society.

However, it is becoming increasingly clear that the tribal way of war against the army of a superpower is not effective. Those commanders who are doing a good job, along with their other tasks, have invented new ways of organising and fighting a modern guerrilla war. Their ideas are progressively becoming more common among Afghans. The main factors in this new type of organised warfare are:

1. Volunteer recruitment
2. Training, ideological and military
3. Wearing of uniform
4. Organised logistics
5. Avoidance of unreasonable regional and tribal loyalties

It is a very hard task, and it calls for extensive educational work. Surprisingly Afghans have shown that they are capable of assimilating non-traditional concepts readily and are making them their own.

Now that I have mentioned some of the features of the resistance let us see what some of its achievements are.

Resistance Achievements

The Afghan resistance has numerous achievements to its credit, both in the military and political fields.

From the military point of view the resistance has become stronger than ever. When the Soviets invaded Afghanistan the resistance was in a weak position, ill-armed and disorganised. It had no experience of fighting a war against the professional army of a superpower. Almost all the world expected the resistance to suffer a crushing defeat in a matter of a few weeks. However, after seven years the resistance is still in control of more than 80 per cent of the land and has the support of the absolute majority of the population. This surely is a sign of strength.

The number of fighters increases steadily. There

are more people waiting for weapons than there are weapons available. The saturation point has not yet been reached. In some areas as a result of repeated air and ground attacks, the women, children and elderly have been forced to leave their homes, leaving young volunteers who must wait for arms to enable them to join the resistance.

There has been a relative improvement in the quantity of the arms the mujahideen possess. Most of their arms come from captured enemy equipment. Mujahideen parties also buy weapons from the free world market. From the point of view of quality there has been no remarkable change during these long years. Except for one or two items the mujahideen are using weapons which they were using five years ago. The political considerations of the neighbouring countries, and of those who are in a position to help, have prevented the mujahideen from obtaining more effective weapons.

War, like any other phenomenon, has rules. To be able to fight one has to learn or develop these rules. Since the Afghan resistance does not follow any model from outside, it must develop them through experience.

At this moment I can say with full confidence that the knowledge of our people about the art of war has improved considerably. They are not only knowledgeable about tactics but also about strategy.

Afghans now know their war is a protracted one. They know that it is not just a military war, but a military-political one which must be fought on every front. They are aware of the importance of natural defence, the importance of bases, the weak points of the enemy, propaganda and economic war. They know all these things without knowing their terminology because they learn them from experience and not from books.

The mujahideen have gained a lot of experience in different types of weapon. There is not a single enemy weapon which has been captured that has not been used against the enemy.

The mujahideen understand the importance of having training. All mujahideen groups have a training programme even if they are not all advanced. There are also elementary programmes.

One of the mujahideen's achievements in the military field has been the introduction of organisational structure. Although it is not a uniform organisation covering the whole of Afghanistan, this development, proving its usefulness, is spreading throughout the country.

As previously stated the most popular and successful types of developments in the resistance are based on volunteer recruitment, training, wearing a uniform and engagement in real combat. Some of these things contradict the normal way of life and they must be introduced gradually and with patience.

Leadership in the Jehad is a natural process. Those who have shown ability and have gained the confidence of the people survive. All the good commanders have achieved their positions through hard work and natural abilities in war. The war situation has trained a chain of leaders who fill gaps when the need arises. We believe no non-native leader can run Afghanistan after liberation, not even for one week.

The mujahideen's achievements in logistics are remarkable. Transporting supplies over hundreds of miles and storing them in a war situation is a formidable task. Mujahideen tunnels, which are used for storing supplies and which also act as bomb shelters, are impressive and these have been dug with very primitive tools.

The mujahideen have also improved their urban guerrilla tactics. They use time-bombs very effectively against selected targets and casualties have dropped with the improved tactics, though lack of proper equipment hinders further improvement in this sphere.

The mujahideen have developed their intelligence network considerably. On the organised fronts no enemy activity goes unnoticed. In occupied territory there are numerous volunteers to help the mujahideen.

In the political field the mujahideen have made progress both inside and outside the country.

Inside the country the mujahideen have been able to keep up popular support for the cause. People from all ethnic groups, in every walk of life, support the struggle of the resistance for freedom. No one doubts this absolute support. This explains why the resistance has survived and even improved. The main reason for this is the common ideology of the people and their firm belief in the justice of their cause. This

Resistance - Achievements and Problems

support is necessary for the survival of the resistance. It is not an unchanging static support, a lot of hard work must be done because the enemy is trying to minimise this support through propaganda and terror.

The mujahideen have made several achievements in the civil organisation field which is necessary to keep the people interested in the cause. The people now choose their leaders to run their affairs. For the first time in the history of our country a type of real election is taking place.

There are judicial committees, usually headed by respected religious scholars. In some areas these judges are more powerful than the military commanders or civil administrators, since religion provides justice with protection.

The mujahideen have established refugee committees to take care of the thousands of people who have been displaced inside the country. They have medical committees to aid wounded civilians and protect them.

Cultural committees publish papers, record songs, run schools and organise mass meetings as well as special political and ideological classes.

The mujahideen have also made some progress outside Afghanistan. They have gained the confidence of the world as a popular and serious fighting force.

At the beginning of the invasion nobody believed the present leaders or commanders would be so successful. This is a big achievement without which no cooperation can take place outside Afghanistan.

The resistance has been able to maintain the political balance between different conflicting forces and still remain independent. Everybody wants to have good relations with a neighbour like Iran and a superpower like the USA, but, at the same time, it is not an easy task to walk this tightrope.

Although our achievements in propaganda and the mass media are not very extensive they cannot be ignored. Mujahideen parties have opened offices in several of the world's capitals. We have gained experience in working with international news agencies and broadcasting companies. We have developed good working relations with international relief organisations.

Finally, we have proved that if a nation is

determined to defend its faith and country it can be done even if it fights alone. In the past the big powers have helped movements against other powers, but we are fighting a superpower without any real effective support.

Problems of the Resistance

As well as its achievements the Afghan resistance also has its problems. One of the major problems of the resistance is the lack of unity among all the fighting forces who oppose the Soviet invasion. There are natural factors that account for this but there are also some artificial factors which divide the mujahideen.

The geographical structure of the country, the lack of good contacts and communication between people of different religions, and the misguided policies of the past government which the resistance has inherited, are some of the natural factors which divide it.

Rivalries between parties, shortsightedness and enemy infiltration are some of the artificial factors which divide the resistance.

I think there is no immediate solution to this problem. The problem of unity, the co-ordination of actions and co-operation among the parties and fronts is improving in proportion to the development of the war. In the past there was very little practical cooperation at all. It is better now and will improve as time passes.

The second major problem is the uneven development of the fronts inside the country. Among the mujahideen there are commanders who have military and political knowledge and use it in an effective way. There are also commanders who have one or the other of these skills but not both. I think the major purpose of our struggle is to make the Soviets tired of their occupation by continuous attacks on their military and economic targets and to make use of these events to create political problems for them both inside and outside the Soviet Union. While there are strong motivations and the will to make sacrifices, all mujahideen are not aware of the importance of this type of work.

If there are only a few developed fronts the

Resistance – Achievements and Problems

enemy concentrates all its powers to destroy them. Panjshir is a case in point.

In addition to this, practical unity is not possible unless all the fronts have reached a minimum level of organisational development.

The long-term policy of Sovietisation is a threat to the resistance and to Afghanistan. After their failure with the present generation the Soviets are trying with the next generation and are sending thousands of children to the Soviet Union to win their hearts and minds, thus permitting the further Sovietisation of our education and economic system. This is all part of their long-term plan.

It becomes more dangerous too when the resistance does not present an alternative to the people because of its preoccupation with the constant war and the need to work persistently to get supplies to fight this war.

Lack of finance for the war is another major problem the resistance faces. As time passes the country is becoming more and more destroyed and the people poorer and more dependent on the resistance for help. With the escalation of the war and the use of new tactics and weapons the need for outside support increases.

I have myself seen that 60 per cent of the time and energy of the commanders is spent on humanitarian causes and the rest of their time on combat activities. Today the resistance is in desperate need of military and non-military aid.

In the military field we lack enough weapons and ammunition of every kind. In particular, the lack of an effective weapon against enemy aircraft is a major problem.

The shortage of food, medicine, clothing and other necessities for the displaced people inside the country is a big headache for the commanders.

The flow of a large number of refugees to neighbouring countries is a problem. The more people who leave the country, the less support there is for the resistance. Efforts by the resistance to keep people within the country have not been successful because the resistance is not able to offer sufficient help for them to be able to stay.

Lack of effective external support is also a

major problem. The Afghan resistance, contrary to what some people may think, has not been helped effectively in either the military or the political field. There are many reasons for this.

Afghanistan belongs to the Muslim world. Because of historical events and developments around Afghanistan which are not seen to be favourable to the West, the West has been hesitant to help whole-heartedly. Although the situation has improved there are still problems.

A poor information service is one reason for the lack of interest and support. If people do not see the terrible events that happen in Afghanistan on their television screens they do not remember what is happening. Restrictions by neighbouring countries, rough terrain, lack of experienced Afghan journalists and shortage of funds for publicity, are some of the problems and reasons why more exposure is not given in the Western mass media.

Soviet intimidations and lack of moral courage prevent countries from actively supporting the cause of Afghanistan. One can see this in the UN resolutions which do not name the Soviet Union as an aggressor.

Any cause wishing to gain widely based support must win the support of the intellectuals first. Intellectuals have in the past played an active part in anti-war movements. Afghanistan is a new situation. Now the aggressor is the Soviet Union, a so-called socialist country. This development has changed the theory of what an imperialist is, i.e. it contradicts the traditional concepts of imperialism, colonialism and empire building. It disturbs the left-orientated intellectuals and challenges their very understanding of socialism. Hence they hesitate to take a firm stand against Soviet oppression and hegemony.

This war is about Soviet oppression, hegemony, aggression, imperialism, colonialism and plain old-fashioned empire building.

13

AN ASSESSMENT OF THE NEW MUJAHEDDIN ALLIANCE

Sabahuddin Kushkaki

The purpose of this chapter is not to give an account of attempts by Afghans in the past to unify their ranks against the Soviet-installed communist government of Afghanistan and the invasion of their country by the Soviet Union in December, 1979. Instead, I am aiming at assessing the consequences of unity, or lack of unity, on the future of the resistance.

At present, the main groups of Afghan mujaheddin have pledged themselves in a loose alliance or coalition, which was formed on 16 May 1985. The new unity, formed among seven Peshawar-based resistance groups, (1) was established after the dissolution of the two old alliances which were formed in the summer and autumn of 1981.(2) These alliances were dissolved in May 1985, primarily for the following reasons:

1. Lack of concord among the leaders of what is known in the West as the 'fundamentalist' groups. These groups, although constituting the most powerful mujaheddin organisations, failed to co-operate effectively within the framework of their alliance. They were expected to dissolve their own offices and instead establish an Office of Unity. But they were not able to do so. Day-to-day relationship had also worsened between most of the leaders belonging to this group leading to serious clashes among their mujaheddin groups inside the country.
2. The two alliances - the Fundamentalists and the Liberals - failed to build between themselves

bridges of co-operation in a number of fields including the appointment of a single spokesman to speak on their behalf and that of the resistance in the world community, and co-operation in a number of military fields inside the country.

Neither the Afghans, the rest of the Islamic world nor other countries supporting the resistance were ready to accept any single one of these groups as the sole representative of the Afghan nation.

Both these factors not only threatened to weaken the very basis of the resistance but also presented difficulties for the prospects of a solution to the Afghan problem.

Without doubt the 1985 alliance or coalition among the seven groups of fundamentalists and liberals was created as a result of pressure by a number of Islamic countries, notably Pakistan and Saudi Arabia who had been contributing more than any other source to the strength of the resistance including large amounts of funds for humanitarian purposes to Afghan refugees. The mujaheddin leaders were also under constant pressure from their own compatriots to create a broadly based unity among their groups.

Were it not for such pressure from several sources, the present alliance could not have been established. At the time of the formation of this alliance, both organisational and personal relationships among several groups and leaders were at their worst. The atmosphere for the creation of a new alliance or the strengthening of the old alliances was not good.

And yet the seven leaders announced the formation of an alliance among themselves mainly due to pressure brought upon them by others and due to anxiousness on the part of their majority(3) to do away with their old alliance which, as far as the fundamentalists were concerned, had become obsolete and was a hindrance in the way of the ambition of some of the leaders to strengthen the ground of their own organisations.

Features of the New Alliance

The new alliance was announced by the seven leaders in a 'joint communique' at a press conference, 16 May

The New Mujaheddin Alliance

1985. The communique(4) said that the alliance was primarily established at a time when the Soviets were attempting to find a solution to the Afghan issue on the basis of their own interests and terms. Therefore it was necessary, it said, that

> the history-making resistance of our believing nation should assume its due prestige and dignity in the international community and that the resistance forces, which deal with this one and only issue of the Afghan people, should obtain the official right of representing the Afghan issue and (thus) of providing a broader international perspective to the problem.

For the realisation of this objective, the leaders said that they agreed to:

1. Form a single united front;
2. Put aside their mutual differences for the sake of strengthening the resistance.

And in order to do so, they further agreed:

1. To form a new alliance under the name of Islamic Unity of Afghanistan, Mujaheddin, which had been a name shared by the alliances;
2. Each of the seven organisations of the new alliance, on its own initiative and on the basis of its own administrative and party identity, is to work together with the others on the basis of agreed principles;
3. A 'powerful' council is to be created for the alliance, so that it may adopt measures and an all-out programme for further unity among member parties and for the 'unification of the whole nation in a single rank';
4. To represent the resistance at international gatherings, a single spokesman is to be elected by the council. The council is also to decide on the mode of the election and the tenure of office of this official spokesman;
5. The leaders themselves will lay down 'appropriate' rules regarding the nature of the powers, obligations and methods of the election of

members of the council. A committee, comprised of these seven leaders, will be the highest decision-making authority of the alliance.

The communique pointed out, for the sake of creating further co-ordination in mujaheddin ranks and jointly facing enemy tactics and activities, that certain joint activities and practical steps have already been adopted. This was a reference to the creation of a 'military committee' comprised of the representatives of seven groups. This committee had been created almost two months before the new alliance was officially announced. Before their formal announcement about the formation of the alliance, the leaders had also agreed on the establishment of a 'non-military committee' for the alliance. This committee has so far not been established.

The first problem which the leaders of the new alliance faced was their disagreement on the formation of the 'powerful' council. Once they issued their agreement on the formation of the alliance, they discovered that in a situation where party loyalty and discipline is very loose, the very delegates that a leader sends to the council might rebel against his policies and that of the party. Thus, several leaders refrained from sending delegates to the council. At first, they had agreed to send ten representatives each to the council, which according to the communique was to play a leading role in shaping and promoting the policies of the alliance. However, no such council has as yet been established.

One member who particularly insisted on the immediate establishment of the council was Mr Sayyaf. A number of leaders, notably Mr Hekmatyar, accused him of trying to create rifts among the delegates and their leaders and to woo a number of them to his side and thereby carve for himself a leading position in the new alliance.(5)

Not being able to convene the council, the leaders agreed to elect a spokesman from among themselves on a rotation basis on their own initiative. The first spokesman was Mr Khales. He was succeeded by Mr Hekmatyar.

The decision of the leaders to create a council

The New Mujaheddin Alliance

that might overpower the leaders themselves was interpreted by a number of Afghans in Pakistan as legally defective. After all, they argued, the delegates were expected only to act on behalf of their leaders. They were not expected to act otherwise. They were the creation of their own leaders. Their votes were to be cast in blocks. So why multiply 1 by 10 or 7? To vote contrary to the dictates of the party would amount to rebellion against the party. Furthermore, it would cause disorder and splits which would be contrary to the very aims of the alliance.

Accomplishments of the Alliance

In political fields

As discussed so far in this chapter, despite the fact that many provisions of the agreement reached on the new alliance have not yet been implemented, the very fact that the resistance right now has a spokesman to represent it when needed, is a significant accomplishment and development.

The alliance, during the tenure of office of Mr Hekmatyar as its spokesman, was able to organise a delegation of all seven groups and send it to New York to claim the Afghan United Nations' seat in the midst of the celebration of the 40th anniversary of the founding of that organisation. Although this delegation left for New York quite late and not in time to contest the Afghan UN seat when the credential committee of the United Nations was examining the credentials of member states, it was able to bring up the issue for the first time on behalf of all mujaheddin in public and notify the UN.

The New York delegation, headed by Mr Hekmatyar himself, declined to accept an invitation to meet the US President Ronald Reagan. It is understood that he did so despite the insistence of all other members that the delegation should meet the US leader.

Mr Hekmatyar's position was that the delegation had gone to the United States solely to contest the Afghan seat at the United Nations. Furthermore, supporters of Mr Hekmatyar's decision in Pakistan said that establishing closer contacts during the visit with the US leadership, including high-ranking

The New Mujaheddin Alliance

Congressional leaders, might have given face value to a baseless Soviet argument that the resistance was collaborating with the US against the Soviet Union or that it was a puppet of the US. Both these arguments, though relevant and sound, should also be examined in the light of Mr Hekmatyar's position vis-a-vis international Islamic movements.

In the military field

As already stated, the seven Peshawar-based mujaheddin leaders had established a joint military committee even before their agreement to form the new alliance. the committee was assigned in particular to work on:

1. Stopping mujaheddin interfighting
2. Co-ordinating efforts in patrolling mujaheddin supply routes
3. Exchanging information on elements in communist service believed to have infiltrated the mujaheddin ranks.

Mujaheddin interfighting has still continued, though far less than in previous years. It is difficult and too early to conclude whether the reduction in interfighting has been a result of committee efforts or increased mujaheddin consciousness inside the country about the futility of such clashes.

As a result of some of the biggest and most aggressive Soviet assaults so far against mujaheddin supply routes, the routes have become very difficult for the mujaheddin to cross. The Russians have not only peppered these routes with a great number of mines and other types of explosives, but they have also been able to build more military posts along some of these routes, notably in the province of Logar in the south, and Konar in the east.

However, despite such partially successful Russian moves, the mujaheddin are still able to carry their supplies through these or alternative routes. One successful operation against such Soviet tactics was reported in early November this year by Herat mujaheddin under the command of Ismael Khan. The resistance forces in Herat reported that they were able to eliminate communist military posts in the

The New Mujaheddin Alliance

upper zones of Afghan territory which border Iran.

The most spectacular and important instance of mujaheddin co-operation in the battlefield was observed in August-September of this year (1985) when all important groups fought the communists in the southern province of Paktia. For almost three weeks, the mujaheddin forces, comprised of some of the best veterans of this war, fought against a big communist offensive in the Khost region. For a time, Mr Hekmatyar commanded these forces.

Other instances of mujaheddin co-operation in battlefields had nothing to do with the efforts of the joint military committee. Such co-operation had existed and still exists on the basis of local arrangements within the country.

The Future of the Alliance

To summarise, the new alliance, since its establishment, has been able to establish a military committee to co-ordinate mujaheddin war efforts and appoint one single spokesman on behalf of all major resistance groups. But the new alliance has been expected to do more. It has so far been unable to implement most of the provisions of the agreement reached by the seven leaders.

It should be recalled that the purpose of the new alliance has NOT been to completely unify the ranks of the mujaheddin. As specified in the 17 May communique of the seven leaders, the groups were expected to cooperate in a number of military, political and humanitarian fields. The breaking up of the old alliances have also resulted in the dissolution of a number of educational and cultural organisations which had been set up within each alliance by member parties.

Right now, each group is reorganising itself by its own efforts. Some parties have been able to make swift moves in this direction, others have been lagging behind. There seems to be a tendency on the part of some of these parties to think that, as a result of their independent moves aimed at expanding and solidifying their own ranks, they will eventually emerge as the strongest group and thus either eliminate or, at least, overshadow other groups.

But, despite such efforts and tendencies, the

parties seem to be unable to cope with a number of issues independently. For instance, no one party can cope with the enemy in all parts of Afghanistan independently. None of them can deal alone with the problems of education and the immense task of bringing up an educated generation conscious of its responsibilities within the context of present Afghan realities. No single group can cope alone with the problems of health and agriculture inside the country, etc.

For some time to come, it seems as though the resistance leaders will have to agree to have a single spokesman to act on their behalf in the international community. The sources which have induced them to join the new alliance may not let them discard this part of the accord. But unless a number of concrete and meaningful steps are adopted, the new alliance will play no other positive role in the life of resistance. The new steps would be to include the creation of a permanent body to implement the decisions of the leaders. The creation of a so-called 'powerful' committee suggested in the 16 May communique of seven leaders, if established, might very well start a new phase of splits and confusion within the resistance. I have already referred to this in the first part of this chapter.

A number of Afghan observers in Pakistan are of the opinion that, instead, a secretariat should be established for the new alliance. This secretariat should (a) carry out the decisions of the leaders who are to form the supreme council of the alliance, and (b) devise plans and programmes and refer them for the approval of the leaders and then implement them.

The Peshawar-based mujaheddin leaders are very sensitive to seeing any other person or organisation acquiring greater powers than themselves. Mostly for this very reason they are not willing to establish the 'powerful' council which they themselves had advocated at one time. The creation of a secretariat may well become an alternative to the impasse.

One of the greatest virtues of any leadership is to build bridges and eliminate the gaps between itself and the people. A primary motive behind moves for unity among mujaheddin groups has been to satisfy the urges of the grass roots of the resistance. These

The New Mujaheddin Alliance

grass roots demand dynamism and logical action from their leadership. It has been held by many Afghans, including this writer, that under the present circumstances, it is neither practical nor, perhaps, advisable for the resistance to be completely merged together. Instead there should be special areas and spheres of co-operation among members of an Afghan alliance. The new unity among the seven groups has been established on this very concept. In order to enable this new alliance to move ahead, those very forces which once played an effective role in establishing it must nourish it as well. To leave the leaders to themselves to achieve the basic objective of the alliance will in many ways be counterproductive.

Notes

1. They are: The Ittehad-e-Islami of Abd Al-Rasool Sayaf, Hezb-e-Islami of Gulbuddin Hekmatyar, Jamiat-e-Islami Afghanistan of Buhanuddin Rabbani, Hezb-e-Islami Afghanistan of Mohammad Yunus Khales (All these four groups were members of the now defunct alliance of what in the West is usually called the Fundamentalists), Harakat-e-Enquelab-e-Islami of Mohammad Nabi Mohammadi, Jabha-e-Melli Nejat of Sebghatullah Mojaddidi and Mahaz-e-Melli-e-Islami of Sayuyed Ahmad Gailani (the latter three groups were earlier united in the alliance of 'Liberals').
2. The alliance of 'Liberals' was formed in the summer of 1981 and that of the 'Fundamentalists' in the autumn of 1981.
3. Only Mr Sayyaf tried until the very last minute to avoid the dissolution of the alliance of the Fundamentalists. He was the spokesman for that alliance and his refusal to dissolve the Fundamentalist union delayed the official formation of the new alliance for almost two months.
4. Translated by this writer from the Dari text of the communique.
5. These charges were published in an interview which Mr Hekmatyar gave to the Wahdat-e-Islam, a mujaheddin newspaper published in Peshawar.

PART IV

ECOLOGY

14

ECOLOGY AND THE WAR IN AFGHANISTAN

Terje Skogland

Abstract

Afghanistan belongs to the zone of recurrent drought typical of the arid Sahel belt of Africa and the Middle East. During the last 7,000 years of domestication and adaptation of pastoralism and agricultural settlements, man's impact on the environment in the form of overgrazing, soil degradation and erosion has accelerated, mostly within historic time. In part of the Sahel belt desertification has accelerated at an alarming rate. In the western part of the Himalaya range, including Pakistan, deforestation has led to serious soil erosion (the highest on record in the world today) with increased unpredictability of floods and siltation of arable land. There are no indications that these changes over time are caused by climatic deterioration.

Afghanistan is situated between the zones of deserts and the forested Himalayas. Against this ecological background I shall try to assess the situation in Afghanistan in relation to that in the rest of this ecological zone. Animal stocking rate and degradation of the environment appears to be higher in most other countries within the zone. There are in the main three causes of continued degradation: increasing human populations, disruption of cultural land-use patterns affecting the practice of pastoralism, and warfare. Increased human populations is the main ecological problem in Pakistan and most countries of the Sahel. Disruption of nomadism by the former

Ecology and the War

Shah Reza regime in Iran led to serious overgrazing due to human concentration. Afghanistan appeared to have one of the most favourable land-use practices within the zone before the Soviet invasion and apparently within ecological carrying capacity. I shall discuss some disease problems resulting from Soviet destruction of the ancient irrigation systems in Afghanistan and assess some alternatives to food production.

Introduction

In the arid zone the natural vegetation is undergoing rapid regression as a result of clearing, overgrazing and the collection of firewood, wood for charcoal, etc. Erosion and desertification progress at a terrifying rate (Le Houerou, 1973). Natural vegetation is currently regressing at a rate of 1 to 2 per cent per annum.

One may ask oneself whether this progressive degradation of vegetation during the historical epoch may not in part be due to the worsening of a climate which is becoming more arid. Many authors (more than one hundred) belonging to some ten scientific disciplines, have concerned themselves with this problem over the past half century. Several bibliographical reviews - some critical, others not - have been devoted to it (Monod, 1958; Le Houerou, 1968; Rapp, 1974).

The specialists are unanimous in recognising that aridification of the climate in the arid zone took place between 3000-2500 BC. They are equally unanimous that there is no proof, nor even any serious presumption, in favour of any worsening of the climate since the beginning of historical time (Figure 14.1). Monod (1958), in one of the most in-depth bibliographical reviews on the subject, concludes thus:

> It seems that, as knowledge of the regions in question, of their past, and of the evidence, written or otherwise, regarding it, becomes deeper, general opinion is inclined to the view that, since the beginning of historical time - say, broadly, for the past five to seven thousand years - there has been no appreciable, signifi-

cant nor general change in climate.

Later literature, particularly abundant since the droughts of 1970 to 1973, has very largely confirmed this analysis, which is already 24 years old (Le Houerou, 1981a). Within SW Asia the historic records from the Quetta station indicate a stable climate during the last 100 years (Figure 14.2).

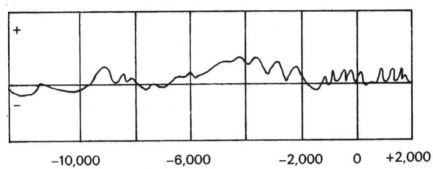

Figure 14.1 The main trend of precipitation (hypothetical) in the Near East since 14,000 years before present (from Butzer (1961)

Arid Ecosystem Dynamics

Man has been part of the ecology of arid zone ecosystems since prehistoric time. It is therefore fair to call this region a 'cultural landscape' (Barth, 1975). Man has been blamed for creating deserts, cf. Reifental's dictum 'the nomad is not so much the son of the desert as its father'. I shall try to analyse this dictum to see whether it holds true or not in view of modern ecological theory.

To illustrate the historic process I shall use a microcosm represented by data on the introduction of sheep into arid brush steppe in Australia as an example (Figure 14.3). Over a period of about 100 years introduced sheep expanded in numbers far above ecological carrying capacity, bouncing back down to below half initial peak numbers due to starvation mortality and diminished initial plant production levels. Subsequent oscillations have been confined around one-half the initial peak with mortalities

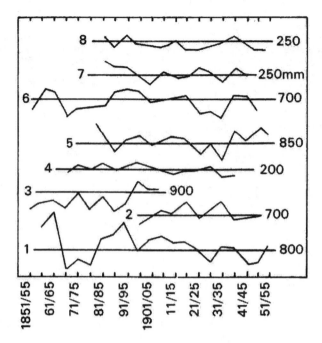

Figure 14.2   Five-year precipitation means from Gibraltar (1) to Quetta (8) in the Near East basin. Vertical scale is uniform relative to approximate median value at right (in millimetres) (from Butzer, 1961)

bringing numbers down from around 7 million (the new ecological carrying capacity). The drawn line indicates the maximal economic sustainable carrying capacity at around 5 million sheep. For this region of the arid zone, that would be about 0.42 sheep/ha of pastoral land (Williams, 1981). The upper and lower confines around this maximum sustained capacity (line) is the stability domain of such a system, while maximal production is obtained at one-half the oscillatory pulse (Skogland, 1985; Fowler, 1981). Since the ancient start of man's use of domestic animals, a similar process can be visualised to have taken place over a time scale of thousands of years where the upper stability domain is set by periodic drought, since water in such ecosystems is an essential part. Arid or desert ecosystems are understood here as regions with less than 300–500mm annual rainfall (Noy-

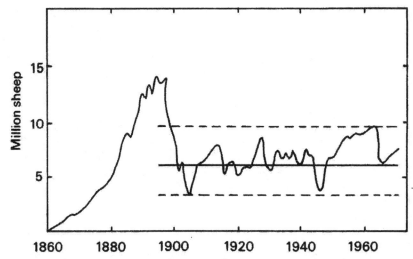

Figure 14.3   Trend of numbers of introduced sheep in one part of arid Australia between 1860 and 1972 (from Butlin, 1962 and subsequent data)

Meir, 1973). Such regions are characterised by three factors,

1. The main limiting factor for most biological processes is the water input by rainfall.
2. This input is variable and infrequent.
3. The timing and magnitude of the rainfall pulses are to a large extent unpredictable.

These three factors in no way mean that desert ecosystems are unstable. When viewed on a time scale of decades and millennia, most biological components of arid ecosystems show remarkable 'stability' or rather 'resilience' (Holling, 1973). This apparent paradox is not surprising if we consider that they have evolved in an environment where the normal pattern is more or less random alternations of short favourable periods and long stress periods.

What then are the stabilising features of arid ecosystems?

1. Drought resistance of plants; ephemeral plant growth; water conservation by grazers like the camel that can go a week without water; and fat-

tailed sheep that can catabolise water from fat deposits.
2. Adaptability for rapid recovery of plant reproduction and growth following rainfall, i.e. 'a pulse and reserve paradigm' whereby a trigger (a rain event) sets off a reproduction pulse in annual plants. Much of this pulse is lost rapidly through mortality or consumption by grazers, but some is directed back into plant reserves (e.g. seeds). This reserve is lost only slowly during the no-growth period or when inaccessible to grazers and from it the next plant growth pulse is initiated. This pattern explains the long-term stability of the system.
3. Stability is ensured by flexible and opportunistic feeding habits (camels, fat-tailed sheep and goats).
4. Nomadic migrations by human pastoralists and their stock to avoid the dry zones ensures maximal utilisation of wet season zones.

The adaptations of desert plants and the stocks of human pastoralists increase their resilience to stress and that of the ecosystem as a whole. But there are also some characteristic susceptibilities in arid systems. Destabilising features are:

1. Sensitivity of plant reserves to damage by overgrazing or trampling.
2. Sensitivity to time lags. If animal or plant species are introduced that continue to reproduce during droughts, it may amplify oscillations with important side-effects on the rest of the ecosystem (e.g. rabbits and merino sheep introduced to Australia, or cattle in Africa).
3. The proximity of pastoral lands to areas of irrigation or water holes. Most experience with new artificial water holes in East Africa has shown that domestic stocks increased instead of spreading out. Catastrophic overgrazing has resulted.
4. Sensitivity of topsoil erosion to overgrazing. Studies by Charley and Cowling (1968) have shown that overgrazing can reduce plant production by between 40 and 90 per cent. In some areas 40

years of protection have not led to plant recovery and plant succession. Furthermore, heavy overgrazing reduces the germination possibilities of trees or shrubs and increases the river siltation loads.

The Indus river in India and Pakistan today carries the heaviest siltation load in the world (McVean and Robertson, 1969; Eckholm, 1975). Through the Northern hills, after passing through India, the Indus river is Pakistan's jugular vein. The water of the Indus and its six major tributaries is about all that stands between the bristling, densely populated civilisation and deserted, sandy wasteland. With such a high rate of erosion in the uplands, the exceptionally heavy silt load carried by these rivers is rendering the country's expensive new reservoirs useless with startling rapidity. The FAO survey of land and water resources in Afghanistan concluded already in 1965 that this upper catchment area of the Indus is remarkable for its sparseness of vegetation with almost no soil cover left. The report from the FAO forestry projects in Paktia also showed that the forests of Afghanistan covered only 0.1 per cent of the land area and that the cedar trees were no longer germinating due to lack of topsoil. During the recent Soviet offensives in Paktia some of these remaining forests have been burnt down.

The combination of all these four above features will add to the destabilisation of arid ecosystems.

Adaptations to the Arid Zone by Man

I shall now look at the human use of arid zone plant production in some more detail. The development within the different countries as regards sedentarisation of nomads and its consequences have been dealt with by anthropologists at length elsewhere (i.e. Barth, 1975; Ghallab, 1975 and others cited by them). However, one clear distinction should be made. The pastoralists of the Middle East and SW Asia are closely tied to the markets and are dependent on market transactions to sell their animal produce. The subsistence cattle herders and agriculturalists of East Africa on the other hand are less dependent on

Ecology and the War

open markets and subsist to a larger extent on their stocks' milk or on crops. This makes them susceptible to the effects of overexploitation of pastures and loss of stock, while the pastoralists of Middle and SW Asia remain more flexible in their options such as nomadism, semi-nomadism, and transhumance combined with farming and trading, etc., since they historically have been a much more integrated part of the national economies in their countries.

In arid and semi-arid regions of the world the division between pastoralism and other forms of agriculture is based on water availability. Where water is available, the higher potential value of cultivated crops dictates that the land be used for crop production. Where water is unavailable, the land is used extensively for livestock grazing, often with low capital investment.

Nomadic Pastoralism

Pastoralist economies which evolved in the arid zones of Asia and Africa are characteristically nomadic, with movements being either wholly opportunistic (central Sahara) or partly cyclic-seasonal (most other areas). The pastoral economies introduced into arid Australia (and partly America) became sedentary after a nomadic stage, but retained options of 'motorised nomadism' in droughts.

As mentioned in the introduction nomadism has been charged with 'deterioration' of the desert ecosystem (or even its 'creation'). Theoretically, this claim seems absurd. The nomadic habit of many desert animals is an excellent adaptation to the environment, which is likely to increase resilience. Nomadic grazing facilitates a more flexible use of regional resources than strictly sedentary grazing, and prevents extreme local grazing pressures. However, one destabilising side-effect is often the competitive use of common grazing lands and the lack of incentive for any individual to use them conservatively or to limit herd size.

The nomadic pastoralist ecosystems in Asia and Africa seem to have fluctuated for thousands of years within the same well-defined stability domain (Monod & Toupet, 1961). This is probably different from the pre-pastoral domain, but there is no evidence for progressive deterioration until recently. Stock populations generally fluctuated consequent to climatic fluctuations (though perhaps with greater lag and amplitude than wild populations) and were prevented from 'explosion' by incident droughts. Thus arid ecosystems with nomadic pastoralist economics have shown considerable long-term resilience.

A definite and accelerating trend of range deterioration and erosion has been observed in arid and semi-arid zones in Asia and Africa within the last decades (Pearse, 1970, Le Houerou, 1974). It is associated with transition from a nomadic to a sedentary system, extension of cultivation, and increased contact with non-arid and urban systems (veterinary care, supplementary feeding). Examples are from Pakistan and India. These developments have removed previous restrictions on human and stock populations, and allowed them in many cases to exceed the 'carrying capacity' of the resources of the region, so that now they can be maintained only with inputs from other regions. The trend is stronger in the semi-arid fringe than in more remote arid regions.

Sedentary Pastoralism Farming

Such economies allow a more direct, efficient and complete utilisation of plant production by man than nomadic pastoralism, and hence higher population densities. The integration of cultivation and livestock allows some stabilising complementary and compensatory practices (Tadmor, Eyal and Benjamin, 1974): grazing of stubble and, in drought years, of the whole crop; storing of grain; rotation; use of manure. Private ownership of grazing lands (or at least more permanent rights on them) can provide an incentive for conservative use and even improvement (though often this does not happen), and for the management of local water resources by run-off farming.

But there are also destabilising factors. The loss of stock mobility and its permanent concentration near settlements and waters may increase grazing pressure there, particularly in drought to a point where the vegetation-animal balance 'crashes' (Morley, 1964). A new balance may be attained but with much lower productivity and palatability (Le Houerou, 1974, see also Figure 14.3). This is not prevented by supplementary feeding in drought since the handfed stock usually continue to graze. Thus large areas of productive range are turning into mere 'exercise grounds' (Pearse, 1970). This is often accompanied by accelerated erosion of devegetated rangelands and of wrongly cultivated land.

Settled people usually require or expect a higher and more constant standard of living than desert nomads, i.e. they have higher and less flexible 'maintenance costs' which are difficult to bear in droughts (insofar as the economy is based on the resources of the arid zone alone). This requirement for higher 'persistence' reduces the economical (and psychological?) 'resilience' of the society in an environment where droughts are normal rather than exceptional.

These factors lower the stability-resilience of sedentary grazing-farming ecosystems in arid and semi-arid zones and increase the probability that a long drought will cause an irreversible 'crash' or at last a severe crisis (more severe than in nomadic systems). In semi-arid regions such systems have existed successfully for long periods despite the incidence of such crises. But attempts to extend them beyond a certain lower limit of rainfall (or of crop success-probability) have often collapsed, causing abandonment or return to pastoralism. Improved management (erosion control, range conservation and improvement, proper integration) can certainly increase the chances for long-term success. But it would be dangerous to underestimate the strong geological constraints, in particular the large and random fluctuations in productivity.

The desert ecosystem, always being pushed around by the climate, thus bounces continuously back and forth within a large 'stability bowl', but the walls of the bowl are steep and the system is unlikely to be bounced out of it. The introduction of man, and then of domestic animals, further widened this bowl and changed its shape, but in nomadic systems the probability of being pushed out of it remained low. The transition to a more sedentary and intensive agriculture, in an attempt to move the bowl to a domain of

Ecology and the War

higher production and to reduce its diameter, often also lowers its walls.

Thus the aim of arid zone agronomy by constancy of animal production is directly contrary to the ecological realities, and therefore reduction of the <u>variance</u> of production has in most instances been done at the expense of long-term resilience, be it within the frame of Western capitalism or Soviet Marxism.

Thus the dictum quoted in the beginning of this chapter that the nomad is 'not the son of the desert but its father' must be rephrased since all experience today indicates that if he is the father of the desert it is not so much by choice as by political dictum, often strongly contrary to his own traditional adaptations to desert life.

The Present Ecological Situation Within the Arid Zone

In Figure 14.4 I have compiled data on livestock numbers in selected countries within the arid zone in relation to total available land area usable for pastoralism. Although the figures are necessarily rough they give an indication of the actual stocking rates and degree of exploitation of the pasture resources. For comparison, figures from 1979, before the Soviet invasion of Afghanistan, are used (FAO Production Year Book, 1979).

The figure shows both sheep and goats as well as cattle densities. Sheep are the most drought-resistant of the three, while goats are the most flexible in terms of terrain use and being better able to cope with brush. Cattle are the least adapted of the three to arid conditions and among nomads the least used stock (except some East African tribes, foremost the Masai) (Lee Talbot, 1974). In most cases cattle are an indication of sedentarisation while sheep and goats are the nomad's and pastoralist's basic stock. The highest densities of sheep and goats are found in Pakistan while Afghanistan has a much more favourable ratio of stocking density indicating maintenance of a traditional pastoralism adjusted to ecological conditions. The ecological stability domain for regions with 100-150 mm annual rainfall is between 0.12-0.7 sheep equivalents/ha of pastoral land with an economic maximum of between 0.2-0.5 (Le

Houerou, 1981b; Williams, 1981).

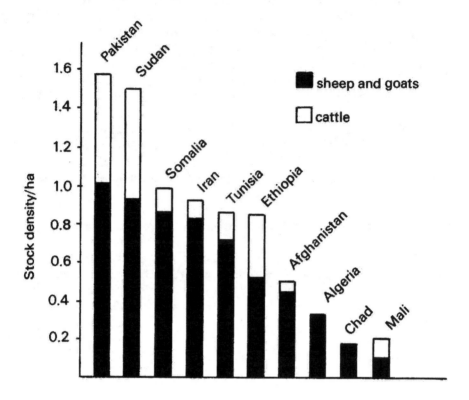

Figure 14.4   The population density of sheep, goats and cattle per ha of pastoral land in various selected countries within the arid zone. Data from FAO Yearbook, 1979

One cow eats the equivalent of 4 sheep and requires daily water intake. The actual grazing pressure within the selected countries would therefore best be shown as total densities of grazers in sheep equivalents (Figure 14.5). Sudan and Pakistan show the highest ratio in the worst ecological imbalance while Afghanistan appears to have the most favourable situation. Since the largest contribution to ecological imbalance is made by cattle, which primarily indicate sedentary households, the localisation of

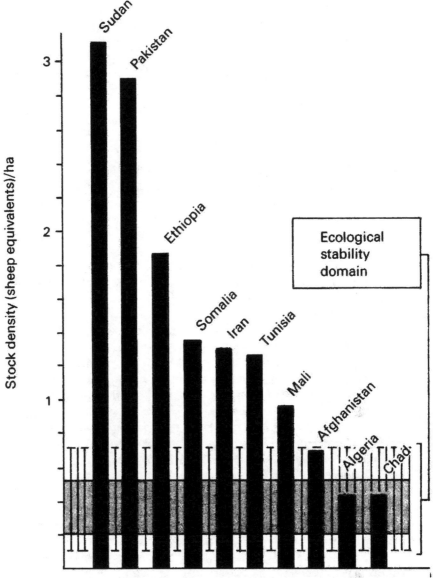

Figure 14.5   The population density of sheep, goats and cattle calculated as sheep equivalents per ha of pastoral land. Data source same as Figure 14.4. The hatched area indicates the economic carrying capacity within the 100-500 rainfall zone while the upper and lower stippled areas indicate the approximate ecological stability domain

overgrazing with cattle will be even more localised than for pastoral economies. For pastoral land-use the figure suggests that most countries other than Afghanistan are far above the ecological carrying capacity. Since the upper stability domain is set by periodic droughts, the consequences will first appear at full force when such droughts appear. If this hypothesis holds true we should expect a density-dependent effect of food limitation to lower condition of pasture animals (e.g. Skogland, 1983). In order to test this I took figures from goats which are most prone to such an effect (they do not have the fat deposits of fat-tailed sheep) from regions of similar genetic stock of goats from SW Asia (Figure 14.6). The results suggested bodyweights are halved in high density regions. A corresponding diminished recruitment due to juvenile mortality as a result of increasing population density has been reported for most large ungulates that have been investigated (e.g. Skogland, 1985). The data support the hypothesis that Afghanistan had stock densities within carrying capacity.

We are all aware of the ecological problem causing starvation in the Eastern Sahara where several million people have starved to death in the last two years and 25 million people are in imminent danger. Yet Pakistan is still able to feed its people despite an extremely high population density for both animals and people. This must be related to the more integral part of the national economy contributed by pastoralist and social consciousness inherent within the Islamic tradition. Also, Baluchistan stocking densities and traditional pastoralism are still in a similar ecological balance as Afghanistan (Buzdar and Jameson, 1984). The ecological dangers already mentioned in Pakistan are closely tied to the Indus river basin and the north western border zone with Afghanistan.

In Ethiopia, under the pressure of an increasing human population, farmers started ploughing up lands formerly reserved for grazing. This has accentuated overgrazing and consequent erosion of the remaining pastures, and has also resulted in a lower cattle population. Fewer cattle meant less manure which in turn meant lower yields and greater requirements for arable land which necessitated further ploughing of

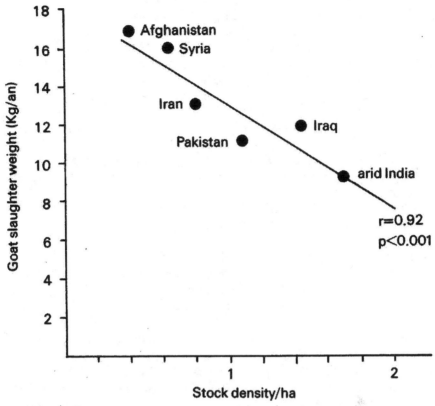

Figure 14.6   Domestic goat slaughter weights in relation to livestock densities from 6 countries in the Near East (data from FAO Yearbook 1979 and Mackell and Norton, 1981)

pasture land, thus completing the cycle of degeneration. The villagers were violating their own land management rules and they knew it but saw no alternative (Eckholm, 1975). Formerly the land in Ethiopia was owned by the Church, the Royal Family and a powerful aristocracy. There is no question that the economic and political conservatism slowed modernisation of agriculture in Ethiopia. The forced resettlements and collectivisation of the mountain village people in new areas without proper socio-ecological planning has not been able to solve the agricultural problems. This together with the civil war created by the new Marxist regime that took power in 1975 has led to the tragic mass starvation in the last two years which followed of drought.

In the Sudan the Kababish tribes of Northern Kordofan and other Arabian tribes have been transferred into semi-settled life, having abandoned pure pastoralism and settled in villages following the government policy of ploughing the pasture land, but retaining their herded cattle. The concentration of extreme grazing pressure, with desertification as a result, as well as ploughing with consequent topsoil erosion, plus a rising number of cattle due to an improved veterinary vaccination practice, are the major contributing factors to the present catastrophic situation in that country.

Within the zone of arid lands where starvation is happening today we see the results of political turmoil compounding unsound ecological land-use policies, in addition to sedentarisation and water management failures. Because of war this leads to increased human suffering and starvation. One may ask the question whether Soviet policy in Afghanistan has the same aim as that of the Ethiopian government of resettlement and land reform. The USSR passed a resolution in 1921 to 'eradicate political economic and cultural backwardness of the nomads in Kazakstan', (Tursunboyer and Potapov, 1959). Today these nomads have been settled and integrated into the urbanised industrial life of the Soviet Union. Their arid lands have been transformed, under the Khrushchev Virgin Lands programme, into ploughed lands for growing crops. The area today is a dust bowl with parts of it a sandy desert due to badly planned ploughing and the clearing of steppe vegetation. I have seen no public reports, although Soviet scientists are quite aware of the problem (e.g. Rodin, 1981), indicating that the USSR has given up this land reform programme. We should therefore fear what lies ahead for Afghanistan under a Marxist regime not adhering to ecological principles. To be fair, Western capitalism has not given better answers either. The stories of sheep overgrazing and desertification in Australia and the USA are part of the same tradition of mismanagement of nature under modern agronomy. Results from the ploughing of the _Artemisia_ steppe in Jordan were equally disastrous (Le Houerou, 1981). The relatively high stocking density of sheep and goats in Iran is the result of the modernisation of Iran under the former Shah regime with forced sedentarisation of nomads and imprisonment of nomad leaders so that the 1979 stock density ratio of Iran became less favourable with concentrated overgrazing around resettled areas.

Water Management in Afghanistan

The traditional water management systems of Afghanistan with at least a 2,000 years' history of adaptation appear to be well suited to small-scale agriculture in valleys within the major drainages of the Hindu Kush mountains. The bombardment of the Afghan irrigation systems by the USSR with almost complete destruction in many provinces has had severe implications for the crop production and the nutrition of the people. I shall not deal with this food problem here but address a less well-known ecological consequence of the destruction. The estimated global incidence of malaria in the 1940s and 1950s was 300 million cases with one death every 10 seconds (MacDonald, 1957; Nielsen, 1979). In Afghanistan malaria has been one of the principal diseases and the mosquito Anopheles culicifacies has been one of the major carriers of the disease (Russell, 1971). A. culicifacies like in many other regions of the arid zone live in standing or running water of irrigation channels and the major rivers.

A major conclusion from the history of land use in the arid zone is the many instances of public health tragedies due to defective and careless irrigation practices. That irrigation is a source of malaria has been clearly observed for many years. Recent examples have occurred in India, Mesopotamia, Egypt and elsewhere (Russell, 1961). The extent to which malaria contributed to the failure of the irrigation systems in ancient times can only be conjectured since specific historical records on this point do not exist. It is not unlikely that malaria was an important factor in the failure of ancient Mesopotamian irrigation schemes that were so successful at first and such utter failures in the end. A point to be made is that, as a rule, the more intensive the cultivation of land and the more careful the use of irrigation water, the lower will be the incidence of malaria. Malaria-carrying mosquitoes thrive in water collections created by sloppy irrigation practices. Very likely, when the civilisations of the Euphrates and Tigris, as well as those of the Indus and Nile basins, were flourishing the irrigation systems were well maintained, with careful attention to the canals and to the conservation of water. But then the irrigation systems began to be neglected and no doubt malaria began to increase. This sort of phenomenon in modern times sets off a 'chain reaction': the more neglect – the more malaria – the more neglect. Thus great ancient civilisations have probably disintegrated as a result of malaria.

In Afghanistan the Soviets' systematic destruction of the ancient irrigation systems, which are a vital part of the Afghan agricultural economy, has led to stagnant water pools, and as indicated by medical reports, a sharp increase in malaria in the population has taken place. Thus the destruction of the irrigation systems not only makes food production difficult, but introduces malaria which is a most serious disease making the population less able to work and fight and also causing death.

Are There Alternative Ways to Enhance Food Production in Afghanistan?

I have been asked the question: Is there any way to produce agricultural crops in the mountains away from the destroyed irrigation areas in Afghanistan? Around all the sedentary centres of farming by intensive irrigation, overgrazing is almost total. Topsoil erosion has led to a drastic decrease of plant production around such settlements. Fertilisation is not able appreciably to increase the rate of recovery of the plant cover. It is only within the remote regions of extensive pastoralism in Afghanistan that the vegetation is in better shape with the topsoil more intact. But here too brush and wood cutting for fire has caused soil erosion. The sad history of the dry land ploughing of the Artemisia steppe and the reports from other regions of the world (USSR, Jordan, Tunisia, SW USA; the Artemisia steppe is the major vegetation type of Afghanistan; Breckle, 1983) indicate that this is unfeasible for most areas of Afghanistan outside the higher reaches of the Hazarajat and the Hindu Kush in Nuristan. Also, within the alpine tree line in Nuristan, corn crops had traditionally been raised for stock feeding in winter and these have already, and can also in the future, be better converted to production of faster-growing legumes that can be used for human consumption. Outside these areas there are severe ecological constraints to the expansion of dryland farming by ploughing.

The best alternative I can see at the moment is to provide the people of the Mujaheddin-controlled provinces with water-well drills and water pumps so that water can be drawn from the ground water table and quickly pumped on to small plots of ploughed land.

Conclusion

Although Afghanistan, like the rest of the arid zone countries, shows the scars of man's exploitation of plant resources, the adaptation of man and his domestic stock there was still confined within the stability domain of the predominant Artemisia steppe vegetation. The traditional tenure of land use, the grazing by fat-tailed sheep adapted to survival under arid conditions developed over thousands of years of selective breeding, and the interaction of nomadism, transhumance, trading and valley village agriculture based on intimate management of snow melt water from the upper catchment basins of the Hindu Kush and Hazarajat mountains, represent a culture of high resilience. Critical analysis of the available data furthermore indicates that countries that have adopted Western modernisation programmes uncritically, or have been under the influence of imperialistic colonisation, or which come under the influence of Soviet land reform programmes have all suffered from the severest ecological repercussions when coupled to a rapidly increasing population. Most of this has taken place during the last three decades. Until 1979 Afghanistan had been spared the consequences of such effects, with the exception of the Helmand project.

References

Barth, F. (1975) Socio-economic changes and social problems in pastoral lands; some concrete factors, Ecol. Guidelines for the use of natural resources in the Middle East and South West Asia, IUCN meeting, Persepolis, Iran, p. 9

Breckle, S.W. (1983) 'The temperate deserts and semi-deserts of Afghanistan and Iran', Ecosystems of the world 5. Temperate deserts and semi-deserts. ed by N.E. West, Elsevier Scientific Publishing, Amsterdam, pp. 271-320

Butlin, N.G. (1962) The simple fleece, Barnard, A (ed), Melbourne University Press, Melbourne, pp. 281-307

Butzer, K.W. (1961) Climatic change in arid regions since the Pliocene. A history of land use in arid regions. Stamp. L.D. (ed.), UNESCO, Paris, pp. 31-56

Buzdar, N.M. and D.A. Jameson (1984), 'Range management and shepherds in Baluchistan, Pakistan, Rangelands 6(6), pp. 243-6

Charley, J.L. and S.W. Cowling (1968) 'Changes in soil nutrient status resulting from overgrazing and their consequences in plant communities of semi-arid areas'. Proc. Ecol. Soc. Austr., 3, pp. 28-38

Eckholm, E.P. (1975) 'The deterioration of mountain environments', Science, 189 pp. 764-70

FAO Production Yearbook 1979, FAO, Rome, 1980, vol. 33

Fowler, C.W. (1981) 'Density dependence as related to life history strategy, Ecology, 52, pp. 602-10

Ghallab, M.E.S. (1975) Socio-economic changes and social problems in pastoral lands, Ecol. guidelines for the use of natural resources in the Middle East and South West Asia, IUCN meeting, Persepolis, Iran, p. 6

Holling, C.S. (1973) 'Resilience and stability of ecological systems', Ann Review Ecol. and System, 4, 1-24

Le Houerou, H.N. (1968) La desertisation du Sahara systentrional et des steppes limitrophes (Algerie, Tunisie, Libye) Ann. Alger Geogr., 3(6), 2-27

--- (1969) Principes, methodes et techniques

d'amelioration pastorale et fourragere. Tunisie, Paturages et cultures fourrageres, etude no 2. FAO, Rome, p. 291
—— (1973) 'Ecologie, demographie et production agricole dans les pays mediterranes du Tiers Monde', Options Medit., 17, pp. 53-61
—— (1974) Principles, methods and techniques for range management and fodder production, FAO, Rome, p. 214
—— (1981a) 'Impact of man and his animals on Mediterranian vegetation', Ecosystems of the world II. Mediterranean type shrub lands di Castri, F., Goodall, D.W. and Specht, R.L. (eds), Elsevier, Amsterdam, pp. 479-517
—— (1981b) 'Long-term dynamics in arid-land vegetation and ecosystems of North Africa', in Arid land ecosystems: structure, functioning and management, Vol. 2, Goodall, D.W, Perry, R.A. and Howes, K.M.W. (eds), Cambridge University Press, Cambridge, pp. 357-86
MacDonald, G. (1957) The epidemiology and control of malaria, Oxford University Press, London p. 201
Mackell, C.M. and B.E. Norton (1981) 'Management of arid-land resources for domestic livestock forage', in Arid-land ecosystems: structure, functioning and management, Goodall, D.W., Perry and Howes, K.M.W. (eds) Cambridge University Press, Cambridge, pp. 455-78
McVean, D.N. and Robertson, V.C. (1969) 'An ecological survey of land use and soil erosion in the West Pakistan and Azad Kashmir catchment of the river Jhelum', J. Appl. Ecol., 6(1), pp. 77-109
Monod, T. (1958) Parts respectives de l'homme et des phenomenes naturels dans la degradation du paysage et le declin des civilisations a travers le monde mediterranum lato sensu les deserts aux semi-deserts adjacents, au course des derivers millenaires, C.R. 7 ene Reunion IUCN Athens, pp. 31-69
Monod, T. and C. Toupet (1961) 'Land use in the Sahara-Sahel region', Arid Zone Research, 17, pp. 239-53
Morley, F.N.W. (1966) 'Stability and productivity of pastures', Proc. N.Z. Soc. Anim. Prod., 26, pp. 8-21

Nielsen, L.T. (1979) 'Mosquitos, the mighty killers', Nat. Geogr., 156(3), pp. 426-40

Noy-Meir, I. (1973) 'Desert ecosystems, environment and producers', Ann. Review Ecol. System, 4, 25-52

Pearse, C.K.P. (1970) 'Range deterioration in the Middle East', Proc. 10th Intl. Grassland Congress, pp. 26-30

Rapp, A. (1974) A review of desertization in Africa: Water, vegetation and man, Secretariat for International Ecology, Stockholm, Sweden, p. 77

Rodin, L.E. (1981) 'Central Asia', in Arid-land ecosystems: structure, functioning and management, Vol. 1, Goodall, D.W., Perry, R.A. and Howes, K.M.W. (eds), Cambridge University Press, Cambridge pp. 273-98

Russell, P.F. (1971) Public health factors. A history of land use in arid regions, Stamp, L.D. (ed) UNESCO, Paris, pp. 363-72

Skogland, T. (1983) 'The effects of density-dependent resource limitation on size of wild reindeer', Oecologia (Berl.), 60, pp. 156-68

—— (1985) 'The effects of density-dependent resource limitation on the demography of wild reindeer', J. Animal Ecology, 54, pp. 359-74

Tadmor, N.H., E. Eyal and R. Benjamin (1974) 'Plant and sheep production on semi-arid annual grassland in Israel', J. Range Management, 27(6) pp. 427-32

Tursunboyer, A. and A. Potapov (1959) 'Some aspects of the socio-economic and cultural development of nomads in the USSR' International Social Science Journal, 11, pp. 511-24

Williams, O.B. (1981) 'Australia', Arid-land ecosystems structure, functioning and management, Vol. 1, Goodall, D.W, R.A. Perry and Howes, K.M.W. (eds), Cambridge University Press, Cambridge, pp. 145-212

15

EFFECTS OF THE WAR ON AGRICULTURE

Mohammad Qasim Yusufi

Introduction

With the invasion of Afghanistan by the Soviets, agricultural activities have declined very sharply. Agricultural production factors such as the labour force, commercial fertilizers, improved seed varieties, agricultural machinery, animal power, irrigation, agricultural extension services, etc. have been disturbed by the war. Bombing of villages, gunning down of farmers and animals, destruction of the irrigation systems, lack of security in the villages, and finally the destruction of the whole agricultural infrastructure, have forced the farmers to leave the villages. The farmers' access to agricultural inputs such as improved seed, fertilizers, agricultural machinery, etc., is difficult or impossible.

The Russians have tried to create famine, poverty and starvation in the villages by destroying harvests and burning grains and other food-stuffs in houses. They also try to buy food-stuffs from villages with higher prices to increase their own food supplies and create food shortages in rural areas.

Because of all these problems, the Mujahideen may suffer from food shortages in rural areas. Attention should be paid to the re-establishment of agricultural projects in areas under the control of Mujahideen. Besides sending food-stuffs, farmers who are still inside the country should be encouraged and assisted by providing them with agricultural inputs to continue their agricultural activities. In addition, starting

The War and Agriculture

agricultural projects for refugees in Pakistan would be very useful.

Area and Land Use of the Country

Afghanistan is an agricultural country. About 72 per cent of the total labour force of the country is directly or indirectly involved in agricultural activities.

The total geographical area of the country is 65.2626 million hectares, 62.61 million of which is agricultural area. The arable land occupies an area of 7.91 million hectares and 54.7 million hectares are permanent pastures and meadows. The total irrigable area is 5.3 million hectares, but because of the unreliable nature of the water supply, only 2.5 to 2.6 million hectares are actually irrigated in any given year. About 85 per cent of the total irrigated land is irrigated by canals and the other 15 per cent is irrigated by sources such as springs, karezes and wells. The actual cultivated area in any given year is about half of the area available. See tables 15.1 and 15.2.

Table 15.1   Classification of land use (000 hectares) (1)

	Years 1976-77	Years 1977-78
1. Agricultural area	62,610	62,610
(a) arable land	7,910	7,910
(i) land under temporary crops	3,851.6	3,746.5
(ii) land under permanent crops	140	140.3
(iii) uncultivated land	3,918.4	4,023.2
(b) permanent pastures and meadows	54,700	54,700
2. Forest and woodland	1,900	1,900
3. Other area	752.6	752.6
Total geographical area	65,262.6	65,262.6

The War and Agriculture

Because of variations in soil type, topography and climatic conditions, most cool and semi-temperate crops can be grown in the country. Table 15.2 shows total cultivated area under principal crops and production of various principal crops grown. From Table 15.2 it is clear that wheat is the staple crop in the country and occupies about 60 per cent of the cultivated land. Other important crops grown in the country are corn, rice, barley, cotton, sugarbeet, sugarcane, oilseeds, fruits and vegetables. Fruit trees and vines are an important part of Afghan agriculture which take years to reach maturity and need careful watering and pruning to survive and keep high yields.

Table 15.2   Area under principal crops and production of principal crops

Crops	Area (000 hectares) Years 1976-77	Years 1977-78	Production (000 tons) Years 1976-77	Years 1977-78
Wheat	2350	2345	2936	2652
Corn	482	480	800	760
Rice	210	210	448	400
Barley	310	310	400	300
Other cereals	42	43	40	35
Total cereals	3394	3388	4624	4147
Cotton	128	128	159	136.5
Sugarbeet	4.75	5	90.9	97
Sugarcane	3.5	4	68.1	64
Oilseed	106.4	50	62	36
Total industrial crops	242.65	187	380	333.5
Total vegetables	139	95	918.2	660
Potatoes	19.8	19	354	200
Total fruits	140	140.3	900	692
Grapes	70	70.1	471	430
Other crops	76	76.5	415	413
Total crops	3991.6	3886.8		

The War and Agriculture

Animal husbandry

Animals and their products play an important role in the economy of the country, especially in the economy of the nomads who constitute about 10 per cent of its population. Animals contribute to both the welfare of the people and to the exports of the country. Among these animals, ordinary and Karakul sheep are primary sources of meat for domestic consumption. Extensive herds of sheep and goats are an important source of meat, milk and wool. Karakul skins and wool contribute to domestic and export incomes. Though some cattle are used as a source of meat and milk, most oxen, cows, donkeys, mules and horses are beasts of burden and are used for ploughing, threshing and transportation.

These animals, particularly sheep, use natural public grazing land and pastures. Low precipitation, poor range management, inefficient grazing of the natural pastures and high demand for meat cause a considerable reduction in the number of these animals, particularly sheep. Table 15.3 shows the livestock population in Afghanistan in 1968.

Table 15.3　Livestock population in Afghanistan in 1968 (1)

Livestock	Local owners	Numbers (000) Nomads	Total
Ordinary sheep	11,361.08	3,602.00	14,963.08
Karakul sheep	6,491.89	-	6,491.89
Goats	3,114.73	72.00	3,186.73
Cattle	3,390.52	209.00	3,599.52
Camels	169.15	130.00	299.15
Horses	367.92	35.00	402.92
Donkeys	1,236.40	92.00	1,328.40
Mules	41.35	-	41.35

Irrigation Practices

Afghanistan has a continental climate. Because it is a long distance from large bodies of water and because of the presence of desert area, the country has a dry climate. In general, the amount of precipitation is not enough for most dry farming purposes. Still, dry farming is practised, especially for wheat and barley cultivation. Annual precipitation in most parts of the country is 100-400 mm. Besides the low amount of rainfall, the distribution pattern of rainfall is also a problem. The country generally gets the least amount of rainfall during the summer season which is the growing and ripening period for many crops (see Table 15.4 (1)).

Table 15.4   Seasonal distribution of precipitation. Approximate percentage of the annual rainfall

Season	Months	\multicolumn{4}{c}{Annual rainfall percentage}
		1974-75	1975-76	1976-77	1977-78
Spring	Apr-Jun	30.5	25.4	33.0	21.0
Summer	Jul-Sep	4.8	4.5	8.7	4.8
Autumn	Oct-Dec	14.4	11.5	11.8	25.1
Winter	Jan-Mar	50.3	58.6	46.5	49.0

A traditional surface irrigation system is very common among Afghan farmers. The source of surface water is mostly snowfall. There are about ten river systems or major sub-systems in the country, of which the Helmand, Kabul, Oxus (or Amu Darya), Konar, Hari Rud and Khash Rud rivers are the most important. The water from most of the systems is highly variable and silt laden, especially at high flow. The Afghan farmers, however, do a good job of levelling and applying water to their fields within the constraints of the tools and the water supply and distribution systems available to them. Afghan farmers mostly divert water from the rivers into irrigation canals and streams by building brush, stone and mud diversion dams.

At high river flows the uncontrolled intakes admit so much water that the canals often overflow and are washed away. The intakes are usually filled with debris to such a point that, as the rivers recede, the canals are left high and dry until the intakes can be cleared and perhaps relocated. It takes from ten to a thousand workers (depending on the size of the canals and inlets) to shovel the debris from the inlets. Canals also suffer from washouts and silting due to summer storms.

In every area the villages are divided into small units. In each unit a few farmers will share a given water right. Water rights were determined by the farmers or their parents a long time ago, based on farm sizes and traditional agricultural laws and regulations. A farm size of 20 jeribs (four hectares) is called one Qulba land. Qulba literally means plough, but in this context it means that if a farm family has one pair of oxen and works full-time, it will be able to cultivate 20 jeribs of land annually. Greater land acreages give access to more water rights and vice versa.

There is no special arrangement for the management and upkeep of canals. Generally, the farmers themselves select one person to take care of the irrigation canal and to warn the farmers in case of any damage or silting problem. This man is called Meraw or Meraab (water caretaker). There is no pay for Meraws but during harvest every farmer will give him 1/80 of his yield (mainly cereal crops such as wheat, rice and perhaps corn). Why should he have a share only of cereal crops? Perhaps, because of the traditions of the farmers. Since farmers mostly grow cereal crops in that area, their pay is based on this type of crop. Some of the main duties of Meraws are as follows:

(a) To cut the grass and shrubs which impede the movement of water in the canal.
(b) To repair minor damage to the canal banks.
(c) After contacting the farmers, to regulate the amount of water flow from intake into the canal.
(d) In case the diversion dam is broken or damaged or

the intake is filled with debris, he tells the farmers to repair the dam or to clean the debris from the inlet. He does not do this personally; instead he beats a drum (Naghara) early in the morning. Whenever the sound of Naghara is heard by the farmers, they gather together to repair or clean the dam, intake or channel. Normally, the farmers remove silt from the irrigation canals once or twice a year.

(e) Sometimes he schedules irrigation hours among the farmers. In some places this scheduling is not done by Meraws, in that case the scheduling of the irrigation hours having been decided by the farmers many years ago. The farmers could decide to change their irrigation hours at the end of the year but mostly water rights are more or less fixed and do not change often. If any farmer does not follow or obey the determined water rights, he will be penalised according to the traditional laws and regulations of the farmers.

In some areas (for example, Logar) besides Meraws, there are other groups of water caretakers called Merkhada. In these areas Meraws are also in charge of water distribution for flourmills built along the irrigation canals. They do not get paid for this but may be given some flour by the owners of the mills. At harvesting time, they may also get a very big bundle of harvested wheat from each farmer. The size of this bundle of wheat, which is called Gawinda, might be so big that it would yield about 60 kgs of grain. Merkhadas have the same duties designated (a, b, c and d above) as Meraws. To select a Merkhada, farmers from each group of a few Qulbas will nominate one person for the post of Merkhada. Out of these nominees only one will be selected. Whenever the farmers work on the irrigation canals, the Merkhada keeps an attendance record for each of the farmers. When a farmer is absent, he will not be marked absent for that specific day, but the Merkhada will take a shovel or some other tool from one of the farmers in the missing farmer's Qulba group. If the absent farmer does not come the next day, the Merkhada will henceforth own the tool which he had taken the day before. If the absent farmer comes the next day, then

The War and Agriculture

he will be penalised in cash, say 50 Afghanis, for one day and this money will go to the Merkhada.

Besides streams and canals, a considerable amount of land (about 35,500 hectares) is irrigated by the springs and the Kares (Qanat) system.(4) The Karez system was developed centuries ago by the Persians. It consists of a series of holes about 50 feet or more apart, dug in line through an underground channel beginning on a hillside and going to a lower elevation. The lower end of the Karez is connected by a channel having a more gradual upward slope than the surface terrain, leading it up to the surface. About 12,000 hectares are irrigated by Persian wells.(4) In some areas the Karez system can be owned only by one farmer but in others Karez systems are used jointly by a group of farmers.

Farming Status After 1978

It is a well-known fact that the production of agricultural products is affected by many different factors such as land, labour, capital, agricultural technology and inputs such as fertilizers, water, improved seed varieties, agricultural machinery, pesticides, herbicides, farming practices and so on. In this part of the report, it will be explained how these agricultural production factors are influenced by the present war-time conditions.

Under the present conditions it is very hard or even impossible to get reliable data on agricultural production. There is not much written information about the agricultural situation in the country. In addition, neither relief committees nor parties nor UN organisations in Pakistan have tried to collect and distribute written information about Afghan agriculture. Dr Azam Gul, former Professor of the Faculty of Agriculture, Kabul University, is the only agricultural expert who has written a report about the present agricultural situation. In it he has tried to determine the average farm sizes, agricultural production of common crops, and yield factors such as seed, fertilizers and irrigation water, and to compare these data with those of 1978 which he uses as a base. Data for the year 1978 are considered 100 per cent in all calculations.

The War and Agriculture

According to Dr Azam Gul, the average farm size was 140 jeribs (5 jeribs = 1 hectare) in 1978, 131 jeribs in 1981 and 134 jeribs in 1982. The smallest average farm size was 10 jeribs in Kunar and the biggest was 1,226 jeribs in Farah. The average number of full-time farm workers was 4.6 in 1978, 2.9 in 1981 and 2.2 in 1982.

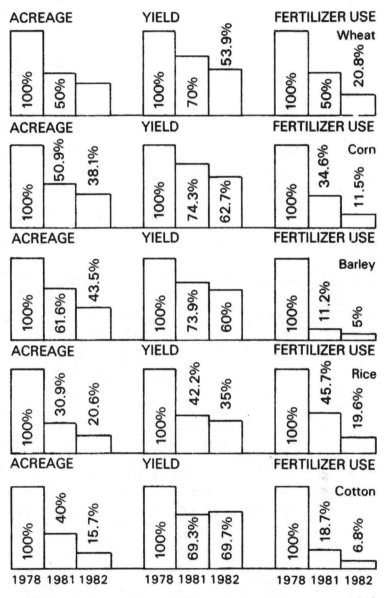

Figure 15.1   Acreage, yield and fertilizer use (4)

Table 15.5   Average acreage, yield, production and fertilizer use

	Acreage (jeribs) 1978	1981	1982	Yield (seer/jerib) 1978	1981	1982	Average farm production (in seers) 1978	1981	1982	Fertilizer use (seer/jerib) 1978	1981	1982
Wheat	37.3	18.7	13.9	60.1	42.1	32.4	2,084.6	796.5	425	4.8	2.4	1.0
Percentage change from 1978	100	50	37.2	100	70	53.9	100	38.2	20.4	100	50	20.8
Corn	5.5	2.8	2.1	58.5	43.5	36.7	345.8	129.4	78.1	2.7	0.9	0.3
Percentage change from 1978	100	50.9	38.1	100	74.3	62.7	100	37.4	22.6	100	34.6	11.5
Barley	7.3	4.5	3.1	45.3	33.5	27.2	316.6	132.7	81.4	0.8	0.09	0.04
Percentage change from 1978	100	61.6	43.5	100	73.9	60	100	41.9	25.7	100	11.2	5
Rice	9.7	3.0	2.0	140.6	59.4	49.3	417.3	183.7	108.2	1.53	0.7	0.3
Percentage change from 1978	100	30.9	20.6	100	42.2	35	100	44	25.9	100	45.7	19.6
Cotton	4.4	1.8	0.7	49.6	34.4	34.6	258	73.1	31.4	4.4	0.8	0.3
Percentage change from 1978	100	40	15.7	100	69.3	69.7	100	28.3	12.2	100	18.7	6.8

Table 15.5 shows the acreage, yield, production and fertilizer use for wheat, corn, barley, rice and cotton. It is clear from the table that the acreage devoted to wheat, corn, barley, rice and cotton in 1981 and 1982 was sharply reduced in comparison with the base figures of 1978. Regarding the figures for 1978 as 100 per cent, then the average wheat acreage has dropped, in percentages, to 50 in 1981, and to 37.2 in 1982; that of corn to 50.9 in 1981 and to 38.1 in 1982; that of barley to 61.6 in 1981 and to 43.5 in 1982; that of rice to 30.9 in 1981 and to 20.6 in 1982; and that of cotton to 40 in 1981 and to 15.7 in 1982. See also Figure 15.1.

The main cause of this acreage reduction is the continuous shortage of the farm labour force. The reasons for this farm labour force reduction can be summarised as follows:

(a) Military drafting of all males between the ages of 15 and 45.
(b) Escape of some people to the mountains or to the resistance.
(c) Flight of about five million Afghans (about one third of the population of the country) to Pakistan, Iran and other countries.
(d) Killing of farmers. Military action has forced many farmers to farm only at night. Farmers working in the fields are frequently gunned down by Soviet helicopter gunships or jets. Those who do not flee have been forced to reverse the traditional working day, sleeping by day and working in the fields after dark.(3) Lala Dad, a farmer from Dasht-e Guhar, Baghlan, said in a 25 September 1984 interview in Peshawar that Soviet jets usually came between 10 and 12 in the morning when the people were in the fields. They were killed whenever and wherever the Soviets found them. Rostam was killed – he was a farmer – while he was weeding.(3) In late 1984, while Russian convoys were coming from Behsood, Nangarhar, they gunned down many people in the village and killed two farmers (Mr Khwaja Mohd and Mr Hazrat) in their fields (an interview with Yar Mohd, August 1985). In the same way, there are many reports about how the Soviets kill

The War and Agriculture

farmers, burn their fields and destroy their harvest and grain in store houses.

(e) In addition, the price and scarcity of oxen has greatly increased. The shortage of gasoline and repair mechanics has rendered many tractors idle. It is reported that one barrel of gasoline, selling for 500 Afs. in 1978, now may cost as much as 6,000 Afs. and in many areas is not available at all.(4) It is estimated that in 1977 the Agricultural Development Bank (ADB) gave out 1,400 million Afs. in agricultural loans. In 1981, the total had come down to 600 million Afs. and in 1982 (by September) only 100 million Afs.(2) According to Syed Abdul Rahman Hashimi, a former senior official of the ADB who defected to Pakistan in October 1982, the ADB had announced loans of 10 million US dollars earlier in 1982 but there was no one to receive them and only 30,000 US dollars (about 3 million Afgs.) had been distributed.(5)

(f) Lack of security and tension created by the government in villages have forced civilians and farmers to leave and seek security in cities. Farmers are ordered by the government to use weapons for so-called 'self-defence' against the Mujahideen. However, farmers reject this order. In some areas, for example in Nangarhar, farmers were asked to grow a special kind of crop, for instance rice, and not to grow other crops, for example corn. Whenever a farmer rejects these orders, he puts his life in danger and has to leave the village.

Russian attacks have rapidly increased during the last two years. Their latest heavy attacks caused thousands and thousands of families to flee the country and seek refugee status in foreign countries. Many Afghan farmers arriving in Pakistan say that there is very little agricultural activity in the country or perhaps none at all. Mohammed Tahir, a graduate of the Faculty of Agriculture who was in Surkh Rud and Hesarak, Nangarhar, early in 1985, said in an interview on 16 October 1985:

Generally, most of the land is uncultivated and

has been bare for the last 4-5 years. Wild plants like camel thorn and other shrubs have replaced the cultivated crops. About 80 per cent of fruit and other trees are dry because of bombing and a shortage of water. Most big trees have no branches at all. Irrigation canals and streams are filled with sand and clay and in some places even the streams are not visible. Because of heavy military attacks and movement of tanks on agricultural fields, the soil structure has deteriorated and boundaries of farms have vanished making property lines indistinguishable. The number of farm animals has also decreased substantially. Farmers mostly grow wheat and not vegetables because of a shortage of water and labour. People living in the area try to cut down the green trees of farmers who have emigrated rather than cutting down their own dried trees. Since most civilians have left the villages, the area looks like a desert and you can find wild animals, insects and desert birds (such as wolves, wild honey bees and other bees, partridges, etc). In the villages one farmer had sprayed DDT over his farm to get rid of the birds. Whenever the Russians come to the area they destroy cultivated fields, burn harvests, grain and houses. Improved seed and commercial fertilizers are not easily available. If fertilizer is available, the farmer cannot afford to buy it because of high prices and transportation costs. The transportation cost of 7 kg of fertilizer from the city to the village (a few kms in distance) is 25 afghanis.

Also from Table 15.5 and Figure 15.1, it is obvious that the yield of most common crops has decreased considerably since 1978. By 1982, the yield of wheat dropped to 53.9 per cent of the 1978 level, of corn to 62.7 per cent, of barley to 60 per cent, of rice to 35 per cent and of cotton to 69.7 per cent of the 1978 level.

The main causes of these low yields are shortage of improved seed varieties, chemical fertilizers, labour, irrigation water and disruption of other agricultural services and technology.

The War and Agriculture

There were many improved seed production centres in the country (Kabul, Ghazni, Kandahar and Helmand). After the Sour coup in 1978, the efficiency of these centres decreased rapidly. Most of them are now under the control of the Mujahideen. The import of improved seed may not be a problem for the government, but their delivery to farmers is very difficult, to some places even impossible. Farmers living close to Kabul may receive imported improved wheat seed but the seed can never reach the farmers farther away. Due to the seed shortage, improved seed is eaten rather than used for farming.

In comparison with the level of 1978, fertilizer used for wheat production in percentages has dropped to 50 of its level in 1981 and to 20.8 in 1982, of corn to 34.6 in 1981 and to 11.5 in 1982, of rice to 45.7 in 1981 and to 19.6 in 1982, of barley to 11.2 in 1981 and to 5 in 1982, of cotton to 18.7 in 1981 and to 6.8 in 1982. This decrease in fertilizer use (by 1982 for wheat it dropped to 21, for rice to 20, for corn to 11, for cotton to 7 and for barley to 5) still continues because of the very high price of fertilizer and its transportation. The average fertilizer price per seer (one seer = 7 kg) was 502 afghanis in 1978, 717 afghanis in 1981 and 843 afghanis in 1982. According to recent reports received from farmers, fertilizer is not available at all in most provinces, especially in those provinces which are far away from Kabul and the fertilizer plant in Mazar-i-Sharif.

Irrigation water is another yield-limiting factor. In order to maintain the irrigation systems in working order, a large labour force is needed. Therefore, because of a severe labour shortage, most irrigation systems are blocked and not working properly. Reports from inside the country tell of the bombing and destruction of irrigation dams and canals as well as destruction of Karezes by grenades.

Farmers from inside the country have also reported the cutting down of fruit trees such as vines, apple, apricot, pomegranate, etc. along main roads and in orchards as well as the destruction of agricultural fields by the Soviets as a precaution against Mujahideen attacks.

Figure 15.2 shows agricultural production for wheat, corn, barley, rice and cotton. Crop production

The War and Agriculture

figures have been obtained by multiplying the acreage cultivated by the yield. Wheat production, in percentages, decreased from the 1978 level to 38.2 in 1981 and to 20.4 in 1982, of corn to 37.4 in 1981 and to 22.6 in 1982, of barley to 41.9 in 1981 and to 25.7 in 1982, of rice to 44 in 1981 and to 25.9 in 1982 and of cotton to 28.3 in 1981 and to 12.2 in 1982.

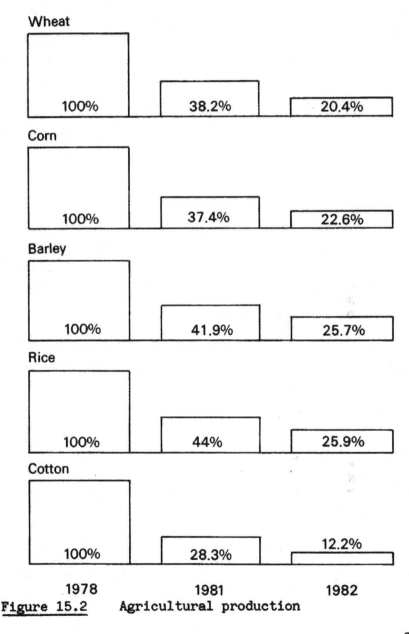

Figure 15.2   Agricultural production

The War and Agriculture

As previously mentioned, agricultural production is interrelated to many factors such as farm acreage, labour force, fertilizers, water, agricultural machinery, improved seed varieties, pesticides, herbicides, farming practices, proper management and maintenance of the land, qualified agriculturalists, and so on. Because of the war and direct and indirect interferences by the Soviet and Afghan government army, all the above-mentioned production factors have been disturbed in one way or another. Although agriculture engages over 70 per cent of the working population, the 1982/3 Development Plan gives priority to mining, industry and power (37.6 per cent) and transportation (27.4 per cent) and allocates only 10.4 per cent of resources to agriculture.(5) As a result, agricultural production has declined substantially and food imports have increased sharply since 1978.

Conclusions and Comments

With the invasion of Afghanistan by Soviet troops, all aspects of life for the people in both cities and rural areas changed. They faced various social, cultural, religious, economic, educational, health, industrial, commercial, agricultural and other problems.

Because of war conditions, agricultural production factors such as labour force, fertilizers, irrigation water, improved seed varieties, agricultural machinery, proper farming and management and maintenance of land have been greatly disrupted on the one hand, and the government pays very little or no attention to the agricultural sector of the country on the other. (It has allocated only 10.4 per cent of its resources to agriculture in the 1982/3 Development Plan.) After the invasion of the country, all Western and Muslim countries stopped their aid to Afghanistan. The country lost most of its experts and highly educated personnel. From the Faculty of Agriculture in Kabul University alone, about 70 per cent of its highly qualified professors left their jobs. Because of military attacks by the Soviets, even the ecological system of plants and animals has changed. Wild

The War and Agriculture

plants have taken the place of cultivated ones. Many wild animals, birds and insects have left the mountains and deserts and occupied the villages. Wild life and natural resources such as forests and soils have deteriorated.

The Russians try to create famine and starvation in the rural areas of the country. They have tried to destroy and burn food stuffs and to kill farmers, other civilians and animals. According to a report covering the period 1980 to 1984, about 5 million animals were killed by Soviet troops, and agricultural productivity dropped to 30 per cent of the year 1978.(6) The contamination of food products and water in springs and Karezes by poisonous chemicals have also been reported. In this way, the Russians try to force civilians to leave their villages for cities or to surrender themselves to the government. Afghan government troops and their agents have also tried to purchase local grain at very high prices in order to create inflation and seasonal scarcity of grain in rural areas. The prices of most food items have gone up 3-4 times in comparison with 1978.(6)

In order to satisfy the needs of people in the cities, the government has to import a large amount of food, mainly from Russia. In a statement on 15 October 1982, Babrak Karmal admitted that people faced food shortages and malnutrition. He said current annual imports were 150-200 thousand tons of wheat, 30,000 tons of rice, 17,000 tons of edible oils and thousands of tons of dairy products. Actual figures may be much higher, according to foreign observers; wheat imports are believed to have risen from 100,000 tons in 1978/9 to 240,000 tons in 1980/1.(5) Also, according to Bakhtar, the official news agency, on 18 May 1982, sugar imports for that year would be 15,800 tons, up to 61 per cent over 1981.

Unfortunately, in the beginning of the war, the Mujahideen did not realise that the Russians intended to create famine and starvation in areas outside their (Russian) control. News reports from most fronts always talk about food shortages in the country. I think the existence of agricultural projects inside the country is a very supportive tool for the Afghan Jehad. Besides weapons, food supply for the fronts is an important factor which can influence the failure or

The War and Agriculture

success of the Jehad. Therefore, I would like to respectfully request that all peace-loving and human-loving people of the world pay attention to the agricultural situation of the free areas of the country and to save, to some extent, the life of millions of homeless, futureless and innocent Muslim people in Afghanistan.

So far none of the relief committees in Pakistan has paid much attention to the agricultural situation of the Afghans. The exceptions occur in foreign-supported projects in Wardak and probably in Paktia and Panjsher. In addition, the Swedish Committee for Afghanistan will start an agricultural survey in the near future. I would like to add the following brief reflection on agricultural projects inside and outside the country.

Agricultural projects inside the country

In order to avoid food shortages inside the country, food could be sent inside or people inside could be assisted by giving them cash to buy food. However, it would be hard to continuously send food inside. Also, it is not easy to find or purchase food in rural areas. I would like to suggest the following:

(a) A detailed survey of agricultural production, livestock and the availability of agricultural inputs could be very useful.
(b) After a brief survey of topography, soil types, weather conditions, labour force availability, etc., the establishment of various agricultural projects in different provinces could be recommended.
(c) Among agricultural inputs, improved seed and pesticides and other possible inputs should be sent inside. By teaching farmers proper land management and good cropping practices, the productivity of lands could remain high.
(d) Among the crops which are less sensitive to burning, root crops, vegetables and potatoes could be recommended. Since growing of vegetables needs more labour and regular irrigation, it might not be too realistic under certain circumstances. Potatoes are rich in

starch and could easily compensate for cereal crops. Also, the yield of potatoes per unit area of land is higher. With a few jeribs of potato cropping, sufficient food for a large number of people could be provided.
(e) In areas with severe shortages of labour and irrigation, the growing of cereal crops such as wheat and barley could be recommended.
(f) Poultry programmes could be useful; they are easy, cheap and productive. One person can easily handle a project of a few hundred chickens. Again it is important to have a survey of the area regarding feed available for chickens.
(g) In areas with no agricultural possibilities, the sending of dried and conserved food such as milk powder, powdered eggs, fish and beef meats, would help.
(h) Teaching conservation methods for fruit, such as apples, and vegetables would be helpful to the farmer.

Agricultural projects for Afghan refugees in Pakistan

Refugee life and its problems are completely different from those of the Mujahideen and other civilians remaining in Afghanistan. Under refugee situations they have no land but plenty of labour and more security which is the reverse of the situation inside the country. In order to improve self-sufficiency, UNHCR and other relief committees in Peshawar have tried to establish income-generating projects for the refugees. Unfortunately, again, I must say no one has paid attention to agricultural projects among the refugees. The Afghan Refugee Commissioner has some agricultural and veterinary science activities in the camps. The International Rescue Committee under its income-generating programme has recently started some agricultural activities for the Afghan refugees in the Kohat and Hango areas. As far as I know, hundreds of agriculturalists (mostly BSc graduates) are looking for jobs. To make some refugees self-supporting, to reduce increasing food prices for Pakistani and other refugee communities, and to provide some job facilities for qualified agriculturalists, it is of

The War and Agriculture

great importance that some kind of agricultural project for Afghan refugees in camps be established. Among these projects, priority should be given to:

(a) Poultry and dairy farming.
(b) Gardening of vegetable crops.
(c) Teaching conservation methods for vegetables.
(d) Research projects in Peshawar for qualified agriculturalists and communication with the outside world's specialists and research institutes.

Notes

1. Afghan Agriculture in Figures, Central Statistics Office, Ministry of Planning, December 1978.
2. Afghan Information Centre, Monthly Bulletin, for November 1982, Peshawar, Pakistan.
3. Laben, Y. and B. Rubin (1984), Tears, Blood and Cries. Human Rights in Afghanistan since the Invasion 1979-1984. Helsinki Watch, New York.
4. Gul, A., Agricultural Survey of Afghan Farmers in Pakistan, Peshawar, NWFP, Pakistan, March 1983.
5. Fullerton. J. (1983) The Soviet Occupation of Afghanistan.
6. National Committee for Human Rights in Afghanistan, Five Years of Blood, Five Years of Resistance, Feb. 1985, Peshawar, Pakistan.

PART V

THE EXILE

16

WHAT HAPPENS TO HONOUR IN EXILE?
CONTINUITY AND CHANGE AMONG AFGHAN REFUGEES

Inger W. Boesen

When the Afghan refugees speak about themselves, they do not use the Persian term 'refugees' - panohand - but 'travellers', muhajereen. This designation expresses the refugees' desire to return, as well as their hopes that the circumstances that drove them into exile will end in a foreseeable future. But the prospects of returning are still uncertain, and by now many have been refugees for more than six years. New refugees are still crossing the borders of the neighbouring countries of Iran and Pakistan, fleeing from bombed villages, massacres, napalm-burnt crops and ruined irrigation systems, anti-personnel mines, repression by the government, forced conscription, and a famine that is rapidly assuming disastrous proportions.

Today, the proud Afghan people, who have never had to face real colonialisation of their country, constitute the world's largest groups of refugees. Out of approximately 15 million Afghans (in 1978), between 2.8 and 3 million are now refugees in Pakistan,(1) in addition to approximately 2 million in Iran. The best-educated and wealthy Afghans seek refuge in Europe, the USA, and even Australia, whereas those remaining in Pakistan and Iran are predominantly lower middle-class shopkeepers and 'white-collar workers', bazaar craftsmen, as well as the rural population, small farmers and tenants, and village artisans. In particular, the rural population has very limited alternatives to living in the refugee camps, surviving with the help of relief goods. The middle-class, on the other hand, generally try their

Afghan Refugees

best to survive on their own in the cities, trying to avoid living in the camps, where the 'rural' setting is very alien to their urban background.

Today, approximately every fourth Afghan is a refugee in an alien country. To this comes an estimated number of approximately 1 million Afghans who have been forced to leave their homes in the areas in Afghanistan devastated by war and to take refuge in the mountains or the cities of their own country.

Exile

For refugees all over the world, the problem is the same: how are concepts of identity and self maintained in the refugee situation, when so many of the points of life to which one's concepts of identity have been anchored are lost? Which cultural elements can be maintained in the new surroundings, perhaps providing strength and support for the refugees, and which are changed with the change of environment?

This chapter does not attempt to provide definite answers to all the questions. At the present time, it is only possible to point out trends and raise questions - the answers still lie in the future.

The Afghan refugees in Pakistan

On one important point, the situation of the Afghan refugees in Pakistan differs from most refugee contexts, at least as far as the Pashto-speaking refugees are concerned. These refugees, the Pashtun (or Pakhtun) come from South and East Afghanistan, from provinces adjoining the borders of Pakistan; ethnically, they belong to the same people, living in the border regions of North-West Pakistan, and basically they share the same culture. Superficially, no major conflicts or problems of identity seem to exist, neither in the eyes of the observer nor in those of the Afghans themselves. Nevertheless, at the present time, seven years after the Soviet invasion of Afghanistan, and eight years after the arrival of the first refugees, a picture of conflicts and tensions is emerging which may, over time, cause changes in the culture and identity of the Pashtun, both in their own eyes, and in relation to the Pakistani Pashtun.

The ideal harmony:
Common language, religion, and cultural system

The Pashto-speaking Afghan refugees and the local population in the host country share three elements fundamental to their society: language, religion, and the Pashtun cultural system, sometimes termed by themselves Pashtunwali ('the Pashtun Way').

Obviously, such a shared cultural base is of extreme importance to the understanding and co-existence between refugees and the local population. Until recently the co-existence between the two groups has remained relatively free from conflicts, compared to refugee situations in other parts of the world. However, the idyllic image of 'Muslim and Pashtun brotherhood' presented by refugees as well as by locals is in itself part of the culture - harmony and unity of family, agnatic group and tribe, is the ideal - but deep rifts have emerged in the 'brotherhood'.

Religion - Islam

The all-dominating experience shared by Afghan refugees and local Pakistanis is religion. Islam constitutes a spiritual as well as a moral system that offers not only interpretations and perspectives of metaphysical and spiritual questions, establishing a cosmic order to human existence, but also a detailed set of regulations to worldly life, laying down concepts and rules of good and bad, correct and wrong, in almost every aspect of living.

The most important aspect of this religious community, which exists despite variations of interpretation in different sects and traditions (Shi'a/Sunni, which is of little importance in the NWFP, the Sufi schools, and different local religious sects), is that the local Pakistanis basically regard the Afghans as their brothers in faith - Muslim brothers - to whom they consequently owe help and hospitality. The common religious values also mean that most Pakistanis share the Afghan view of the war against the communist government and the Soviet invasion forces in Afghanistan as a 'Holy War' - jihad. In jihad, the Afghans fight not only a territorial war to defend the Afghan homeland, but also an ideological war, against a

Afghan Refugees

foreign and 'unbelieving' invasion force threatening to destroy the central Islamic values and creed. To lose one's life in jihad, in defence of Islam, is considered martyrdom, shaheed, and, since a shaheed goes directly to heaven without the usual preliminary ordeals, the religious aspect of the war provides the Afghan resistance with a powerful ideological motivation.

Language

The second important cultural element shared by Afghan refugees and the local population in the border areas of Pakistan is the language, Pashto (or Pakhto), which is understood by all Pashtun despite local variations of dialect. However, this obviously only holds true for the Pashtun groups among the refugees. Other groups (Persian-speaking Tajiks and Hazaras, as well as Uzbek and Turkoman groups speaking Turkic languages), have great difficulties in communication, and some, mostly living in the cities of the NWFP, make great efforts to learn Pashto.

The Culture - Good and Bad in the Pashtun Universe

The third basic common element between refugees and local population is the Pashtun cultural system: an ordered set of values and concepts termed Pashtunwali (Janata and Hassas, 1975). The central elements are the concepts of honour (namus), notions of dishonour (pighur) and shame (sharm), equality (siali) - in principle - held by all Pashtun, coupled with the freedom and autonomy of (male) individuals and agnatic family groups and households (azadi); and values pertaining to the types of behaviour defining a person as a 'good' or 'bad' Pashtun (kho or kharap) - something that has to be constantly demonstrated during daily existence, notwithstanding the fact that a person is a Pashtun by descent.

A person who continually manages to demonstrate, through his or her behaviour in different contexts, that he or she fulfils the expectations of Pashtunwali, is said to be a 'good' man or woman, whereas, in the opposite case, he or she will be termed 'bad' (kharap), or 'black' (tor), through behaving 'shamefully'. The terms 'honour' and 'Pashtunwali' are rarely, if ever, used in everyday living. If at all, they may be used in 'theoretical' discussions about Right and Wrong, Good and Bad. A 'good' person (of either sex) is often termed aql'i, in the Afghan understanding of the Arabic idea 'open to God's Wisdom'.

In the Pashtun social universe, like in many Middle Eastern societies with related cultures, central values are defined basically as focused on men, in relation to 'male' qualities and 'male' activities. Although there exists a strict sexual segregation, 'institutionalised' in the form of purdah, the seclusion and veiling of women, the 'rules', values, and behavioural norms of the women's universe are largely - but not completely - congruent with those of the male world.

Purdah and honour

Purdah (curtain) is the physical and symbolic isolation of the Pashtun women from the outside world, through confinement to the home or screening-off by a veil or all-covering garment (bourqa).

The primary function of this seclusion is to prevent any contact or interaction with 'strange' men - i.e. men outside the close family circle - for the purpose of preventing any breach of the married women's sexual fidelity to their husbands, and ensuring the virginal chastity of unmarried girls.

Control of the women is one of the central elements of the basis of a man's and an agnatic family's honour. The honour of the family is embodied in the honour of its women. The maintenance of family honour requires control as well as protection of women and family, house, and land. House, women, and land are all subsumed under the same concept of honour, namus. The namus of a family household is the embodiment of its socially recognised existence, its autonomy in short its social identity as 'proper Pashtun'. It is the common property(2) and the common cause for all its members to defend against the outer world, that is to say in the Pashtun social universe primarily against other households of similar structure and ideally of equal status.

As a vital element of the family's control of 'property' in the Pashtun world, women are structurally part of the possessions of the agnatic family group – women are perceived as the passive property of men, a view that is, directly and indirectly, widely expressed and shared by Pashtun men. Throughout their lives, women are dependent on men (father, husbands or sons) for their material and social existence; men control land and other productive resources, as well as marriages and lineage affinity (defined by agnatic descent).

'Woman is a Witch
May God not Create a House without its Witch'

(Pashtun proverb)

Why this emphasis on the control of women, not only through seclusion, but also through the rights of the husband to use physical means of control, corporal punishment, and even the right to kill his wife in the case of adultery (but, along with this right, also the obligation to kill the lover, in order to 'prove his case' and avoid alienation from the wife's family)?

Purdah, which is shared by many other groups throughout and even outside the Middle East, may take different forms in different contexts. I have argued elsewhere (Boesen, 1977), that the practice of purdah can be structurally correlated with interests in private property, primarily land, in a competitive social context, for economic as well as political reasons. Another important function of purdah can be the social delineation of the family group in a socially and/or ethnically mixed context (cf. e.g. Pastner, 1972). The functions of purdah as 'symbolic shelter' of the women and the family against an alien and potentially hostile outer world are particularly pertinent in this context (cf. e.g. Papanek, 1973).

Among the Pashtun, seclusion in purdah is an ideal, closely connected with the concept of family honour, despite the fact that not all groups in society are able to achieve it in practice. The 'necessity' of confining women to the house in order to protect the honour of the family seems to be related to a male view of women as socially immature and not fully responsible for their own actions, and consequently not trustworthy of defending the family's interests of their own free will. This distrust is structurally most acute in marriages where the wife is an 'outsider', for instance, marriages arranged to confirm an alliance between distant or non-related families, or to confirm the settlement of a feud.(3)

This attitude towards women on the part of the men obviously reflects their awareness that women are not entirely the 'passive property' of the agnatic family, to be subsumed under the control of the men, but that they are able to act against family honour (as well as family peace!) - an ambivalence which is expressed in the numerous proverbs and sayings about women as 'witches' (bala) - and corroborated by the popular ideas of romantic love across the boundaries of matrimony, shared by Pashtun of both sexes (Boesen, 1981 and 1983).(4)

Pashtunwali as a cultural system

The concept of honour is closely related to the notion of equality (siali) of all male Pashtun, since they all belong to the same descent system and thus ultimately can trace their descent through a common ancestor. Honour is thus expressed through the demonstration of equality towards all other Pashtun (cf. Christensen, 1984).

On the other hand, as we have seen, honour is closely connected with man's, or an agnatic group's autonomy based on its ability to control and defend the vital elements of the family's social and material existence, embodied in its house, land, women, and family honour.

In actual living, this central emphasis on autonomy often encourages the pursuit of individual or family interests vis-a-vis the interests of other family units or even family members (e.g. rivalling brothers or agnatic cousins), striving towards dominance and control.

The conflicts and dilemmas between the values of equality and agnatic solidarity versus the struggle for autonomy, rivalry, and relations of dominance even within the agnatic group itself, are integral elements of the Pashtun social universe. 'Pashtunwali ...

contains ambiguity, because the maintenance of honour may pose the dilemma of choice between autonomy and agnatic solidarity, both of which are considered important values by the Pakhtun' (Christensen, 1984: 19).

Pashtunwali cannot be understood as a homogeneous and consistent cultural system, but must be seen as a heterogeneous system, based on a set of core values, containing inherent perceptual dilemmas and choices of interpretations of these core values, choices which must be understood in the contexts of specific interests and the process of 'practice'.

This heterogeneous cultural system, with all its built-in ambivalences, open to alternative situational interpretations of its basic values, appears flexible enough to adapt to varying conditions of living. Is it also able to cope with the fundamental changes of a life in exile, deprived of the vital elements of Pashtun identity, Pashtun land?

Reality: Tensions and Conflicts Between Refugees and Pakistanis

Competition for resources in ecology and economy

Despite the common value system of the Afghan refugees and the local population in Pakistan, tensions and conflicts, as well as cultural changes, perceived as such by the refugees themselves, have developed.

The roots of this apparent paradox is obviously the new situation where an additional population of between 2.5 and 3 million refugees is crowded into Pakistan, which is itself a developing country with serious problems of unemployment and scarcity of arable land.

The refugees are primarily settled in the North-West Frontier Province (NWFP) (1.8 million registered refugees), 500,000 in Baluchistan, 100,000 in Punjab (mostly resettled to ease the pressure in the NWFP), and c. 600,000 living unregistered scattered in Pakistan. The registered refugees live in camps of between 10,000 and 100,000 families; the largest camp, with c. 125,000 refugees, being the largest concentration of refugees in the world. Many have brought livestock with them, an estimated total of c. 3

million head.

There is a growing resentment in the population of Pakistan against the Afghans who have 'invaded' their country, competing heavily with the local population for basic and scarce resources, water, fuel (firewood), and pasture for the livestock. Particularly in the border areas - the so-called 'tribal areas' with local semi-autonomy - and Baluchistan, the ecological balance is and has always been extremely precarious. In many of these areas, the presence of the additional population has destroyed this balance, causing 'desertification' and consequent soil erosion. The nomads, in particular, who used to cross the border seasonally with their herds, using the pastures temporarily, but now being 'trapped' in one place due to the closing of the border, have contributed considerably to this process. The tensions and the conflicts exist and are continuously being aggravated despite the efforts on the part of UNHCR and a considerable number of relief organisations to alleviate the pressure on ecology through alternative supplies of water and fuel.

Competition for work

In addition to the competition for the resources of the physical environment, the Afghan refugees constitute serious competition in the local labour market. The presence of large numbers of refugees seeking employment causes a decrease in local wages, to the detriment and bitterness of the Pakistani population.

A mitigating factor is that many Pakistanis have migrated to the Gulf States in later years for employment in the oil industry (along with many Afghan refugees). This has caused a gap in the Pakistani economy and provided a niche for the refugees 'at the bottom' of the labour market, offering them the lowest-paid and most despised unskilled jobs such as street vendors, shoe-shiners, construction workers, etc.

However, far from all Afghan refugees constitute a destitute labour force, ready to accept any work at any wage. Quite a few have managed to bring some valuables, which are used as starting capital for establishing themselves in, for instance, bazaar trade in the cities as well as in the refugee villages.

One very important and lucrative activity is the illegal trade across the Afghan border by Afghans using Afghan vehicles, bringing down cherished items to the Pakistani market and the refugees, such as fruit, vegetables, nuts and dried fruit, cloth, timber, etc. Lately, however, this traffic seems to have been impeded by the growing control of the border passes, especially the Khyber pass, by Afghan military forces.

Other important trade items are the popular Afghan carpets, which are continuously brought out of Afghanistan. Many refugee families of the carpet-weaving ethnic groups, especially the Turkoman, continue to produce carpets in Pakistan, on their own, as well as supported by various relief organisations including UNHCR. The carpets are mainly sold in the streets and bazaars in the major cities, but also (the old and expensive carpets) in exclusive carpet boutiques.

Many Afghans are involved in the transport business with trucks or minibuses brought from Afghanistan. To some extent, the trade across the border is in the hands of wealthy nomads, who have invested in modern trucks instead of the traditional camel caravans.

The need for establishing transport services for the refugees, for example in the refugee villages, of which many cover large areas, has also offered a niche for Afghan bus owners.

These trade and transport activities result in serious competition in this sector of the local Pakistani economy. Estimatedly, more than 6,000 Afghan vehicles are now plying the roads on Temporary Registration licenses, and probably just as many are Afghan-registered. It is no wonder that this is one of the most important causes of resentment towards the Afghans in the Pakistani population.

Another aspect of the entrepreneurial Afghans' economic activities are the shops and bazaars flourishing in the refugee camps and the neighbourhoods of the cities where the refugees are concentrated. In the city of Peshawar, the capital of NWFP, it is possible to find almost everything that was to be found in Kabul: Afghan restaurants, tailors, jewellery, leather-work, regional food specialities – and Afghan music cassettes.

Emergent crisis

A picture is gradually emerging of a deep rift between the Afghan refugees and the Pakistani population, despite the common culture and their common 'Pashtunness'.

However, the crisis does not exist only in the relationship between refugees and Pakistanis, but also among the refugees themselves, caused by the very conditions of refugee existence.

The majority of the refugees, small farmers and tenants from the rural areas, have been forced to leave their homes and land, to see it occupied or destroyed by napalm or bulldozers by the invaders. The very foundation of their material and social existence as cultivators – their land – has been swept away.

Because of the Afghans' special situation as refugees in Pakistan, which does not permit permanent asylum but only temporary refuge, even the refugees who could afford it are not able to buy land in Pakistan. The only solution to the problem of getting access to land for cultivation is to arrange, on an individual basis, for the lease or tenancy of land from a local landowner.

In fact, the refugees who were formerly non-cultivators, such as tradesmen and skilled artisans – who were groups with much more inferior status than farmers in the Pashtun social universe – are now in a better position than the cultivators to earn a living on their own in exile. The majority of the farmers, except for those who have succeeded in finding some unskilled – and low-paid – job, remain idle in the camps, having turned into passive receivers, dependent on aid.

This situation is threatening to the core values of Pashtun self-conception and their identity as Pashtuns, their honour and autonomy.

For the men, the loss of their land means that they have nothing left to do throughout the day except discuss the situation, 'What can we do – we have no land – time just passes'.

Afghan Refugees

Their only answer to this crisis is to return to Afghanistan, as soon as the snow melts in the passes, and fight in the resistance forces, leaving their family behind until next autumn in the care of an old male family member such as their father. Many mujahedeen also seize the opportunity to cultivate their land back in Afghanistan, provided the area is peaceful enough.

The women refugees in the camps still have their housework to do: the family must be fed, children looked after, clothes such as they are, washed and kept in order, the tent or mud-house (katcha-house) must be swept, and the few possessions tidied away. The family may own a goat or a few chickens which must be looked after. But even these chores are not enough to fill their days. The women, too, have plenty of time to sit and talk, to grieve their fate, to worry about their husbands or sons fighting in Afghanistan, to mourn their dead family members – and to worry about the future.

To the burdens of idleness and dependency come the problems of maintaining the central elements of their culture and moral system and to transfer them to the young generation. Most of the young children are born in Pakistan and have never seen the Afghanistan of which their elders speak with such longing. The elder generation is deeply worried about their possibilities of bringing up the young ones as 'good Afghans', teaching them the norms and values of the Afghan cultural traditions. Who is there to exercise paternal authority to sons as well as daughters, when the grown-up men are either absent or dead? How will the girls ever have a chance to get properly married when they are allowed to grow up without the strict hand of a father, in a group of women perhaps too preoccupied with their own worries to be able to control the whereabouts of young girls? How can the sons grow into responsible husbands and fathers, learning to work hard to provide for their family, when there is no work and practically no chance of education above the primary level?

One example that shows how the conditions of refugee life may work against the moral values of the Pashtun is the widespread corruption of the distribution of rations in the camps, which may make it necessary for a family to lie about the real number of family members in order to receive a minimal covering of the family's needs. The elder Afghans themselves shake their heads in worry and despair over the bad example the parents are forced to give to the growing generation. 'We teach them to lie' - which is 'shameful' and socially unacceptable in Afghan culture.

Another serious problem which is also against Pashtun moral values, is the increasing addiction to drugs, mainly among the young men with no work or educational possibilities. Hashish, heroin and opium are relatively cheap and easy to get in Pakistan. The youngsters who want it get the money mainly through selling part of their rations in the camp bazaars.

Together with the very limited possibilities of secondary education and vocational training, these tendencies towards a weakening of the traditional Afghan values of honesty, independence, industry, and 'soberness', are the most negative prospects for the future of the Pashtun culture, and of Afghanistan, since they affect the young generation most seriously.

Women and Purdah

The functioning and continuity in exile, and also potentials for change, of purdah, are reflected in the situation of the refugee women.

The first thing a Pashtun refugee family will do when installed on its small plot in a refugee camp is to construct some kind of wall or screen of straw mats or sacking around their new home, even if it only consists of a tent. Later, if and when the family can afford it, they may build a proper mud wall and perhaps a house within. As refugees, the Pashtun feel even more obliged to protect and delimit the family and the family house in the strange environment than at home. In the refugee villages, neighbours are often complete strangers, belonging to different sub-tribes and originating from different regions of Afghanistan, whereas in the home village the social environment was generally familiar, everybody knew everybody, and people were widely united through a common kinship network. Above all, the surrounding Pakistani society is considered as the most serious threat to the Pashtun women and family, despite the fact that the local Pakistanis share the Pashtun culture and its concepts regarding women and purdah.

To the women and girls, this strengthening of purdah means that their possibilities of physical freedom of movement are even more restricted than at home. In their home village, they could leave the house, for example, to visit friends and relatives, and in families which were not rich enough to afford hired labour to fetch water and help in the fields. As refugees, the women's social network also tends to be narrower, since they often live separated from their relatives. The possibilities of school education for the girls are much reduced, at least in comparison with some areas of Pashtun settlement (Eastern Afghanistan), due to different factors in the development of the conflict in Afghanistan, mainly the attempts at forced education of rural women on the part of the socialist regime after the coup in 1978, which has probably meant a serious setback to the Afghan attitudes towards the education of girls, for a long time to come.

The importance attached to purdah in the refugee situation and the problem it causes, such as preventing women from leaving the house to get necessary food supplies in the absence of the male family members for prolonged periods, is illustrated by the following story of a family the author of this chapter knows well.(5)

> Shera Gul lived with his old mother, one unmarried sister, and his pregnant sister-in-law in a camp near Peshawar. The family was very poor, the father was dead back in Afghanistan, and Shera Gul, perhaps 18 years old, had sole responsibility for the family (his only brother had joined the resistance and was fighting in Afghanistan). For some reason they were unable to obtain rations, not uncommon in the case of 'weak' families like this, consisting of a widow and a son either too young or not strong-willed enough to insist on their rights. Shera Gul succeeded in finding a job as chowkidar, a watchman, in Peshawar city, in order to support his family.
>
> However, because of the nature of the job,

he had to stay away for the week, his only day off being Friday. During the whole week, the women were left alone in the compound, not allowed to leave, but also afraid of leaving it to fetch water or buy food. They mostly sustained themselves on supplies brought by Shera Gul on his day off, or by the assistance of neighbours.

Their living quarters were very poor, consisting of a worn-out tent and a small mud house with no roof, since the money for building materials had run out too soon. The narrow compound was surrounded by a low mud wall. The family, the women, as well as Shera Gul, expressed their deep anxiety about thieves and intruders being able to climb the wall, and said they felt insecure. During the week, at his job, Shera Gul was constantly preoccupied with worry about his family, and even collapsed physically several times from the nervous strain, until, faced with the coming of autumn, cold nights and winter rains, he decided to explain the situation to his employers, an international refugee relief organisation, and ask them for help. This resulted in a roof for the house, built by Afghan volunteers employed by the same organisation, on their own initiative and in their spare time, and the employment of an additional watchman to work in shifts with Shera Gul, allowing him an opportunity to stay with his family, which was now endowed with a baby, Shera Gul's niece.

Single women in the refugee camps, widows, or women whose husbands are in Afghanistan, without any male relative to take care of them, have had to assume duties and responsibilities that would normally have been taken over by their husbands or kinship network. These women, 'heads' of 'mother-centred households', have to cope with many difficulties, for instance, in obtaining rations for themselves and their children, because of purdah and the social taboo against a woman negotiating with strange men. On the other hand, it seems that war and refugee life have contributed to a change of roles for these women. In recent years, this category of women has received increased attention from several relief agencies, giving, for example, support through special widow programmes, income-earning opportunities, and so on. Future development will show to what extent women, who have taken over the traditionally male role of provider for the family, and who perhaps are able to support themselves on their own income, are ready to give up their social and economic independence in relation to the traditional sex-role pattern, in the event of repatriation.

The daily routine in the camps where most of the men are idle, doing nothing to help the women with the household chores is also slowly changing. It is becoming increasingly common to see a father taking loving care of babies and giving a hand with cooking, cleaning, and fetching water. Whether this change of the traditional division of labour will have lasting effects probably depends on the duration of the exile, and the opportunities for work and education for the young generation.

Pashtunwali in Exile

What can be concluded about the development of Pashtun culture among the refugees - which tendencies can be identified against the background of the problems outlined above? And, first of all, how can the Pashtun maintain their social identity as Pashtun, their honour, when the basis of the autonomy of the Pashtun family, control of land, no longer exists?

Obviously, anxiety, insecurity, and lack of work are heavy burdens to the refugees. In particular the dependency and its mental consequences are a serious threat to the Pashtun concepts of moral and self-respect, based as they are on self-reliance and ability to look after one's family. The worry of many Pashtun elders about this threat to their basic moral values reflects a consciousness of this tendency and a will to prevent it, first of all through striving for economic independence. The refugees' efforts to achieve this can be seen in their multitudinous entrepreneurial activities, exploiting different niches in the local Pakistani and refugee economy. However, we have seen that the non-agriculturalists are much better equipped than the people who used to be highest ranked in Pashtun society: the cultivators, whether landowners or tenants. The non-cultivators are in a better position to use their various skills as, for example, tradesmen or specialists. The cultivators have become reduced to the lowest-paid unskilled jobs, if they can get any.

Nevertheless, the refugees seem to have no problems in defining themselves as 'proper Pashtun', at least in relation to the local, Pakistani Pashtun, whom they tend to look down upon even though they belong to the same ethnic group and share the same basic values.

Generally, this seems to be related to the fact that most Pakistani Pashtun are far more integrated in the Pakistani state and urban culture than most of the Afghans from the rural areas ever were. The spreading 'Pakistani' culture, containing many elements of Punjabi culture and even its language, contributes to a gradual weakening of the distinct Pashtun identity in North-West Pakistan. The Afghans tend to look down slightly on the Pakistanis, as 'traitors' to the basic values of Pashtunwali: honour, autonomy, and cultural integrity. On the other hand, the Pakistanis widely consider the Afghans as 'rural boors'.

Particular causes for the growing rift between Afghans and Pakistanis are the real tensions and conflicts of interests outlined above, which to a growing extent result in open clashes and harassment of the refugees by the locals, especially in the cities. Other irritants are the corruption of many Pakistani relief administrators regarding the distribution of rations, admission to local hospitals, etc. All these factors contribute to the Afghans' opinion of the Pakistanis as kharap - 'bad' - just as the Pakistanis increasingly consider the Afghans as kharap due to the problems caused by their presence in the local communities.

This mutual distrust is, for example, reflected in the stricter practice of purdah in both groups, each explaining it by the untrustworthiness and 'bad character' of the male members of the other group. The Pakistanis consider the Afghans, especially the young single men in the cities, as a threat to 'their' womenfolk, and complain that they 'have to be more careful now', just as we have seen that the Afghans claim the same thing.

But, what about the refugees' conceptions of Pashtun identity and status among themselves?

It seems that the refugees try to solve the problems of honour in relation to autonomy and control of land in various ways:

'The family land at home is not lost, it is only temporarily occupied'

The refugees still speak about the land at home as 'their' land; in defining the family's status, the present deprivation still does not seem to be final.

'Jihad, the defence of our country, is our most important namus'

The common cause of defending Afghanistan against the invasion forces and the 'marionette regime' in Kabul is perceived as the ultimate obligation of honour, an extension of the obligations of defending the land and house of the agnatic family and lineage, for all Afghans including non-Pashtun ethnic groups.

This growing sense of Afghan nationalism is mainly an effect of the war. Before the invasion, feelings of nationalism were weak in the provinces of Afghanistan, in relation to the sense of ethnic distinction and local and regional interests. The Pashtun especially, with their emphasis on equality and family autonomy, have had extreme difficulties in organisation and co-operation in the resistance. The split and division among the Afghans has been a serious problem for the organisation of the resistance, and still is. On the other hand, the sense of unity in jihad, as well as the sense of a common fate as refugees, seem to have grown out of the years of war. As an old refugee woman said in reply to a question concerning the special problems of the refugee women: 'What does it matter, women or man, Pashtun or Tajik - we are all Afghans, and we are all fighting the same war.'

Purdah and control of women

In the refugee situation where the family is

(although, in their own eyes, temporarily) deprived of the control of land, the control of the family's house and women seems to have assumed an even more important role than at home, in the symbolic expression of family identity and honour. It could thus be argued that the stricter practice of purdah among the refugees has two functions: protection and defence of the family in an environment which is experienced as more alien and dangerous than at home; and the symbolic demonstration of the agnatic family's social and ethnic identity, in a situation where the male Pashtun are deprived of their 'normal' means of demonstrating identity and social status, through economic and social autonomy.

Considering this multifunctional characteristic of purdah, it might be concluded that not only is the practice of purdah not always positively related to, or convergent with interests in landed property (Boesen, 1977), but it may even function as a 'compensation' for the loss of land in the symbolic maintenance of honour and status of the family.

The Future

Despite the examples of flexibility and 'adaptability' of Pashtunwali described here, it must not be forgotten that it largely depends on the duration of the war and exile whether the central elements of Pashtunwali will be maintained among the Pashtun refugees. Dependency and passivity are central problems and their demoralising effects are strongly felt, particularly by the old generation, who are left in the camps to look after the families, the men too old to fight or to embark on an economic activity. The only thing to do is to wait and hope that one will be able to see Afghanistan once again in this life, but, as the Afghans say, 'it is all in the hands of God'.

Crucial to the future of Pashtun culture and of Afghanistan are the opportunities offered to the young generation, of education, training, and work, learning skills that are useful in exile as well as in Afghanistan in the event of repatriation, and gaining and keeping self-respect and their sense of identity as Pashtun and Afghans.

Afghan Refugees

Notes

1. The uncertainty is due to the mobility of the Afghan refugees in Pakistan, and to gaps and double-registration in the registration system.
2. Cf. the phrasing of honour as the family's 'symbolic patrimony', in relation to another tribal Middle Eastern society, the Berber in North Africa (P. Bourdieu, 1977: 40ff).
3. This was not frequent among the Pashtun of eastern Afghanistan, according to field material from Kunar, 1977-78; but it is reported concerning the Swat Pashtun in northern Pakistan by Lindholm & Lindholm, 1979.
4. Cf. Rosen, 1978 and 1984, regarding male-female relations in Morocco.
5. The author of the article spent 20 months in Peshawar and in various refugee camps in the NWFP, in connection with a relief programme for Afghan refugee women (Danish Refugee Council).

References

Boesen, I.W. (1977) 'Purdah og Magt. En komparativ analyse af kvindens situation i den islamiske mellemostlige verden' ('Purdah and Power. A Comparative Analysis of Women's Situation in the Muslim Middle East') Thesis (magisterkonferens), Danish, University of Copenhagen

--- (1981) 'Women, Honour, and Love' Folk, vol. 21-22, Copenhagen

--- (1982) 'Conflicts of Interests in Pakhtun Women's Lives', Conference paper, Bielefeld, published in: 'Forschungen in und uber Afghanistan', Breckle & Naumann (eds.), Mitteilungen in des Deutschen Orient-Instituts, no. 22, Hamburg

--- (1983) 'Conflicts of Solidarity in Pakhtun Women's Lives', In 'Women in Islamic Societies', Studies on Asian Topics no. 6, Scandinavian Institute of Asian Studies, Bo Utas (ed.), Copenhagen

--- (1985) From Autonomy to Dependency: Aspects of the "Dependency Syndrome" among Afghan Refugees, in Migration Today, vol. XII, no. 5, New York

--- (1985) 'Vi er alle afghanere, og vi kaemper alle

den samme kamp' ('We are all Afghans, and we are all fighting the same War'), Danish, in Jordens Folk, vol. 20, no. 3, Copenhagen

Bourdieu, P. (1977) Outline of a Theory of Practice, Cambridge Studies in Social Anthropology, Cambridge

Christensen, A. (1980) 'The Pashtun of Kunar: Tribe, Class and Community Organization', in Afghanistan Journal, vol. 7, no. 3, Graz

--- (1984) 'When Muslim Identity has Different Meanings: Religion and Politics in Contemporary Afghanistan' paper prepared for Symposium on Islam: State and Society, University of Arhus, Denmark

Janata, A and Hassas, R. (1975) 'Ghairatman - Der gute Pashtune. Exkurs uber die Grundlagen des Pashtunwali', Afghanistan Journal, vol. 2, 3, Graz

Lindholm, C. and Lindholm, C. (1979) 'Marriage as Warfare', Natural History, Oct. 1979

Papanek, H. (1973) 'Purdah: separate worlds and symbolic shelter', in: Comparative Studies of Social History, 15

Pastner, C. Mc.Cl. (1972) 'A Social Structural and Historical Analysis of Honor, Shame, and Purdah', Anthropological Quarterly, 45, 4

Rosen, L. (1978) 'The Negotiation of Reality', in Women in the Muslim World, L. Beck and N. Keddie (eds.), Harvard University Press

--- (1984) Bargaining for Reality, Chicago

17

AFGHAN NOMADS TRAPPED IN PAKISTAN (1)

Bernt Glatzer

In the autumn of 1981 an officer of the Pakistan Commission for Afghan Refugees in Peshawar gave me an unofficial estimate that 100,000 Afghan Powindahs were in Pakistan awaiting the end of the war. Pakistan does not consider them refugees unless they register themselves and stay in one of the officially established refugee camps. Such a figure is difficult to judge because a Powindah in Pakistani or in former British terminology denotes an itinerant Afghan who seasonally crosses the Durand Line either in order to find winter pastures for his livestock in the Indus Valley or to trade wood, clothes and other merchandise to and from Afghanistan, or to seek seasonal wage labour all over the subcontinent. Afghan moneylenders, caravaneers and camel drivers are also included in the term 'Powindahs'.(2) What concerns us here are the pastoral Powindahs, also called Kuchis in Eastern Afghanistan.

The great majority of Kuchis remained within Afghanistan migrating seasonally with their flocks of sheep and goats between the lowlands and the mountainous central or north-eastern Afghanistan. They raised sheep and goats for sale, with milk products providing additional food and cash. As beasts of burden they used camels and donkeys. Many east-Afghan Kuchis combined a pastoral life with trading and seasonal labour. Ethnically more than 90 per cent are Pashtuns; the major tribal branches are the Ghilzays in the East and Durranis in the West.(3)

Only a smaller portion of the Afghan nomads or

Kuchis actually crossed the Afghan-Pakistan border. In the spring of 1972 Janata counted about 80,000 pastoral nomads who had crossed the border that year (Janata, 1972, 1975). He estimated the maximum number of nomads in Afghanistan (Pashtun and non-Pashtun) at one million (Janata, 1975). The number of transborder nomads varied annually according to climatic changes as well as to the changing political conditions in both countries. In times of drought or severe cold more nomads could be expected to seek relief in the mild winter climate of Pakistan. Such were the winters of 1970-2 when Janata counted the nomads subsequently returning to Afghanistan. During the early 1960s Pakistan had closed the border to the Powindahs in retaliation for Afghanistan's Pashtunistan irredentists. This caused heavy losses to the nomads' herds caught on the Afghan side of the border (Janata, 1972). The figure of 80,000 nomads seemed to Janata to be a maximum; many of them told him that in future they would prefer not to go to Pakistan because they felt harassed by the administration there (Janata, 1972). Another factor may have been that in the severe winter of 1971/2 more than half of Afghanistan's livestock was lost (Mir Aqa et al., n.d.); this allowed the pastures to recover from previous overgrazing making it possible to feed the surviving herds in Afghanistan during the following years.

Although afterwards livestock numbers in Afghanistan increased quickly (Clark, 1984), transborder nomadism never recovered and in 1978 the first serious census of nomads ever carried out in Afghanistan came to a figure of only 3,000 (three thousand!), Afghan nomad families having spent the winter that year in Pakistan (Balland, 1982).(4) Even if some of the Powindahs had escaped the census, the figure of 100,000 estimated by Pakistani officials a few years later seems to be grossly inflated even if we take into account the new situation in Afghanistan. I would guess that a figure under 50,000 would be closer to reality.

However, as a matter of fact, at present there is a considerable number of Afghan nomads in Pakistan who have not returned to Afghanistan for years. In the spring of 1980 while travelling with a team from the Austrian Relief Committee for Afghan Refugees through

Afghan Nomads in Pakistan

North and South Waziristan I saw the spring migration of Afghan nomads back towards Afghanistan. I could not make out whether they were more or less numerous than in other years, nor whether they actually entered Afghanistan or tried to find summer pastures on the Waziristan side of the border. I could not get reliable answers to my questions. At that time it was not impossible for nomads to reach agreements with the local population: e.g. in the same year a number of Gomal nomads, formerly spending the summer on the Afghan side of the border, migrated to Waziristan where they purchased agricultural land and obtained grazing rights (Ahmed, 1982). The relationship between Afghan nomads and the Wazirs and Mahsuds of Waziristan has been traditionally hostile, despite their common Pashtun (called Pathan by the Pakistanis) ethnicity; twice a year the nomads had to fight their way through Waziristan. Today the situation seems to be relatively relaxed, due in part to the absence of a large part of Waziristan's active male population, working in the Gulf States.

Since 1980 small camps of one to four typical Afghan nomad tents can be seen all over the northern Potohar Plateau (North Punjab), in the lower valleys of Hazara District (the part of the NWFP east of the Indus), at the foot of the Malakand Pass, and in Lower Swat. In 1982 and 1983 I detected about a dozen Afghan nomad families camping inside Islamabad in the green belts dividing the city quarters. There they found plenty of grazing for their sheep, and their young men found work on the capital's construction sites. Other Afghan nomads could be seen grazing their animals in the vast fallow areas between the twin cities of Islamabad and Rawalpindi or elsewhere on the Potohar plateau between the Margalla-Murree Hills and the Salt Range. These nomads still use tents of the Ghilzay shape (see Ferdinand, 1959/60), consisting mainly of a rectangular tent cloth held up by a varying number of vertical wooden poles. Traditionally the cloth is of goat hair, often patched with pieces of cheaper textiles. Nowadays in Pakistan goat hair is scarce, so industrially manufactured tent canvas is used instead. Goat hair also fell out of use because it is not fully waterproof (own experience) and does not provide adequate shelter in the rainy Potohar where rainfall is around 1,500 mm annually (CDA, n.d.).

Elsewhere in Pakistan Afghan nomads have also found grazing and camping grounds, for instance in the desert east of Bahawalpur (Adam Nayyar, personal communication) and in north-eastern Baluchistan (own observation). Even some former Afghan farmers have taken to pastoral nomadism in Pakistan as a new venture. In April 1982 near Faizabad, a suburb of Rawalpindi, I found ten Afghan tents scattered over a large fallow field. Seven were of the Ghilzay shape while the other three were refugee tents; the stamp of UNHCR could still be seen on the canvas. Beside the three refugee tents a flock of about 60 sheep was grazing, and five donkeys were standing nearby. The occupants of the refugee tents told me in an interview that they were Daulatzay Pashtuns. Before 1980 they had been farmers near Ghazni and had never tried animal husbandry before. In 1980 they sold their farm land in Afghanistan and came as refugees to Parachinar in Kurram (a tribal agency in Pakistan) but soon found life in a refugee camp too dull. They invested their money from the land sale in a new way of life and bought sheep in Parachinar. The pastures in that area were poor and after hearing about greener and freer pastures near Rawalpindi they loaded their refugee tents on their donkeys, and along with their families and their flocks migrated to this place. Here they also found cause for complaints: they found people unfriendly, nobody understood Pashtu, when selling sheep they felt cheated and the police allegedly harassed them regularly, demanding grazing permits which, of course, they did not have (and which officially are not needed). However, they praised the quality of the pasture and intended to stay as long as possible. Only when the summer heat became unbearable would they cross the Margallas for the hills beyond.

No doubt Pakistan offers opportunities to Afghan animal farmers; there is pasture land available and there is a high demand for the products they can offer, such as mutton, butter and wool. The opportunities, however, are limited. There is a marked shortage of summer pastures in Pakistan. Because of high summer temperatures in most of the country (maximum > 40°C), including the Potohar, most of the otherwise rich and plentiful pastures cannot be used the whole year round. Profitable sheep and goat husbandry in this part of the world needs summer pastures above 1,000 m altitude, but these are scarce and already occupied by traditional local shepherds such as the Baluch and local Pashtuns in the south, local Pashtuns in the Tribal Areas to the west, and other local shepherds, mainly Gujars, in the north. This is the bottle-neck of animal husbandry in Pakistan and it does not present a bright future for Afghan nomadism there. From 1980 to 1982 thousands of Afghan nomads succeeded in migrating to the highlands of northern Pakistan in the summer: to Dir and Swat Kohistan, to the lower Indus Kohistan, to the high valleys of the Hazara Division, especially the Upper Kaghan Valley, and to Pakistani-controlled Kashmir. This caused over-grazing in many parts, for instance in Upper Kaghan (Anne Sweetser, personal communication), and clashes between the Afghans and the local shepherds (own information).

In the spring of 1983 the NWFP provincial government blocked the Afghan nomads' access to the main valleys in North Pakistan, in particular to the Kaghan Valley, to Upper Swat and to Dir. In Indus Kohistan locals demanded at gunpoint that not one living Afghan be allowed in (Adam Nayyar, personal communication). However, in August 1983 near Besal in the Upper Kaghan Valley I saw 22 tents of Ahmadzay-Ghilzay. They told me they had sneaked in through a side valley of the Kaghan, circumventing Pakistani police. In general, however, the ban on Afghan nomads in the north is quite effective and has discouraged most of them.

This development is not necessarily the end for Afghan nomads in Pakistan but it limits their prospects. By changing their kinds of livestock they might be able to use the lower-lying pastures for the whole year but this might cause overgrazing and damage as is demonstrated by such experiments in other parts of the world. Until now the practice of most Pakistani shepherds of leaving the low-lying pastures at least for a part of the year allows the pastures to recover.

To conclude this short note, Pakistan offers refuge to a number of threatened Afghan nomads and allows some of them to continue their way of life, but that number seems to have reached its limit. Pakistan will hardly turn into a haven for Afghan nomads despite the increasing demand for nomadic products. Their proverbial adaptability, flexibility and shrewdness combined with endurance will probably enable them quickly to find alternatives even outside nomadic life (for good examples see Ferdinand, 1969b, and Pedersen, 1981).(5) Whatever the result of the present disturbances in the region the Afghan nomads will probably not be the ones ending up at the bottom; or, as a nomad in Badghis (Afghanistan) once said in answer to my question how he and his family survived the drought of 1970/71: 'A nomad doesn't wait around and starve.'

Notes

1. This chapter is based on information gathered during fact-finding trips to the tribal areas of Pakistan and to Baluchistan in April 1980 and September 1981 on behalf of aid agencies, and during a two years' stay in Pakistan (1982-4) as a representative of the South Asia Institute, Heidelberg University.
2. For a full description of the Powindahs seen from the eastern side of the Durand Line see Robinson, 1934.
3. For a comprehensive ethnography of eastern Afghan nomadic life see Ferdinand, 1959, 1959/60, 1962, 1969a, 1969b, 1970; Janata 1972, 1975; for other nomads in Afghanistan see Barfield, 1981; Glatzer, 1977, 1982; Shahrani, 1979.
4. Janata uses an average number of 10 persons per family (tent) (Janata, 1982:30f).
5. 'Kaum eine andere Bevolkerungsgruppe in Afghanistan ist Neuerungen gegenuber aufgeschlossener als gerade die pashtunischen Nomaden' (Janata, 1975:14).

References

Ahmed, Akbar S. (1982) 'The Gomal Nomads: Nomadism as Ideological Expression', The Muslim (daily, Islamabad) 11 June

Balland, Daniel (1982) 'Contraintes ecologiques et fluctuations historiques dans l'organisation territoriale des nomades d'Afghanistan', <u>Production Pastorale et Societe</u>, bulletin de l'equipe ecologie et anthropologie des societes pastorales (Paris), 11, pp. 55-67

Barfield, Thomas J. (1981) <u>The Central Asian Arabs of Afghanistan: Pastoral Nomadism in Transition</u>, Austin, Univ of Texas Press

CDA (n.d., after 1980) <u>Islamabad Guide Book</u>, Capital Development Authority, Islamabad

Clark, N.T. (1984) 'Some Probable Effects of Drought on Flock Structure and Production Parameters in North Western Afghanistan', <u>Nomadic Peoples</u> (Montreal) 15, pp. 67-74

Ferdinand, Klaus (1959) 'Les nomades afghans' in J. Humlum, <u>La geographie de l'Afghanistan</u>, Copenhagen, Gyldendal

—— (1959/60) 'The Baluchistan Barrel-Vaulted Tent and its Affinities', <u>Folk</u> 1, pp. 27-50, <u>Folk</u> 2, pp. 33-50

—— (1962) 'Nomad Expansion and Commerce in Central Afghanistan: A Sketch of Some Modern Trends', <u>Folk</u> 4, pp. 123-59

—— (1969a) 'Nomadism in Afghanistan: With an Appendix on Milk Products', in L. Foldes (ed.), <u>Viehwirtschaft und Hirtenkultur; Ethnographische Studien</u>, Budapest

—— (1969b) 'Ostafghanischer Nomadismus, ein Beitrag zur Anpassungsfahigkeit der Nomaden' in W. Kraus (ed.) <u>Nomadismus als Entwicklungsprobleme</u> (Bochumer Schriften zur Entwicklungsforschung und Entwicklungspolitik 5), Gutersloh, pp. 107-30

—— (1970) 'Aspects of the Relations between Nomads and Settled Populations in Afghanistan' <u>Trudy VII Mezdunarodnogo kongressa antropologiceskix i etnograficeskix Nauk</u>, Tom 10, Moscow, Nauka, pp. 125-33

Glatzer, Bernt (1977) <u>Nomaden von Gharjistan: Aspekte der wirtschaftlichen, sozialen und politischen Organisation nomadischer Durrani-Pashtunen in Nordwestafghanistan</u>, Wiesbaden, Franz Steiner Verlag

—— (1982) 'Processes of Nomadization in West Afghanistan' in P. Salzman (ed.) <u>Contemporary Nomadic and Pastoral Peoples: Asia and the North</u>, Studies in Third World Societies

(Williamsburg, Virg.), 18, pp 61-86
Janata, Alfred (1972) *Nomadismus. Grundlagen und Empfehlungen fur eine Perspektivplanung zum Regionalen Entwicklungsvorhaben Paktia/ Afghanistan*, Bd. 7, Sozialokonomie. Planungsteam Paktia (report for the Ministry of Economic Co-Operation, FRG, 68 pp)
—— (1975) 'Beitrag zur Volkerkunde Afghanistans', *Archiv fur Volkerkunde* (Vienna), 29, pp. 7-36
Mir Aqa *et al.* (n.d., 1972 or 1973) *The Effect of the Last Two Consecutive Years' Drought on Livestock Growers in the Seven Drought-Stricken Provinces of Afghanistan*, Kabul University and USAID, 29 pp
Pedersen, Gorm (1981) 'Socio-economic Change Among a Group of Eastern Afghan Nomads, *Afghanistan Journal* (Graz) 8, pp 115-20
Robinson J.A. (1934, 1978) *Notes on Nomad Tribes of Eastern Afghanistan*, New Delhi, Government of India 1934, repr. Lahore, Nisa Traders
Shahrani, M. Nazif Mohib (1979) *The Kirghiz and Wakhi of Afghanistan: Adaption to Closed Frontiers*, Seattle and London, Univ. of Washington Press

THE ROLE OF THE VOLAGS

Nancy Hatch Dupree

It has been six years. In those six years the numbers of Voluntary Agencies (VOLAGs) assisting the Afghan refugees in Pakistan have increased appreciably. There are now upwards of 35 VOLAGs in Pakistan, but just as no one can say exactly how many Afghan refugees reside in Pakistan, so it is impossible to say definitely how many VOLAGs there are (N. Dupree, 1985).

Yearly we receive 'definitive' lists from several sources, official and non-official. No two have ever been the same. What is important, however, is the fact that these VOLAGs represent a commitment on the part of Europe, Africa, the USA, the Arab world, Japan, Pakistan, and Afghans in exile (both in and independent of the political parties).

Our studies began in 1978 as the mass exodus to Pakistan commenced. We were part of that exodus, arriving in August. We watched as the numbers swelled, as tented encampments evolved into mud-brick villages, still officially called Refugee Tented Villages (RTVs) to emphasise the assumed temporary status of the refugees. We agonised with those who first came to establish VOLAG offices in Peshawar and Quetta. How to cope with the enormous influx? How best to ease the physical and psychological trauma of a nation in exile? How best to lighten the burden on Pakistan and the Pakistani villagers near whom the refugees settled?

These questions are still uppermost in the minds of assistance programmers, but in the summer of 1985 we noted a high point had been reached. With the realisation that the refugee stay will in all probability be a protracted one, goals have broadened beyond emergency relief to include multi-tiered programmes which look towards the future - to the preservation of a culture which may hopefully blossom once again when the refugees return to their homeland.

It is the evolution of this expanded role of the VOLAGs which this chapter seeks to address. To define this role now is of consequence because the well-being of the refugees may well come to depend more and more heavily on VOLAG assistance. At the 36th meeting of the Executive Committee (October 1985), the United Nations High Commissioner for Refugees announced that UNHCR faced a shortfall of 57 million US dollars for 1985 and that there were scant hopes for improvement in 1986. Yet emergency programmes must be continued, because refugees continue to arrive. This is the first priority. Vital care-and-maintenance must be continued, for to overlook their needs would be an 'outrage against civilisation', as the representative from the Holy See succinctly phrased it (UN-A/Ac. 96/SR 370:3). Therefore, the sad conclusion emerges that when funds are limited it is the substantive programmes which are inevitably curtailed by UNHCR. The vital significance of creative VOLAG programming thus becomes acutely apparent and their expertise for stimulating funding crucial.

Goals

The three classic solutions to refugee problems are not fully open to the current Afghan situation in Pakistan: (1) voluntary repatriation, the most desired goal, is for the moment highly elusive, enmeshed in world politics; (2) local integration is not feasible because it would threaten Pakistan's stability; (3) resettlement in a third country cannot be entertained because of the size, composition and desires of the majority of the refugee population. The one exception being the approximately 4,350 Turkic-speaking refugees resettled by the government of Turkey in 1982.

Therefore, while recognising that repatriation remains the only viable ultimate goal, the special requirements of temporary asylum have to be considered. While affording a secure and decent livelihood, programmes must also prepare the refugees for repatriation. At the same time, the local population should not sense it is being threatened by the refugee presence nor penalised by special treatment given to the refugees. The needs of the local population cannot be divorced from the planning processes. Indeed, often the needs of both groups are one and the same.

For instance, several extensive water systems have been installed in both the North-West Frontier Province (NWFP) and Baluchistan Province which benefit both local and refugee populations. Labour-intensive programmes, providing employment for both Afghans and Pakistanis, upgrade/extend roads, irrigation systems, and implement range management/reforestation schemes. Such programmes initiated by the government of Pakistan (GOP)/UNHCR are worthy examples of successful attempts to design solutions which emphasise refugee contributions to Pakistan's development.

Most probably these projects would not have been implemented so promptly without the presence of the refugees. In addition, the sooner the refugees are seen to be making economic contributions, the sooner they retrieve their own self-respect, and the sooner they gain acceptance. This defuses negative Pakistani attitudes before they can erupt into violence.

The aim pending repatriation, therefore, is to introduce programmes of a development nature. This poses both opportunities and challenges.

Access

Although the population is large, access is relatively easier than it was in pre-exodus Afghanistan where there were many small villages scattered in remote, isolated areas. Among the refugees there are a few almost inaccessible groups at the extreme southwestern and northern tips of the 2,400 kilometre 'refugee arc' along the Afghan-Pakistan border. Also, the mobility of some groups who move seasonally to summer grazing areas, or cross the border to farm in the 'free' areas of Afghanistan, present problems for implementation. In addition, uncounted (variously estimated from 130-200,000) refugees live in cities and are generally beyond contact.

Nevertheless, the bulk of the refugee population is served regularly via a well-established refugee administrative infrastructure which can be easily utilised beyond emergency relief. Never before have so many Afghans been so easily reached by development programmes (N. Dupree, 1986).

The Beginnings

Before the government of Pakistan requested UNHCR assistance (May 1979), the Pakistani-based relief organisations met many emergency needs from tents to blankets to basic office equipment for the fledgling refugee administration. It was a chaotic situation. Afghan aid committees sprang up throughout the world and their representatives came to Pakistan where local Pakistani manufacturers of canvas tents and other necessities scrambled unabashedly after the cascades of foreign currency. Hotel gardens in Peshawar and Quetta sprouted with sample tents which were subjected to simulated assaults of wind, dust and rain as harassed VOLAG representatives attempted to determine which would best resist the extremes of nature's wear and tear.

Visiting dignitaries came laden with blankets. So much so, that many refugees were literally smothered with them. Since the aid distribution system was not yet fully in place, many refugees sold their surplus blankets in order to purchase necessities. This created much ill-will and attracted acrid criticism. The seeds of resentment were firmly planted in the minds of some Pakistanis who accused the refugees of being ungrateful opportunists making profit out of the world's generosity. This attitude persists.

The overburdened administration also had to contend with deliveries of inappropriate foods and outdated drugs accompanied by instructions in languages incomprehensible to those who sought to dispense them. The RTVs were dubbed the dumping grounds of irksome national surpluses. This attitude also persists, albeit to a lesser degree.

Several VOLAGs continue to supply emergency relief which is still desperately needed by certain vulnerable groups, especially new arrivals. Most

The Role of the VOLAGs

programmes have moved, however, towards more specialised long-term activities, particularly in the fields of health, education and income-generation.

In broadening their activities, the VOLAGs are assisted by intergovernmental and non-governmental organisations (NGOs) which channel substantial funds through VOLAGs with established offices in Pakistan. Specialised agencies within the United Nations system also assist UNHCR in its support of VOLAG projects. Finally, the VOLAGs receive positive backing from the GOP through their refugee commissioners in the NWFP, Baluchistan and Punjab provinces.

Health

Health has been a high priority since the inception of the refugee assistance programme because there has always been a genuine fear that epidemics could result from the potentially lethal combination of severe overcrowding, lack of sanitation and poor water supplies.

Also, during the initial stages many aid committees found that donors were particularly attracted by appeals for contributions towards the purchase of vehicles, such as ambulances and mobile health units. A plethora of vehicles arrived, but many soon stood idle because of the high price of petrol. This encouraged the establishment of static Basic Health Units (BHU) within each of the 350 or so RTVs. Donors were also highly receptive to fund-raising campaigns eliciting medicines; medical supply houses responded amenably to requests for large quantities of medicinal drugs. It was not long before some people in the VOLAG health system recognised the danger signs inherent in excessive pill-pushing.

Tendencies towards dependency appeared to be developing rapidly as too much time was spent dispensing pills, leaving too few opportunities to concentrate on such important activities as diagnoses, screenings for malaria and TB, evaluations of the nutritional status and basic health care education.

To withdraw that which has come to be expected is to invite vigorous objection. The VOLAG personnel who first discontinued dispensing placebo drugs were regularly subjected to vociferous verbal abuse, mainly from women. The passion with which insults were unleashed only served to emphasise the degree to which drug dependency infected the refugee population. Despite these negative signals, however, it was difficult to convince many in the administration that a change of direction was needed. They held that pills should be distributed generously for psychological reasons – 'to keep the refugees happy'. In addition, many of the doctors resisted moving into health education considering it beneath their professional status. Persistent VOLAG prodding was needed before these attitudes began to change. The present emphasis on primary health care and education is a major accomplishment for which the VOLAGs merit grateful acknowledgement.

Primary health care

Successes in providing more meaningful health assistance have been accomplished through the establishment of Mother-Child Health (MCH) clinics, special care and feeding programmes with emphasis on nutrition education, instruction in oral rehydration therapy for diarrhoea, and health work and dai (midwife or traditional birth attendants) training programmes for basic health services. The programmes are becoming increasingly popular and the women enrolled in them are credited with augmenting attendance at the MCH clinics. Most importantly, they are spreading the word that better health practices can be just as beneficial as pills and injections. Such changes in attitude will have long-lasting effects for generations to come.

Also, the recognition that effective aid, no matter in what sector, must include women as well as men is gradually being accepted, but much remains to be done in this area.

Other VOLAGs have developed effective training programmes for community health workers. After training (2-3 months) in preventive and basic curative remedies, these workers teach basic health in the RTVs and generally co-operate in social programmes related to health. It is their important function to identify cases of malnutrition, unvaccinated children and those who fail to appear for follow-up shots, difficult

The Role of the VOLAGs

birth cases and suspected TB cases to the medical teams at the BHUs.

Training sanitarians responsible for all aspects of sanitation programmes, including community education on the subject, forms an important component of several health programmes.

The importance of these types of training cannot be over-emphasised. Rural health services in pre-exodus Afghanistan were never very efficient, and even the tenuous services which were available are now totally disrupted. Recognising the emergency of this internal situation, several VOLAGs and international medical teams are devoting their energies to providing doctors, medical supplies and food inside Afghanistan. They also train paramedics and medical support personnel.

At the time of repatriation, therefore, these bodies of trained personnel should be able to work together to provide better health for both rural and urban communities. Many illnesses may be ameliorated by changes in poor eating habits, traditional weaning practices, traditional treatments for diarrhoea which withhold liquids, improper water handling and inadequate personal hygiene. These are precisely the areas included in VOLAG training programmes for health workers.

The medical VOLAGs also offer increasing numbers of specialised services. These include: TB control, including contact tracing; obstetrics and gynaecology; pediatrics; physiotherapy; psychiatric referral services; dermatology, eye and dental clinics. Disability screening, and referral has been undertaken in some RTVs. Hospitals for the war wounded and paraplegics, with prostheses workshops, have also been established. The paraplegic unit is designed to benefit Pakistanis as well, and provides otherwise non-existent training for Pakistanis in this field. Several VOLAGs implement vaccination programmes because the GOP's WHO-assisted Expanded Programme for Immunization has been overly strained by the refugee population. The Malaria Control Programme has been similarly overextended, leading some VOLAGs to consider training Afghan malaria supervisors in conjunction with the sanitation programmes.

The present refugee health programmes assure the

well-being of the refugees. There have been no epidemics. Looking beyond the immediate needs, however, the health planning seeks to aid Pakistan and prepare the refugees for a healthier post-repatriation life in Afghanistan.

Still to be adequately addressed, however, is the design and production of appropriate visual aids on health subjects. A few sample cloth posters emphasise the efficacy of such materials and highlights possibilities for a new dimension in health assistance. The designing and mass-production of health education materials could perhaps be initiated as an income-generation project. Certainly the results would also be useful for Pakistan where there is a great paucity of all such teaching materials.

Education

By and large, the state of education for the Afghan refugees floats in a vacuum in which 'the need' is perceived by many, but the 'what and how to do' are, at best, nebulously defined. The subject of 'the correct path' is hotly debated.

During the past year or so, however, the importance of VOLAG contributions to this sector have become increasingly apparent. They took the lead in supporting secondary schools not included in GOP/UNHCR primary education assistance programmes in the RTVs. As was the case with health programmes, they also took the lead in establishing schools inside Afghanistan. Initially the assistance was haphazard and generally lacking in quality, however. The move towards a more central role for the VOLAGs in education includes the upgrading of existing schools, the establishment of new schools, the creation of curricula and syllabi, the writing and printing of textbooks, the construction of instructional models from available materials, and teacher training. Special courses for the handicapped are in the planning stages. Paraplegics, many of whom are young children and teenagers, have lively minds which deserve to be trained for all manner of professional employment. Courses in Basic English and English for Specific Purposes are also recognised as being essential for upper-level education and employment opportunities in Pakistan.

The Role of the VOLAGs

The production of textbooks is among the more important contributions of the VOLAGs. At present teaching materials are practically non-existent, and often teachers have to dictate the day's lesson before instruction can begin. This component, however, is fraught with frustrations and vexatious challenges because of sensitive ideological differences between the various political groupings in the refugee population. It is hard to reach a consensus, but the impartial professionalism of VOLAG mediators encourages progress. The role of the go-between is an important function of the VOLAGs which is not to be underestimated in all spheres of assistance, but most crucially in the field of education. The need for textbooks is urgent and expediting production will benefit both the refugees in Pakistan and those remaining inside Afghanistan, now and following repatriation. They represent a major tool for preserving the cultural heritage of Afghanistan.

Others seek to produce reading materials to counter Kabul's disinformation efforts, including reinterpretations of Afghanistan's history and culture. These cultural organisations operating out of Pakistan are composed predominantly of Afghan educationalists and professionals. They write for various audiences, from new literates to fellow scholars and professionals, inside Afghanistan and throughout the world.

VOLAGs also act as catalysts in the registration and evaluation of Afghan education professionals. The conferences they hold serve as links between those in need and those with resources to offer, in Pakistan and inside Afghanistan. For the first time since the exodus a measure of co-ordinated effort seems to be emerging because of the efforts of the VOLAGs. Added dimensions continually come to light, presenting new challenges. Undoubtedly programmes in this sector will branch out in exciting new directions which will have important repercussions on post-repatriation Afghanistan.

Of particular import are the moves towards providing enhanced education for urban youth, both men and women. Most urban refugees do not qualify for GOP/UNHR assistance because they do not live in the RTVs. Generally from the middle class, they represent

Afghanistan's future educators and implementors. Yet too many are idle and until recently they have been dangerously neglected.

This is doubly distressing for young teenage girls and young women living in the urban areas whose future is cruelly bleak. In pre-coup Afghanistan urban girls had taken an education for granted and looked forward to a variety of career opportunities. These young women now face the ire of ultra-conservative religious leaders who seek to curtail their activities outside the home. Courageous tentative beginnings to provide new opportunities for these women have been taken by certain VOLAGs, but the entire dimension of the problems and potential of education for young urban women among the refugee population is almost totally unexplored and in urgent need of study.

Adult education

Surprisingly, not much has been explored regarding the question of adult education. One VOLAG produces effective literacy teaching materials in Pashto which is a significant contribution because the refugees are predominantly Pashto-speakers and Pakistan has no comparable materials for its Pashto-speaking population. Teacher-training related to the teaching materials and non-formal education is included in this programme which is area-orientated and seeks the participation of an equal number of Pakistanis living in neighbouring villages. Continuing investigations pursue innovative non-formal subjects for implementation.

Education aids

Also still to be considered are the production of educational visual aids, radio cassettes, and the possibilities of radio programming, powerful education weapons. Any public education radio programmes developed now would continue to be of service when the refugees return to their villages in Afghanistan. In addition to instruction in diverse fields from health to the various sciences, the positive aspects of entertainment should not be overlooked. Folk-tales,

The Role of the VOLAGs

for instance, reinforce cultural values. Visual aids can also impart more than simple information. A large majority of young children in the RTVs left Afghanistan as babies and infants too young to visualise their homeland. Many thousands born in the RTVs are now six years old. There are no textbooks which describe the geography of Afghanistan, no posters depict the beauty of its landscape. Education materials such as film strips would enhance both non-formal and formal education programmes, in the RTVs in Pakistan and in the free zones inside Afghanistan, and strengthen ties to their heritage and homeland.

To further this objective a central visual aid depository/library would seem to be a worthy project for future consideration. Films on teaching methods have also proved useful. Such an institution could be combined with a reading library of multi-lingual books about Afghanistan. Composed of materials at all reading levels, it should be centrally located and be open to all.

Income Generation

Exile has forced many Afghan refugees to modify their ideals concerning role and status. Most are from the rural areas. To till the land and be self-reliant in providing well-being for a family is a matter of pride; a symbol of identity, self-respect and esteem for most rural Afghans. The Pashtun, particularly, generally look on trade and service as less desirable occupations.

For those who have not been able to make this transition, idleness and a sense of loss of purpose combine to create a predisposition toward dependency which threatens to demoralise a people long lauded for their self-reliance. Dependency attitudes are insidious, and, because they can so easily become an attitudinal habit, they jeopardise the very essence of Afghan culture.

In all fairness, it must be noted that such attitudes are most noticeable in the 'fashionable' RTVs frequently visited by foreigners dispensing 'freebees' in the spirit of Lady Bountiful – whether for political merit, or simply to assuage consciences. Thousands of rupee notes and other commodities are distributed indiscriminately, and only fools would fail to take advantage of such handouts and seek more from the next visitor. Outsiders must, therefore, share in the blame of these manifestations of dependency.

Even a cursory glance reveals a tremendous dynamism in most of the RTVs, however. The Afghans have initiated numerous self-reliance endeavours. Nevertheless, although the refugees participate in a wide range of economic activities, there is a high rate of underemployment due in part to limited markets, lack of appropriate tools, and poor-quality merchandise related to the unavailability of quality raw materials. Many Afghans therefore seek opportunities in the Pakistani economy. The massive disbursement of refugees seeking employment outside the RTVs has caused some to worry that the concept of an Afghan nation in exile is being eroded, adversely affecting Pakistan politics. To counter this, efforts are being made to develop services which will make the RTVs more attractive and self-sustaining.

Income-generating projects

VOLAG-implemented income-generating projects concentrate on vocational training, supplementary training, and skills development for production-oriented projects. Some emphasise the production of refugee-related products such as quilts and clothing, particularly hospital gowns and school uniforms. Others seek to develop skills which, while generating extra income now, will establish a basis for Afghanistan's future development when the hoped-for return of the refugees takes place. These include auto-mechanics; domestic and commercial electricity; welding; plumbing; carpentry; masonry; construction; tailoring; shoemaking; weaving carpets, blankets and cotton fabrics; women's and children's fashion designing and production; beekeeping. All the VOLAGs are on the alert for new possibilities.

Major efforts are being made to identify and assist skilled Afghans, an estimated 10 per cent of the refugee population. Building on the philosophy that the best solution to many problems is to help the refugees help themselves, some VOLAGs provide tools and capital so that more refugees may extend enter-

The Role of the VOLAGs

prises or establish new businesses of their own.

Special attention is given to the identification of employment activities for refugee women, since several pilot projects have demonstrated that refugee women have the capacity and motivation to participate in income-generating projects. For the moment these emphasise health-related programmes plus embroidery, tailoring and quilt-making, and to some extent poultry and kitchen gardening which are considered to be income-enhancing. The identification, selection of natural leaders and the promotion of responsible leadership development is vital to these endeavours.

Increased production, by both the skilled and the newly-trained, introduces the problems of marketing, a long-neglected component now being addressed in preparation for the opening of a sales depot for Afghan-produced goods.

Relief Substitution

The expected long-term stay and soaring financial burden have led to recommendations that relief aid to all but the most vulnerable groups be gradually decreased. In advocating the substitution of income for relief, it is also recommended that during the phasing-out period, all relief substitution activities initiated by the refugees be fully facilitated, particularly when they complement Pakistan's development sector. Past experience has shown that the most successful projects have been those which included refugees in their design, management and implementation.

Projects on a grander scale are also envisioned. These include training hospitals, truck farms, dairy livestock breeding and industrial estates with their own training components. These would provide employment and products for both the refugees and Pakistanis, but most significantly the policy of substituting income for relief projects stresses training as an all-important complement to income-generation. For instance, the majority of the refugees are farmers/herders, yet they are presently prohibited from substantive private farming because this would compromise their temporary status as refugees. As refugees they are also discouraged from keeping large herds because these ravage Pakistan's ecology. How then are the children of these peasant farmers/herders to survive on returning to Afghanistan if they are denied learning experiences in Pakistan? How will even minimal industry develop? These types of larger projects seek to provide a solution.

To assess the feasibility of these large projects, UNHCR has engaged NESPAK (National Engineering Services/Pakistan), a Karachi-based private firm with over 1,000 professionals, to evaluate the impact of projects on both the refugees and Afghan-Pakistan relations. The initiation of standardised demographic data-collection would greatly facilitate their efforts as well as the implementation of VOLAG programmes (Dupree, 1986). In addition, VOLAG input into data-collection systems could be far-reaching.

There are some who worry about the small numbers of beneficiaries involved in current VOLAG projects. Certainly the quality of individual programmes is uneven. Lack of co-ordination sometimes results in duplication. In fact, there are critics who regard any attempts to achieve self-sufficiency as unrealistic. Even if 60-80 per cent self-reliance could be achieved, would it be politically feasible to institute relief substitution? Many think not. Many believe the effort must be made.

Whichever the point of view, the diverse roles pursued by the VOLAGs are exerting a significant impact on Afghanistan's present, in Pakistan and inside Afghanistan. A laudable foundation has been laid which provides wide scope for future joint action in the battle to conserve this culture so that once again it may flourish. Afghanistan may never be the same. That cannot be denied. But all concerned should endeavour to help retain the essence of Afghan culture. Bodies such as the distinguished Swedish Institute of International Affairs can fulfil a two-pronged mission by influencing mainstream aid agencies to address problems by identifying creative goals, and acting as catalysts for funding so that the goals may be realised.

References

Most of the information in this chapter is based on

The Role of the VOLAGs

personal research and unpublished in-house reports.

Published reports include:

<u>Tradition and dynamism among Afghan refugees</u>, (1983) Geneva, ILO (International Labour Office).
Christensen, Hanne (1983) <u>Sustaining Afghan Refugees in Pakistan</u>, Geneva, UNRISD (United Research Institute for Social Development)
––– (1984) <u>Afghan Refugees in Pakistan: From Emergency Towards Self-Reliance</u>, Geneva, UNRISD

Noted in text:

Dupree, N.H. (1985) 'The VOLAG Explosion', <u>Afghanistan Forum</u> (201 E. 71st St. 2K, NY, NY 10021, USA), 13, 6. 25-7
––– (1986) 'The Demography of Afghan Refugees in Pakistan', in forthcoming volume of 1984 Villanova conference papers, London, Macmillan (St. Martin's, NY), UNHCR Executive Committee Reports - A/AC, 96/SR 370, 9 October 1984

INDEX

Abdur Rahman (Abdurrahman, 'Abdorrahman); Amir 6, 21, 34, 63, 80, 109, 126-7
adultery 151-2
Afghani, Jamal-ad-Din 61n
Afghanistan; agriculture 197-216; culture 20-37; ecology 175-93; education 75-92, 93-104, 106-12, 113-18; ethnicity 3-19, 20-37, 38-54, 55-61, 62-72; exile 219-39, 240-7, 248-62; religion 3-19, see also Islam; war 121-45; new Alliance 164-72; resistance (q.v.) 148-54, 155-63; see also Democratic Republic
Afghanistan Education Committee (AEC) 114-15
Afzal mawlawi 111
agriculture 24, 197-216; and ecology 183-5, 188-9; and water 182-3, 191; irrigation 193, 198, 201-4, 210; land ownership 128-30, 132, 152-3; land use 198-9; projects 214-16; under Soviet occupation 204-14; see also livestock
Ahymad Shah Baba 57
Ahmad Shah Durrani 21
Ahmed, Akbar S. 28, 242
Albert 2
Albiruni 76
Alexander, the Great 20
Algar, Hamid 100
Al Ghazali 80
Aliyev, Rustam 55

Allahuddin 16
Allchin, F.R. 20
alliance, Mujahdin 164-72
Amanullah (Amanollah), King 91, 127-8
Amin, Hafizullah 25,63, 111, 132, 139
Amin, Rasul 104n
Anderson, Jon W. 17n, 105n, 128
animals see livestock
Ansari, Abdullah 56, 57, 80
'aql 41-3, 223
arid zone ecosystems 175, 177-81; farming 183-5; nomadism 182-3; present situation, Afghanistan 185-91; water 191-2
Artimesia steppe 190, 192-3
Assembly of Theologians 95
Australia 177-9, 190
autonomy 6-7, 126, 225
Azoy, G.W. 9

Balland, Daniel 241
Barfield, Thomas J. 245n
Barry, M. 48
Barth, Fredrik 9, 126, 177, 181
Benjamin, R. 183
Bhattacharya, Sauri 104n
Bhutto, Zulfikar Ali 14
Biruni 61n
body 40-2
Boesen, Inger W. 17n, 219-39
Bosworth, C. 21
Bourdieu, P. 238
Breckle, S.W. 193
Butlin, N.G. 179

Index

Butzer, K.W. 177-8
Buzdar, N.M. 188

Canfield, R.L. 9
Caroe, O. 9, 17n
carpets 90, 228
cattle 185-8, 200
Chaliand, Gerard 124
Charley, J.L. 180
Christensen, Asger 3-19, 225-6
civil service 131-2, 150
Clarke, N.T. 241
Cowling, S.W. 180
crops 199, 205-7, 214
culture 20-37; and refugees 31-4, 87-90, 231; and resistance 106-12, 138-41; history 19-22; modern education 82-5; peasant-tribal society 21-5; reactions to the war 25-31; 'Sovietisation' of 85-7, 90-1, 98-9, 124, 162, 256

Dad, Lala 207
Daoud (Daud), Mohammad 14, 25, 32, 56, 150-1
debt 128-9
Democratic Republic of Afghanistan (DRA) 6-7, 11-12, 124; and USSR 8, 22, 25, 124; fundamentalism 94-5, 143-4; land reform 132, 153; revolts against 25-6, 139, 151
Deoband madrasa 77, 94, 109
desertification 175-7, see also arid zone
disorder, concepts of 38-54; honour and shame 45-7; reactions to change 47-52; responsibility 50-1; self and affliction 40-5, 50
Dupree, Louis 20-37, 126
Dupree, Nancy Hatch 20, 32, 248-62
Durrani Pashtuns 38-54; historical change 47-52; honour and shame 45-7; self and affliction 40-5, 50; society 40; views of Russians 42, 52

Echkholm, E.P. 181, 189
ecology 175-93, 212; arid ecosystem dynamics 177-81; desertification 175-6; farming 183-5; food production 192-3; nomadism 182-3; present situation, Afghanistan 185-91; water management 191-2
education; Afghanistan Education Committee 114-15; and resistance 107, 111, 141; during the war 113-18; modern 81-4, 106-8, 113; political culture and resistance 106-12; refugees 87-90, 112, 117-18, 255-8; scholars, saints and Sufis 93-104; traditional 75-81, 100, 108-12; under Soviet occupation 84-7, 116; see also learning
emancipation see modernisation; resistance
Enevoldsen, J. 17n
equality 8, 45, 225
Es'haq, Mohammad 155-63
Ethiopia 188-90

264

Index

ethnicity 62-72; non-Pakhtun groups 64-6; Pakhtuns, politics 63-4; Uzbeks 66-70
Evans-Pritchard, E.E. 154n
evil 40-1, 49
exile; and honour 219-39; nomads 240-7; role of voluntary agencies 248-62; see also refugees
Eyal, E. 183

Farani, Mahmud 145n
farming see agriculture; livestock
Ferdinand, Klaus 242, 245
food; and water 191; imports 213; production 23-4, 192-3, 205-7, 210-12
Fowler, C.W. 178
Franceschi, Patrice 124-5
Frye, Richard N. 55-61
Fullerton, John 133, 141
fundamentalism 94-5; resistance groups 14-15, 164-5, 172n

Gafurov, Bobojan 55-6, 58
Gailani, family 12, 101
Gailani, Sayuyed Ahmad 69, 172n
garavi 152-3
ghadis 79-80, 94
Ghallab, M.E.S. 181
Ghani, A. 6
Gharjestani, Mohammad Essa 133-4
Ghobar 127
Glatzer, Bernt 240-7
goats 185-9, 200
Good, B.J. 41
government see Democratic Republic; state

Grevemeyer, Jan-Heeren 121-45
Gul, Azam 204
Gul, Shera 232-3

Habibi, Abudl-Hayy 56, 98
Habibullah (Habibollah) II 62, 127
hadith 4
Hammond, N. 20
Harakat-e Islami 69, 172n
Harrison, Selig S. 72n, 124
Hashimi, Syed Abdul Rahman 208
Hassas, R. 7, 222
Hazaras 65-6, 133-4, 137
health 191-2, 252-5
Hekmetyar (Hekmatyar), Gulbuddin 13, 142, 167-70, 172n
Hezb-e-eslami (Hizb-d Islami) 13, 107, 139, 172n
Holling, C.S. 179
'homeland' 3, 15-16, 42
honour 3, 6-12, 45-7, 151-2; in exile 229-39; Pakhtunwali 5, 7-8, 16, 28-9, 221-6, 234-8; purdah 223-5, 231-4, 237
Horton, R. 50
Hujjat, 'Abd ul-Vali 96

Ibn Sina 76
imperialism 21-2, 163
Indus, river 181
insanity 43-4
International Rescue Committee 215
Iran 94; Afghan refugees in 65, 139-40; and Kushans 57-8; nomadism 175-6, 191
irrigation 191-3, 198,

Index

201-4, 210
Islam; and evil 40; and politics 3-18, 95; and refugees 221-2; and resistance 12-13, 136, 153-4, 155; and USSR 59-60; education 76-8, 100, 109; variety within 4-6; see also Sufism
Islamic Front (Jamiat-e Islami) 13, 69, 107, 111, 172n
Islamic Party (Hizb-d Islami) 13, 107, 139, 172n
Ismail Khan 16, 169

Jameson, D.A. 188
Jami 57
Jamiat-e Islami 13, 69, 107, 111, 172n
Janata, Alfred 7, 222, 241, 245n
Jansson, Erland 71n
jihad 221-2, 236
Jinnah, Mohammed Ali 88
jinns 40, 43-4
Jordan 190, 192

Kabul; and rural society 126-33; Persian influence 97; revolutionary regime see Democratic Republic of Afghanistan; university 85, 87, 94, 106-7, 110-11, 115-16
Kaftar 46-7
Kakar, Hasan Kawun 7, 21, 71n
Kamrany, Nake M. 125, 142
karez system 203-4
Karmal, Babrak 57, 63, 66, 113, 124, 213
Keddie, Nikki R. 93-4, 105n
Keiser, R. Lincoln 148

KHAD 33
Khales (Khali), Mohammad Yunus 69, 167, 172n
Khalili, Khalilu'llah 97
khanaqahs 101, 103
Kheshtmand, Sultan Ali 66
Khushal Khan Khattak 30, 57
Kohzad, Ahmad Ali 55, 57
Koran, the 4
Kuchis 240-5
Kunar province 7, 14
Kushans 55-61; Afghan interest in 57-58; as 'roots' 58-9; study of 55-7
Kushkaki, Sabahuddin 164-72

land; 'homeland' 3, 14-16, 42; ownership of 128-30, 132, 152-3; use 198-9
languages 96-8, 103-4, 140, 221-2
leaders; local 32-3, 149-50; religious 12-13, 99-103, 135; resistance 16, 135-7, 156, 159, 164-72
learning, traditional 75-81; Sufism 99-104; teachers 79-81
Lee Talbot 185
Le Houerou, H.N. 176, 183, 185, 190
Lenin, V.I. 83, 91
Lewis, I.M. 53n
liberal resistance groups 164-5, 172n
Lindholm, C. and C. 225
literacy 23, 138; see also education
livestock 185-8, 200; and agriculture (q.v.) 183-4; and ecology 175, 177-80; and nomadism 182-3, 240-5

Index

MacDonald, G. 191
Mackell C.M. 189
McVean, D.N. 181
madrasas 75-7, 94, 108-9, 111
Majrooh, Syad Bahaouddin 75-92, 93-4, 96, 98, 110
maktabs 108
Malaria 191-2, 254
maleks (maliks) 32-3, 149-50
Maloney, C. 44
marriage 40, 46-7, 225
Martin, B.G. 100-1
Marxism; and Islam 13, 59-60; and the Third World 83-4; education in Afghanistan 75, 85-7; see also Union of Soviet Socialist Republics
Massoud 16
Masud, Ahmad Shah 137
maulawis 79-80, 94-5, 103, 108-10
Meeker, M.E. 45-6
men 43; and women 45-6, 223-5; role of 50-1
meraws 202-3
merkhadas 203
migration 33-4, 67-8; see also nomadism
Mir Aqa, 241
Mirajuddin maulawi 109-10
modernisation 121-45; and resistance 121-6; cultural 138-41; rural society and Kabul 126-33; Socio-political 134-8; technical and organisational 133-4
Mohammadi, Mohammad Nabi 172n
Mojaddidi, Sebghatullah 69, 172n
Mojaddidi (Mujaddidi) family 12, 101

Moltmann, Gerhard 104n
Monod, T. 176-7, 182
Morley, F.N.W. 183
Muhajerin (muhajereen) see refugees
Muhammad, the Prophet 4, 118
Mujahidin (Mujahideen) see resistance
mullahs 79
Muslim Youth Organisation 107
Mustamindi, Shaibai 56

Naby, Eden 62-72, 99
Nadir Shah 95
Najibullah (Ahmadzai) 66
namus 8, 45-6, 222-3
nang 7
National Fatherland Front 64
National Islamic Front (Mahaz-e melli-e Islami) 13-14, 172n
National Liberation Front (Jaba-e melli-e Nejat) 13-14, 172n
nationalism 29-30, 70-1; see also homeland
Nayyar, Adam 243-4
newspapers, resistance 138-41, 144-5n
Nielsen, L.T. 191
nomads; arid zone 180, 182-3, 185; in Iran 175-6, 191; in USSR 190; trapped in Pakistan 240-5
Noorzai, Gul Mohammad 56
Norton, B.E. 189
Noy-Meir, I. 178-9

Ovesen, Jan 148-54

Pahlavi, Mohammed Reza, Shah 57-8, 176

267

Index

Pakhtuns (Pashtuns, Pathans, Pushtuns) 17n; and honour 5, 7-8, 16, 28-9, 221-6, 229-38; and Islam 4-5, 14; and resistance 3, 16, and state authority 9; autonomy 6-7, 17; culture 222-6; Durranni (q.v.) concepts of disorder 38-54; Kuchis 240-5; migration 33-4, 67-8; Persian influence 97; politics 13-15, 63-4; purdah 224-5, 231-4; refugees in Pakistan 220-38; rivalry 8-9, 17

pakhtunwali 5, 7, 17, 28-9, 221-6, 234-8

Pakistan 89-90; Afghan nomads in 240-5; Afghan Refugee Commission 88, 117, 215, 240; and resistance organisations 15, 64-5, 139-40; ecology 175-92 passim; Pakhtuns and 63; refugees in 31-4, 88, 112, 220-38; voluntary agencies in 248-62

Panj Pirei 14-15, 18n
Papanek, H. 224
Parkin D. 49
Pashai 148-54
Pastner, C. McC. 224
Pearse, C.K.P. 183-4
peasant-tribal society 22-5; and the state 126-33
Pedersen, Gorm 245
Persia, cultural influence 96-8, 103-4
pirs 81, 101-2
Pitt-Rivers, J. 45

poets 30-1, 57
politics; and religion 3-18, and resistance 13-5, 29-30, 106-12, 136-7, 141-3; homeland 15-17; honour 6-13; Islam 4-6; Pakhtuns 13-15, 63-4
possession 40, 43-4
Potapov, A. 190
Poullada, Leon B. 125, 142
powindahs 240-5
publications, resistance 138-41, 144-5n
Puig, Jean-Jose 133
purdah 223-5, 231-4, 237

qadis (ghadis) 79-80, 94
Qaiz 4
qarz 128-9

Rabbani, Burhannudin 13, 69, 111, 172n
Rahman, Mawlawi Jamil 118
rainfall 178, 201
Rapp, A. 176
refugees 162, 219-20; agriculture 215-16, 230; and resistance 31-4, 162; camps (RTVs) 31, 248; competition 226-9; culture 87-90, 230; dependency 229-31, 258-9; education for 87-90, 112, 117-18, 255-8; honour 230-8; in Iran 65, 139-40; in Pakistan 31, 88, 112, 220-38, projects for 215-16, 250, 259-60; religion 221-2; voluntary agencies for 248-61; women 31, 90, 231-4, 260; work 227-9, 258-60

268

Index

Reifental 177
relief see refugees;
 voluntary agencies
religion see Islam
rental system, land
 128-30, 152-3
resistance 16; achievements and problems 155-63; alliances 16-17, 164-72; and education 107, 111, 141; and modernisation 121-45; and refugees 31-4, 162; assistance for 162-3; changes and developments 123-5, 134, 142-3, 157; culture and 106-12; divisions within 12-15, 29-30, 123, 161; fundamentalist groups 14-15, 164-5,172n; ideologies 136-7, 141-3; leaders 16, 135-7, 156, 159, 164-72; liberal groups 164-5, 172n; local perspective 148-54; non-Pakhtuns 64-6; Pakhtuns 3, 63-4; publications 138-41, 144-5n; traditional 126-7; western view of 121-2, 142
revolution 83-4
rivalry 8-12
Robertson, V.C. 181
Robinson, J.A. 245
Rodin, L.E. 190
Rosen, L. 225
Rowland, Benjamin 21
Roy, Olivier 17n, 72n, 96, 101, 105n, 106-12, 125, 134
Russell, P.F. 191
Rywkin, Michael 71n

Sabiullah 16
Safi, Batinshah 113-18

Sayyaf, Abd Al-Rasool 167, 172n
scholars 76-7, 80-1, 94-5, 99
schools; for refugees 87-90, 112, 117-18, 255-8; modern 81-5, 106, 113; traditional 75-81, 108-9; under Soviet occupation 85-7, 116, 141
self, concepts of 40-5, 49
Shahrani, M. Nazif Mohib 245n
Shalinsky, Audrey 67, 72n
shame 45-7, 222
sheep 177-9, 185-8, 200
sheytan 40-1
Shi'a Muslims 4, 12
Skogland, Terje 175-93
Sohrawardi, Shahabuddin 80
'Sovietisation' 85-7, 90-1, 98-9, 124, 162, 256
Spain, J.W. 17n, 71n
starvation 188-90, 213
state 10-11; and autonomy 7,9; and Islam 6; and rural society 126-33; 'revolutionary government' see Democratic Republic
Steul, Willi 28
Sudan 186, 190
Sufism 4, 13, 80, 99-104, 110
Sunni Muslims 4, 13-15
Swedish Committee for Afghanistan 114, 214
Swedish Institute for International Affairs 261
Sweetser, Anne 244

Index

Tabibi, 'Abd ul-Hakim 100
Tadmor, N.H. 183
Tahir, Mohammed 208-9
Tajiks 65
Tapper, Nancy and Richard 38-54
Taraki, Nur Mohammed 25, 63, 66, 111, 132, 139, 151
tariqas 4, 12, 99-102
Tarzi, Mahmud 97
Tarzi, Zemaryalai 56
Toupet 182
Turkestan 66-9
Tursunboyer, A. 190

'ulema (ulama) 76-7, 93, 95, 103, 108-9
Union of Soviet Socialist Republics (USSR); and DRA 7, 22, 25, 124; and Kushans 55-56, 58-60; Central Asian SSRs 65, 97; Durrani view of 2-52; invasion and occupation of Afghanistan; 27, 30, 65, 78, 85-7, 116, 140, 190, 191-2, 197, 207-13: 'Sovietisation' 85-7, 90-1, 98-9, 124, 162, 256; see also resistance
United Kingdom, imperialism 21-2, 28, 125
United Nations (UN); and Mujahdin 168; High Commission for Refugees 215, 249, 252, 261
United States of America (USA) 60, 168-9, 190
university, Kabul 85, 87, 94, 106-7, 110-11, 115-16
Utas, Bo 93-104
Uzbeks 59-60, 65-8

voluntary agencies (VOLAGS) for refugees 248-62; access 250-1; and education 255-8; and health 252-5; and income generation 258-61; and relief substitution 260-1; goals 249-50

Wahhabis 112, 118
war; and agriculture 197-216; and ecology 175-93; and education 84-7, 113-18; see also refugees; resistance
warrior-poets 30-1
water 178, 191-2, 201-4, 210
Wazir Shah 111
Whyte, S.R. 53n
Williams, D.B. 178, 185
women 43; and honour 8, 45-6, 223-5; marriage 40, 46-7; purdah 223-5, 231-4, 237; refugees 31, 90, 231-4, 260
work, for refugees 215-16, 227-9, 258-61

Yugoslavia 29
Yusufi, Mohammad Qasim 197-216

Zadran, Golzarak 145n
Zahir Shah 56

270